David F. Newton

Digging Roots

Lying and Making Liars

David F. Newton

Digging Roots
Lying and Making Liars

ISBN/EAN: 9783337253585

Printed in Europe, USA, Canada, Australia, Japan

Cover: Foto ©Lupo / pixelio.de

More available books at **www.hansebooks.com**

DIGGING ROOTS.*

Lying and Making Liars.

White Lies and Black Lies.

SATAN IN THE PULPIT—IN THE PRESS.

Swords and Fires, Fires and Swords.

Gospel Fires—Fires of the Gospel.

AND

Little Mary in a Nut Shell.

"Home is the resort
Of love, of joy, of peace, and plenty, where
Supporting and supported, polished fiends
And dear relations, mingle into bliss."

Children trained in Wisdom's ways, truth and love from infancy, are happy all the day, cheerful, joyous. "The ways of wisdom are ways of pleasantness, and all her paths are peace."

"Love through all their actions run,
And all their words are mild;
They're like the blessed virgin's Son,
That sweet and lovely child."

ILLUSTRATED.

This new and beautiful volume will contain between two and three hundred pages.

Price per copy, gilt, $1.50; plain, $1.00; in paper covers, 75 cts.

Postage, 15 cents. ☞ Large discount to Agents.

Address *Author of " Sword that Cuts," etc.,*
303 West Twentieth Street, New York.

---

* " And now also the ax is laid unto the root of the trees; therefore every tree which bringeth not forth good fruit is hewn down, and cast into the fire."—MATH. iv. 10.

DEDICATION.

TO

Our beloved Brother Simeon Newton, and his little daughter Mary,

This Volume is affectionately inscribed.

Make your home a little Eden ;
 Imitate her smiling bowers ;
Let a neat and simple cottage,
 Stand among bright trees and flowers.
There, what fragrance and what brightness,
 Will each blooming rose display ;
Here a simple vine-clad arbor
 Brightens through each summer day.

There each heart will rest contented,
 Seldom wishing far to roam ;
Or, if roaming, still will cherish
 Memories of that pleasant home.
Such a home makes man the better—
 Pure and lasting its control :
Home with pure and bright surroundings
 Leaves its impress on the soul."

Entered according to Act of Congress, in the year 1872, by
D. F. NEWTON,
in the Office of the Librarian of Congress, at Washington.

CONTENTS.

	Page
LITTLE Samuel	5
The Christian Mother	6
Little Mary at her Morning Devotions.	7
Little Mary at her Morning Walk	8
Grand Pa Talking	10
The Shepherd and his Flock	11
Little Mary and Aunty	12
Preaching is he?	13
Little Boy behind the Tree	14
The Praying Boy	16
Little Mary and her Father	17
Busy Folks	19
Swords and Fires—Fires and Swords	22
Is this Little Mary?	29
Fiery Serpents	32
Lying and Making Liars—No. 1	34
" " No. 2	44
" " No. 3	53
Wheat and not Chaff	61
Little Mary Reading with Mother	64
Satan in—Satan out.—No. 1	69
The Lovely Susan	75
Satan in—Satan out.—No. 2	80
" " No. 3	88
" " No. 4	96
" " No. 5	104
" " No. 6	111
" " No. 7	117
Little Mary and her Mother	124
Satan in—Satan out.—No. 8	127
Wide Awake and Popular	135
The best Food for the Mind	140
Teaching Little Mary	144
Tables Turned	149
Little Mary at her Bible Lesson	155
Lying Meditated, Calculated, etc.	160
What Book is this?	167
White Lying to prevent Black Lying	172
Satanic Transformations	180
Testimony of T. De Witt Talmage	182
" Dr. W. H. Vandoren	183
Truth and Lying	186
Sacred Music in Public Worship	188
Nursing Little Folks	196
Moulding "	198
Sitting down to Eat, and rising up to Play	199
Amusements	218
A Pious Father	219
Spying the Nakedness of the Land	220
Busy Folks	227
Winning Little Folks	228
November	232
Woman at Home	233
His Fingers are Cold	234
Attempt to Poison Children	235
December	237
Putting Razors to Children's Throats	238
Killed with a Hatchet	240
Educating Little Mary	242
Savor of Life—Savor of Death	243
Can't Folks and Won't Folks	248
Kindling Heavenly Fires	251
" " " No. 2	267
Josiah in Kingly Robes	269
Light Under a Bushel	271
Christ! Christ!	284
Talking without Saying Anything!	292
Educating Little Folks	296
A Closing, Loving Appeal to Editors and Publishers	303
Sowing Good Seed!	311

The Wisdom of King Solomon.—1 Kings iii. 16-28.

"And the king said, Divide the living child in two, and give half to the one, and half to the other."

Little Samuel.—1 *Sam.* i. 28.

See Samuel on his knees! How *very* early he began to bow thus in supplicating a throne of grace is not recorded; but this we do know, his whole life was bright and shining! Please turn to the books of Samuel, 1st and 2d.

This Christian mother *imparting light, spiritual, from the holy Scriptures!* What else? Sweet little Mary is listening, as you see, with ears and eyes wide open. Happy little one! blessed! "They that seek me early shall find me." Prov. viii. 17.

"God is in heaven; can He hear
    A little child like me?
Yes, little child, thou need'st not fear,
    He'll listen e'en to thee.

God is in heaven; can He see
    When I am doing wrong?
O yes, He can! He looks at thee
    All day and all night long.

God is in heaven; would He know
    If I should tell a lie?
Yes, if thou said'st it soft and low,
    He'd hear it in the sky."

Little Mary at her Morning Devotions.

> " Let your first thoughts by morning light
>   Ascend to God on high ;
> And in the evening raise your thoughts
>   Above the starry sky."

LITTLE MARY pray? Go to the Lord for guidance, wisdom and grace? Supplicate a throne of mercy in faith, in the name of Jesus, for herself and for others?

Assuredly, morning, noon and at even tide ; sooner would she dispense with her regular meals—breakfast, dinner and supper. See her at it at early dawn, ere the sun streaks the east.

> " Wake while yet the sparkling dewdrops
>   Gem each flower's tiny bell ;
> Kneel with calm and thankful spirit—
>   Kneel and breathe thy morning prayer."

Little Mary at her Morning Walk.
"'Mid fruits and flowers—the singing of birds."

BEAUTIFUL! What more?

  The lark is up to meet the sun,
   The bee is on the wing;
  The ant his labor has begun,
   And groves with music ring.

 The morning air adds brightness to the blood, freshness to life, and vigor to the whole frame. "The freshness of the lip is one of the surest signs of health." Would you be well, enjoy health, life, vigor of soul and body? have your heart dance joyfully like the April breeze, and your blood flowing like an April brook? Up with the lark! inhale the pure sweetness of early dawn!

LITTLE MARY AT HER MORNING WALK.

> "Wake while yet the sparkling dew-drops
>   Gem each flowret's tiny bell—
> With the joyous woodland warblers,
>   Loud their grateful chorus swell—
> Kneel with calm and thankful spirit,
>   Kneel and breathe thy morning prayer."

See, morever, little "Trip" is keeping sweet Mary company; taking the lead friskingly.

Rise early! Up betimes? Who questions it? Sleep? dozes away the precious golden season—the prime of day—when all nature is alive, and on the wing—the merry songsters,—the tuneful lark, the blue bird and robbin red breast. Wake, *wake!*—wake up, little sleepers—up and on your knees ere the sun streaks the east!

> "Wake! for behold the rising light
>   Of morning gilds the sky!
> Its glories call for thankful songs,
>   For action, prompt and high."

Prayer is called for—searching the Scriptures—the first thing. All the most eminently distinguished for elevated piety and usefulness have been early risers. The Lord Jesus, our great Exemplar, not only spent whole nights in prayer, but, also, "in the morning, rising up a great while before day, he went out, and departed into a solitary place, and there prayed." See Mark i. 25, and no doubt that this was his frequent custom. Mark, too, those who first visited the tomb of our blessed Lord. Who were they? what the hour of this visitatation? before the dawn, "while it was yet dark." Their souls were kindled, lighted up in a flame most holy.

WHAT IS GRANDPA DOING? Talking to these little girls about the way of salvation through the sufferings and death of bleeding Mercy!—the happy land where saints immortal reign! Is little Mary among the attentive listeners? Look and see. Millions on millions of the littlest of the little have been washed white in the atoning blood of the Lamb, and are now tuning their golden harps around the throne of God melodiously.

And one special object of grandpa is, doubtless, to enlist as many little folks and big folks as he possibly can on the side of the Lord Jesus. Happy meeting! Glorious won't it be when both grandpa and these little ones meet face to face in the kingdom above, where parting will be no more!

"Around the throne of God in heaven
    Thousands of children stand,
  Children whose sins are all forgiven,
    A holy, happy band,
        Singing glory, glory, glory."

The Shepherd and the Sheep.

"*Jesus is the good Shepherd.*"—John 10th.

"Jesus loves a little child;
He was lowly, meek and mild."

"He will feed his flock like a shepherd: he will gather the lambs with his arms, and carry them in his bosom."

How sweet it is, dear Mary, to be a little one whom Jesus loves, and how happy must those little ones be that know his love and prize it! How happy a thing it would be, if every little one were a lamb of the great and good Shepherd! And why should it not be so? Each one is invited to come to Jesus. If you would be happy, come to this great and loving Shepherd, who carries the lambs in his arms. Seek now your Saviour in the days of your childhood; you will then be happy for life and prepared for death. This would not be the mere delight of the moment, as your pleasures now are; it would be eternal happiness, eternal joy.

'The Shepherd sought his sheep,
The Father sought his child;
They followed me o'er vale and hill,
O'er deserts waste and wild."

Little Mary and Aunty.

"On that cheek and o'er that brow,
So soft, so calm, yet eloquent,
The smiles that win, the tints that glow,
But tell of days in goodness spent."

WHAT is aunty talking about or saying to her sweet, smiling little niece?

How good and gracious God is! How much the Lord Jesus loves sinners, the biggest and the littlest! How *exceedingly* desirous he is that all should come to him—accept offered mercy through the shedding of his own precious blood!

Is not this beautiful? worthy the imitation of every aunty? The more little folks and great folks talk with Jesus and about Jesus, "the way, the truth, and the life," the more will they delight in it a *great deal*.

Preaching is he? What about?

The Saviour, who died on Calvary, to save little folks as well as the big folks? Is little Mary in the audience? Young friends, do you know how lovingly the dear Saviour—the Lamb of God—welcomes little children to his happy fold? He numbers the lambs among his flock. "Suffer little children to come unto me, and forbid them not, for of such is the kingdom of God." *Luke* xviii. 16.

Dear children, now is the spring-time of your lives, be sure to plant choice seeds, which may burst forth in beauty, bloom, and bear "the peaceable fruits of righteousness." Jesus was as young as any of you, who "never did sin, neither was guile found in his mouth." He is the perfect example for all. Do you not wish, children, like Jesus, to go about doing good? He loves little children, and will *never* refuse to hear their cries.

> "Then lift your little hands in prayer;
> The Saviour bids you come;
> Safe in his bosom he will bear
> The lambs to his bright home."

See this little boy kneeling behind the tree!

A GENTLEMAN passing at the time saw his little hands clasped together, and his face upturned to heaven, evidently in earnest prayer, little thinking that any one was near. Listening attentively, he heard the dear little fellow, in a soft voice, half choked with sighs, say: "Dear Saviour, wash away her sins and save my dear mother."

As he rose from his knees the gentleman stepped forward, and taking his hand, asked him where he lived.

"I live down there in that small house," he said.

"And where did you learn to pray, my dear?"

"At the Sunday-school, where my teacher told me Jesus died for me, and that now He lives in heaven."

"And do you love the Lord who died for you?"

"Oh yes! oh yes! indeed I do, and I so wish my dear mother loved Him too, for she is very ill and may soon die. I try all I can to make her, and I pray to God for her and father."

"And do you think He hears your prayers, and will really save your father and mother?"

"Oh yes, for my teacher tells me that God loves to hear

little children pray, and that whatever we ask in the name of Jesus, He is sure to give us."

Having said this, the little fellow added: "Now I must go; good-bye," drew away his hand, and smiling sweetly, ran off to his home.

About twelve months after this, the gentleman being again in the village, called to enquire after his little friend, and learned from his father, that both he and his mother were dead, and that his wife had found, ere she died, the forgiveness of sins through the words of her little boy. He said, too, that after his mother's death, he used to come to him and tell him all he learned at the Sunday-school, and that thus, through his son's means, he had also been led to believe in Jesus.

The poor father wept as he talked about his dear little boy, and as he wiped away his tears, said: "I am now just waiting to join him and my dear wife above, there to praise the blessed God, that taught us both to love Him through the infant lips of our child."

"Out of the mouths of babes and sucklings Thou hast perfected praise."—*Matt.* xxi. 16.

"O'er the head of listening children
Christ his sweetest blessings gave;
Little hands may aid his mission,
A dying world to save."

The Praying Boy.

He loves prayer—it's his soul's delight. He's at the mercy-seat 'ere the dawning light.

It was about five in the morning when he awoke, and began one of the hymns which he had learned from his mother's lips.

> "Awake, my heart, awake and sing
> The praise of God, who gives us all
> Food, sleep, and every precious thing;
> To God, thy Friend, direct thy call."

This he repeated aloud to himself. The maid, who was about to milk the cows, had heard him; and, touched by these lines, she entered the stable with the lantern in her hand, and wished the lad "good morning."

Little Mary and her Father.

"How many deeds of kindness
  A little child may do,
Although it has so little strength
  And little wisdom, too.

"It wants a loving spirit,
  Much more than strength to prove,
How many things a child may do
  For others by its love."

A LOVELY daughter, clothed with meek humility, abounding in all the Christian graces, polished "after the similitude of a palace." O what a blessing!

"Lips that can praise and pray,
And gentle words of kindness say,
  To please the King of heaven."

Beautiful! Anything more so this side of glory eternal? "Whose adorning is not *outward* but *inward*—the heavenly."—Tim. ii. 9 ; 1 Peter iii. 8. " The hidden man of the heart, in that which is not corruptible. Even the ornament of a meek and quiet spirit, which is in the sight of God of great price."

There are other ministers of love more conspicuous than she, but none in which a gentler, lovelier spirit dwells, and none to which the heart's warm requitals more joyfully respond. She is the steady light of her father's house. Her ideal is indissolubly connected with that of his fireside. She is his morning sunlight and evening star. The grace, vivacity, and tenderness of her sex, have their place in the mighty sway which she holds over his spirit. She is the elation of his heart, the ornament of his hospitality, and the gentle nurse in his sickness.

Early piety is peculiarly pleasing in the sight of God. How lovely do the snow-drop, the primrose, and the daisy, appear in our sight, because they are the first flowers of the year! And what is thus pleasing to us in the field of nature, is equally delightful to God in the garden of piety.

Happy father! happy mother! This lovely daughter is yours—educated for the kingdom—an "olive plant" around your table. "Many daughters have done virtuously, but she excels them all."

"Favor is deceitful, and beauty is vain ; but a woman that feareth the Lord, she shall be praised."

"Wisdom is the principal thing, therefore get wisdom ; and with all thy getting, get understanding. Exalt her and she shall promote thee : she shall bring thee to honor, when thou dost embrace her : she shall give to thine head an ornament of grace ; a crown of glory shall she deliver to thee."—Prov. iv. 7, 8, 9.

Busy Folks—Folks that are Busy.

WORK! WORK! WORK!

"*Whatsoever thy hand findeth to do, do it with thy might.*" Eccles. ix. 10.
"*God gives the bird its food, but does not throw it into its nest.*"

"Let us then be up and doing,
With a heart for any fate;
Still achieving, still pursuing,
Learn to labor and to wait."

A few lines to little Mary on business habits, activity, life, soul, and power in doing this, doing that, running here, running there, flying here, flying there.

DEAR little niece, here you see a whole family, up and doing! Doing what—folding their hands, taking the easy-chair? or lying down crying: "a little sleep, a little slumber—a little folding their hands to sleep?" Not a syllable of it, every one is at her post—even grandma, with her "specs" on, is as busy as she can be.

BUSY FOLKS—FOLKS THAT ARE BUSY.

Paul told the Thessalonians, "If any would not work, neither should he eat." 2 Thess. iii. 10; also, Ephesians iv. 28.

> "Labor with what zeal we will,
> Something yet remains undone;
> Something, uncompleted still,
> Waits the rising of the sun."

Look at the birds—any idlers here? the fishes—any idlers there? Lift your eyes to the starry heavens, the planetary systems, worlds on worlds flying through infinite space—any idlers or dozers up there? Look at the skipping, dancing animalculæ, millions on millions, before the setting sun—any idlers here, dosers or sleepers? Behold, nature dressed in living green—waving fields, beautiful landscapes, fruits and flowers—any idlers, dozers, or loungers—seen or heard of here?

Everything in nature and grace are active, full of life and motion, on the wing. The sun, the moon, the sparkling heavens, the birds, the floods, the rippling brooks and flowing founts; the birds warble on every tree in ecstacy of joy; the tiny flower, hidden from all eyes, sends forth its fragrance of full happiness; the mountain-stream dashes along with a sparkle and murmur of pure delight. The object of their creation is accomplished, and their life gushes forth in harmonic work. O plant! O stream! worthy of admiration to the wretched idler!

Idleness is the bane, the moth, the gangrene, the curse of life.

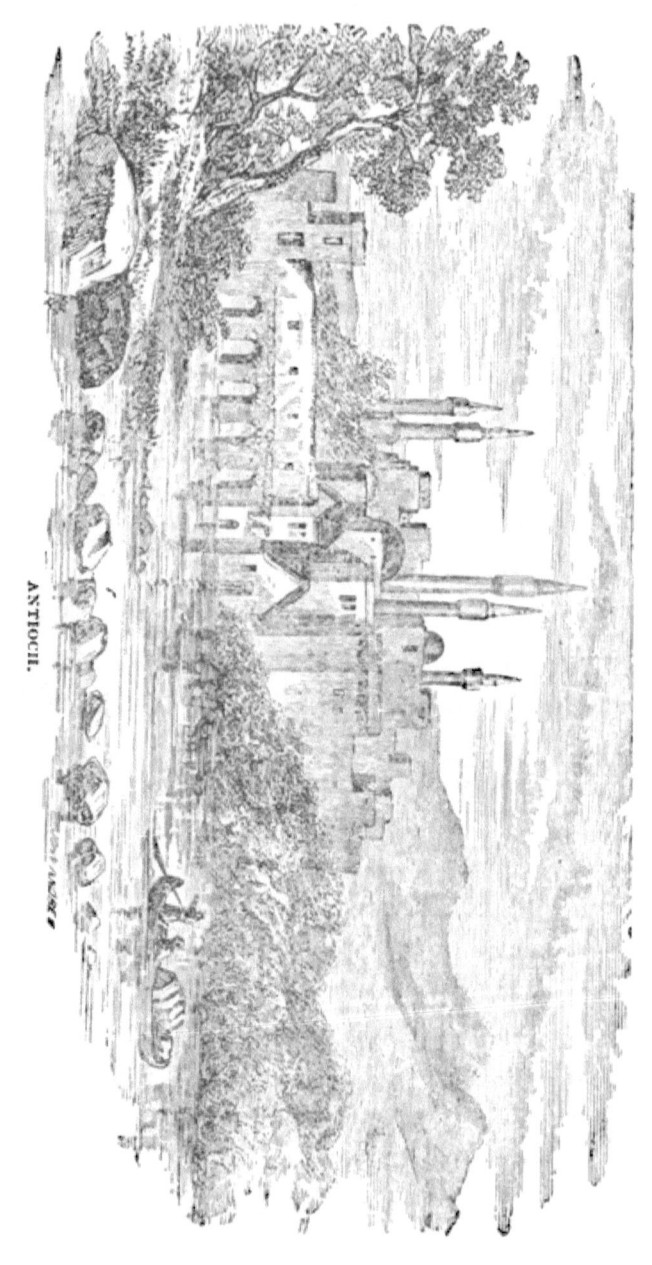

ANTIOCH.

Here Paul and Barnabas preached with great success. "And it came to pass that a whole year they assembled themselves with the Church, and taught much people. And the disciples were called Christians first in Antioch." *Acts.* xi. 26.

SWORDS AND FIRES—FIRES AND SWORDS;

—OR—

Gospel-fire—Fire of the Gospel.

GOSPEL-FIRE should be first, midst, last, *always* in all our religious publications—books, tracts, and periodicals—fire on fire!

Parents and teachers need Gospel-fire, blazing out. Little folks love fire, and will have it. Ministers and editors need fire, sparkling, soul-kindling, and should have it. What! pray, preach, write, without this heavenly Gospel-fire! No marvel we have chaff instead of wheat—cockle instead of barley—dross instead of gold—death instead of life, damnation instead of salvation. Live and breathe without this fire pentecostal in families, schools, pulpits, chairs, editorial, we die the death!

The Waldenses had this fire, wrote it out, preached it out, sung it out, lived it out. Where did they get it? From licentious poets, novels and romances, fictitious tales? or from the Bible—holy inspiration? Their souls were alive in God.*

The holy prophets had fire—fire on fire—blazing out. Where did they get it? From the Bible? Yes; from the Bible. John the Baptist had *fire*, holy fire; Paul had fire,

---

* The more fire, the more love, the more resolutely we fight against sin. It is love kindles fire, and fire kindles love—fire on fire! Without love no holy fire, no true Bible reform. The Lord give us more of it, a thousand fold!

> " Oh! for this love let rocks and hills
> Their lasting silence break;
> And all harmonious human tongues
> The Saviour's praises speak."

Peter, James, and John, pentecostal, baptismal—fire on fire—blazing out. Where did they get it? From the Bible? Yes; from the Bible. Luther had fire, Wesley had fire, Bunyan had fire—fire on fire—blazing out—Edwards had fire, Whitefield had fire, the Tenants had fire, Payson had fire, James B. Taylor had fire—fire on fire—blazing out.

Where did all these Gospel firebrands get their fire—fire on fire? From the Bible? Yes; from the Bible. Oh for this fire—fire on fire! "Man in the pulpit," the editorial chair, will you have this fire—fire on fire—blazing out? Go to the Bible, read the Bible, pray it out, search it out, live it out.

> "Hail! sacred truth, whose piercing rays
>   Dispel the shades of night;
> Diffusing o'er a ruined world
>   The healing beams of light."

Fire and sword, sword and fire, go hand in hand, inseparably. No fire no sword, no sword no fire. The fire is dependent on the sword and the sword on the fire. "The sword of the Spirit, which is the word of God."—Eph. vi. 17. Oh for these heavenly fires—blazing out—swords on swords; swords that cut, fires that burn—Gospel fires!

> "Oh, for the living flame,
>   From His own altar brought,
> To touch our lips, our souls inspire,
>   And wing to Heaven our thought!"

Friend, is your soul thus on fire? kindled to a holy flame, while meditating and conversing about God, his Son, his Word, the home of the weary, the heavy laden, the rest of God's people? Is the subject of religion your chief delight, always, everywhere?

DAMASCUS! HERE IT IS:

ONE of the most ancient and celebrated cities of Asia, and subsisted at the time of Abraham. Gen. xv. 2. One of the streets is called Strait. Acts, ix. 12. Paul was on his way to this city when he was struck down by the Holy Spirit of the Lord Jesus, saying: "Saul, Saul, why persecutest thou me? It is hard for thee to kick against the pricks." Acts, xxvi, 12, 13, 14.

THE BIBLE IN HOUSEHOLD DUTY—THE FAMILY CIRCLE.

"This Book of books I'd rather own
    Than all the gold or gems
That e'er in monarchs' coffers shone—
    Than all their diadems:
Nay, were the seas one chrysolite,
    The earth a golden ball,
And diadems all the stars of night,
    This book were worth them all.

"Yes, yes, this blessed book is worth
    All else to mortals given;
For what are all the joys of earth
    Compared to joys of heaven?
This is the guide our Father gave
    To lead to realms of day—
A *star* whose lustre gilds the grave—
    'The light, the life, the way.'"

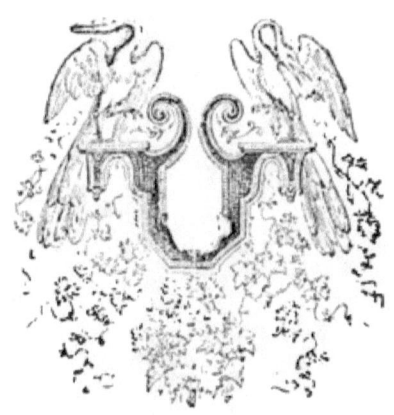

THE BIBLE AND SABBATH SCHOOL TEACHERS.

"Oh speed thee, Christian, on thy way,
 And to thy armor cling;
With girded loins the call obey
 That grace and mercy bring."

OUR *text-book*, the basis of all our attempts to instruct the rising age committed to our care, should be the *Bible*. This book, of all others, is the most lastingly interesting to children. Were it not the depository of *all-saving truth*, still there would be no book to compare with it in power to arrest and retain the attention of the young.

A very interesting and pious writer of the Sunday School Union remarks thus:

"Every Sunday-school teacher, however unlearned in the knowledge of this world, should be well versed in Scripture truth, and be a careful student of his Bible. 'To the law and the testimony' should be his appeal for the truth of every sentiment.'"

THE VERSE-A-DAY SYSTEM. THE LITTLE ONES AT IT.

"Give us this day our daily bread."
"Bread of our souls! whereon we feed;
True manna from on high!"

LITTLE folks, do you commit a verse from the Holy Book daily; repeat it likewise at the table spread with heaven's bounties? How many verses will this be in one year? Three hundred and sixty-five? Yes, young friends, three hundred and sixty-five precious texts from the Sacred Volume, worth more to you, if hid in the heart, than so many gold eagles. Parents, what think you of this system? The responsibility of its success rests on you.

Says the Psalmist: "Thy word have I hid in my heart, that I sin not against thee."

Is this little Mary?

If not, who else can it be? And what is she presenting to dear mamma, smilingly? Guess? No, you needn't.

> "There's nothing lost. The tiniest flower
> That grows within the darkest vale,
> And, like the balm affection brings,
> 'Twill scatter gladness round her head."

This precious little one is now in her fifth year, gentle as a lamb, sweet and smiling. Her mother talks with her frequently about the Lord Jesus—what he has done and is now doing to save everybody that will be saved. On these solemn occasions little Mary is wide awake—all eyes and ears. Every syllable is grasped eagerly. Her godly mother has cheering hopes of her being a Christian, for she is kind, loving, affectionate, obedient, often saying " Mamma, you're tired, I know you are—let me please baby awhile, and help you do this and that." She tries to make every one happy as she is, and always ready to do kind acts, and not tell of them ; never seeming proud of anything she does. These verses she has committed carefully :

> " Not mighty deeds make up the sum
> Of happiness below,
> But little acts of kindness,
> Which any child may show."

The tree is known by its fruit. A good little girl, out of the good treasure of her heart, bringeth forth good things. One day little Mary came to her mother joyfully and said :

"Mamma, if Jesus were here, might I run right into his arms, and hug him, as I do you ?"

" Why do you ask, dear ?" said her mother.

"Because, mamma, I *feel* just as if I wanted to, he is so good."

Then her mother replied, "Yes, my dear, I think you might ; for, when he was on earth, he took little children in his arms ; and they were just such children, too, as now live in the world. Yes, you can go to him, and speak to him, whenever you wish, just as if you knew he was here by your side. Indeed, he *is* here ; only we cannot see him."

Her mother is quite sure this loving, kind, obedient child is one of those little ones whom Jesus calls " His lambs."

We see what Gospel training will do—what an unspeakable blessing a pious, faithful mother is!—the greatest of all earthly blessings. However unseen may be the results of her labors, those labors never are without blessed results in the case of every one of her children.

The influence she exerts is the most excellent known on earth. Children brought up by a godly mother—who knows her duty and does it—who doubts their salvation? She makes the earliest, the deepest, and the most lasting impressions on their hearts. In their minds, religion is associated with all that is kind, winning, and pleasant in home-life. They grow up with reverence for the Bible, the house of God, and the ministers of Christ. They do not remember when first they heard the name of Jesus, or bowed their knees in prayer, or lisped the praises of God. They are instructed to hate and shun vice, and the seductions to it, and to admire and practice virtue. Having been trained up in the way they should go, when they become old they will not depart from it.

How great is their responsibility! God has committed to them the salvation of their own offspring. To secure the faithful discharge of the trust, he has planted in the maternal heart an affection which no toil, care, or sacrifice can exhaust. No mother who studies her responsibility or the interests of her children, can consent to be without the sustaining and guiding influence of Divine grace.

Fashion kills more women than toil and sorrow. Obedience to fashion is a greater transgression of the law of woman's nature, a greater injury to her physical constitution, than the hardships of poverty and neglect.

Here they are with Bible in hand.

Little Mary takes the lowest seat. All ears! Not a word of salvation slips out without her notice. This searching the Scriptures is a daily business. Happy family! a second Paradise!

Here lies the secret of all successful family discipline of "rearing the tender thought."

> "Oh, give me the pious and happy home,
> Where the bond that unites is love,
> Where the will of the Holy One is done,
> And his blessing sought from above."

Fiery Serpents.

"And the Lord sent fiery serpents among the people, and they bit the people, and much people of Israel died."—*Numbers* xxi. 6.

SEE how God deals with folks that murmur. But there are other serpents more fearful and terrible than these fiery flying serpents that bit to death so many of the children of Israel for their wicked murmurings. We mean the serpents in the form of books and papers, sent forth by some calling themselves Christians. Multitudes are dying this very day from the biting and stinging of these vile reptiles. Tell these professed disciples of the Lord Jesus to stop sending these coiled serpents all abroad, that poison the souls of so many little folks, will they do it? Try and see.

But is there no cure for these serpent bites? Nothing, save the blood of the Lamb.

"As Moses lifted up the serpent in the wilderness, even so must the Son of man be lifted up: That whosoever believeth in him should not perish, but have eternal life."—*John* iii. 14, 15.

MANNER OF EXPRESSING CIVILITY, OR POLITENESS IN ANCIENT TIMES. (*See next page.*)

LYING AND MAKING LIARS.

"A lie, how base! how mean! offspring of selfishness—
A lover of darkness, and hater of light."

"A lying tongue is but for a moment."—*Prov.* xii. 19.

CONVERSATION between Mr. Standfast and Mr. Whiffler.—(No. 1.)

Mr. Standfast. "Walk in, sir, walk in—take a seat. Glad to meet you. You're the man I've long desired to see. Your name is Whiffler?"

W. "I'm not ashamed to own it, sir."

S. "I've a word of exhortation for you."

W. "Speak on, Mr. Standfast."

S. "If report speaks truth, you're a liar, Mr. Whiffler, barefaced!"

W. "What do you mean? an insult?"

S. "I'm not double-tongued or double-faced like you; I mean what I say. You're a liar! you write lies, publish lies, sell lies, read lies, and of course you tell lies! You're a double, treble, quadruple liar—a bundle of lies—a liar from head to foot, from top to bottom! Your whole contour, every look, every moving muscle, indicates falsehood or lying. Lying is your trade!"

W. "You call novels lies, do you?"

S. "Novels are lies—and lies are novels. 'A novel,' says Webster, 'is a fictitious tale.' And fiction is falsehood—a lie! Therefore, Mr. Whiffler, take pen in hand, and write opposite your name in capitals, 'LIAR!' Every one is a liar that writes lies, sells lies, or puffs lies, whether in the church or out of it—in the pulpit or out of it—in the editorial chair or out of it! Now, Mr. Whiffler, you see clearly without spectacles to what class you belong, the truthful or the lying—whether you are on the Lord's side or the devil's?

"Do you love truth, talk it, write it, preach it, send it forth to bless the world, or do you take sides with the father of liars—write lies, preach lies, publish lies, send them forth to curse the world? To one of these classes you surely belong. 'No man can serve two masters.' 'He that is not with me is against me; and he that gathereth not with me scattereth abroad.'—Math. xii. 30. Some parents put lies in the hands of their children; they tell us their sons and daughters have no taste or relish for truth, historical, scientific, the Bible, the solid, the virtuous and the pure, that edifies, enlightens the mind and purifies the heart; so, forsooth, they place a lie in their hands—a book or periodical, made up more or less of lies, from the father of liars. And thus children, being fed or nourished on lies, mentally become liars very early—grow up to manhood on lies, become rooted and grounded in lies! When children have once acquired a habit of lying or telling lies, how is this habit to be eradicated? Nothing is so difficult to be removed from a child as lying or telling lies. 'Can the Ethiopian change his skin, or the leopard his spots?' Nothing but grace, superabounding, Almighty, will cure man, woman or child of lying or telling lies when once the habit is formed.

"Lying in families and communities increases, just in proportion as you, Mr. Whiffler, and other liars, continue to write, puff and sell lies—novels, romances, fictitious tales! *What* a curse—*what* a curse!

"Lies beget lies. One liar makes other liars—not a few. The man that writes lies, preaches lies, publishes lies, puffs lies—sells and reads lies. What next? Steal, rob, cut your throat? Look out! The man that tells lies—makes a business of it, as you do—is he any too good to steal or rob?"

Merchants, have you liars in your employ! novel-reading clerks? *Beware!*—look well to your safes.

Young men that have their minds vitiated, and their moral sensibilities perverted by reading lies, will not endeavor to procure wealth in the ordinary way, by labor and patience; this is too slow a process to satisfy the fevered excited mind. Fortune must be made at once. It drives young men to the gambling-table, the theatre, the intoxicating bowl, and to the house of ill-fame. Novels are liars! Lying and thieving go hand in hand. And what sin meaner, more despicable, hateful, devilish, than the one now under consideration?

Barnum, P. T., with all his humbuggery, witchcraft, and devilisms, whom you commend to the public, bid "God speed," is not to be compared for mischief, ruin, desolation and damnation, with what Satan is doing through the medium of a corrupt press. Religious novels, "coiled serpents," mixed publications, partly good, partly evil, sugared pills—the devil's baits—which you, Mr. Whiffler, are endorsing, clasping to your bosom. These serpents bite you, sting you to death, by and by! "With what measure ye meet it shall be measured to you again."

W. "Are you not aware, Mr. Standfast, that the best literature in the market, the most exquisitely fascinating and sparkling, takes the form of stories, tales or novels? By decrying these you defeat the very thing you are aiming at."

S. "That is, there are not specimens of fine writing, beautiful, majestic, heavenly, extant, without resorting to story-telling, liars, and writers of lies! This smells pretty strong of brimstone! These tales or religious novels, eulogized by you and sent forth to curse the world, may not all of them contain anything coarse, gross or vulgar; far better if they did. Evil that comes in the form of grossness or vulgarity, is not so dangerous as that which comes veiled in gracefulness and exquisite sentiment. Subjects which are better not touched upon at all, are discussed, examined, and exhibited in all the most seductive forms of imagery. Parents would be shocked to see a son in a fit of intoxication; and yet, I solemnly aver, it would be better to see a son reel through the streets, in a fit of drunkenness, than to see the delicacy of a lovely daughter's mind injured, and her imagination inflamed with false fire! Twenty-four hours will terminate the evil in the one case, but twenty-four years will not exhaust the effects of the other. You must seek the consequences at the end of very many years. 'Behold, how great a matter a little fire kindleth.' 'Keep thy heart with all diligence, for out of it are the issues of life.'— *Prov.* iv. 23.

"The first step in a downward course should be shunned as a deadly serpent! None become abandoned at once: we cannot have too clear an idea of the *danger* of the 'first steps' in any sinful career.

"Truths of the most important character, of life, science, art, geography, history, ethics, and religion, can be set forth in a style that will interest while it instructs, and will be even more fascinating to young minds than the sensational stories and sugar-coated nonsense now placed in their hands by you and others.

"Children should be encouraged to read works written for their seniors. Youths of ten or twelve years old would get far more help and intellectual health and vigor from reading histories, biographies, books of travel, art, and even of sciences, than almost any juvenile works. But the Bible first, midst, last, always.

"Yet after all, you tell me and the public brazen facedly that we are dependent on novel-scribblers—writers of lies—for the best and finest specimens of human composition! Shameful! This assertion of yours is a libel! What softer name give it? The truth is well known, that the style of writing of the very best of these novelists, is generally below mediocrity—weak, puerile, silly, uncouth, unchaste, and very often positively gross, vulgar. This you see in most of the stories or tales inserted in religious weeklies and monthlies. How otherwise, penned as they are under the influence of the satanics?"

W. "Your assertions are broad and sweeping. Will you not, *do* you not admit of exceptions, Mr. Standfast?"

S. "Satan does, in very deed, *sometimes* help his faithful servants marvelously in composing, especially those given *exclusively* to his service."

"A novel was a book,
Three volum'd, and once read; and oft crammed!
Of poisonous error, blackening every page;
And oftener still, of trifling, second-hand,
Remarkable and old, diseased and putrid thought,
And miserable incident, at war
With nature, with itself and truth at war;
Yet charming still the greedy reader on,
Till done—he tried to recollect his thought,
And nothing found but dreaming emptiness."

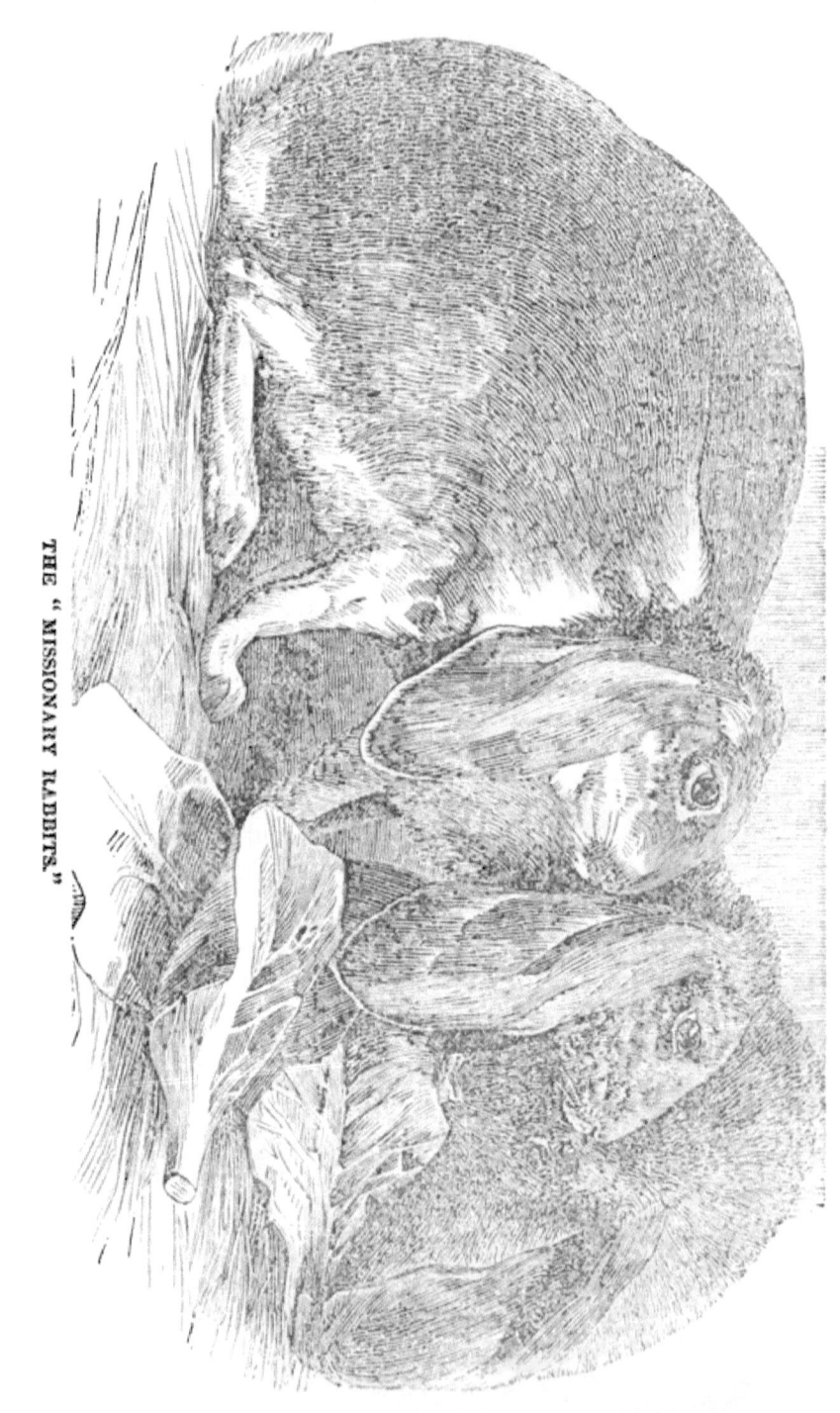

THE "MISSIONARY RABBITS."

This is Naaman, the Leper.

But who is Naaman, and what was he? Turn to 2d Kings, chap. 5, and the secret is disclosed. Elisha said to Naaman, "Go and wash in Jordan seven times, and thy flesh shall come again to thee, and thou shalt be clean." But who told Naaman that Elisha could cure sick folks? A little captive girl! Hark! "And she said unto her mistress, Would God my lord *were* with the Prophet that *is* in Samaria, for he would recover him of his leprosy."—2 *Kings* v. 3.

You see what little hearts of love can do, the Lord helping—not bigger than little Mary—by dropping kind words. Every little boy and girl born from above, full of faith and the Holy Spirit, as all little folks should be, will drop kind words—they can't help it! And what more beautiful, praiseworthy?

"Little children, Jesus loves you,
  He invites you to his arms;
To his breast he waits to fold you,
  There to shield you from alarms."

Abraham and Isaac.

Who are these walking up hill briskly? Abraham and Isaac! Turn to Gen. 22, and you will see how it is—who it is. They are on the way to Mount Moriah. Isaac is to be offered for a burnt sacrifice. God told Abraham to do this, and that was sufficient. Whatever God told him to do, whether pleasant or unpleasant, for life or for death—what now, stop? parley, hesitate, question proprieties? Not a *breath* of it; the very *instant* duty was plain—staring him full in the face—he was off in the twinkling of an eye. His invariable motto was: "*Speak, Lord, for thy servant heareth.*" Fear consequences? Indeed what had Abraham to think, say or do about consequences? He knew full well God takes care of consequences. Duty is ours, consequences or results God's. "*Go forward.*" Why was this blessed patriarch called the father of the faithful?

1. Because he was strong in faith, giving glory to God. His faith was not a dead faith, without works. It was faith and do, do and faith, but faith first—*all the time*—and works followed *instantly*, after faith! "Faith wrought with his works, and by works was faith made perfect. And the Scripture was fulfilled which saith, Abraham believed God,

and it was imputed unto him for righteousness : and he was called the Friend of God. Ye see then how that by works a man is justified, and not by faith only. But wilt thou know, O vain man, that faith without works is dead ?"— *James* xx. 23.

2. Abraham was called the father of the faithful, because of his faithfulness in household duty. Here, everything was clock work. No family in the whole region was more orderly or better disciplined. " I know him," saith the Lord, " that he will command his children, and his household after him, and they shall keep the way of the Lord, to do justice and judgment, that the Lord may bring upon Abraham that which he hath spoken of him."—*Gen.* xvii. 19. You see he resorted both to persuasive and coercive measures. When mildness failed, gentleness, sweet as heaven—what then ? let things slide ? Satan rule the day ? yield to false tenderness, sickly charity, as most parents do ? Spare the rod, spoil the child ! Had Abraham thus healed slightly, daubed with untempered mortar, " conferred with flesh and blood ;" or, like Eli, suffered the inmates of his house to do vile things, and restrained them not—would he have been highly honored as he was ?

" Them that honor me, I will honor ; and they that despise me shall be lightly esteemed." 1 Saml. ii. 30.

What sin greater, what more God-dishonoring, than the neglect to train our children in the " way they should go," or to " bring them up in the nurture and admonition of the Lord ?"

" Oh, it is a sadd'ning sight,
    When children go astray,
Forsaking what is good and right,
    To walk in Satan's way."

"Mark the Perfect Man and Behold the Upright
for the end of that Man
is
PEACE."

"LET ME DIE THE DEATH OF THE RIGHTEOUS."

LYING AND MAKING LIARS.

Conversation between Mr. STANDFAST *and* Mr. WHIFFLER.
(No. 2.)

"They flattered him with their mouth, and they lied unto him with their tongues."—*Psalms* lxxviii. 36.

W. "WHAT shall we do, then, Mr. Standfast, if we take away the story? The appetite is not satisfied. The mind is left empty, swept, and garnished, and for one story cast out by parental authority, seven others worse than the first will creep in. We can only defeat bad stories by good ones."

S. "That is, don't feed children on bad lies but on good lies—not on black lies but white lies! See the cloven foot, do you, Mr. Whiffler? Could a cunning, crafty, devilish devil do up anything better to his liking to ruin the souls of little folks? This smells stronger of brimstone than anything yet! What will not the old serpent do next?

"Here's the snake in the grass, the 'serpent coiled.' Because children in their natural state, at enmity against God, in the gall of bitterness and bonds of iniquity, crave lies, the food of Satan, you fill them to the full of this food, gratify their depraved appetites to surfeiting. It's natural for the carnal heart to crave lies, while the heart is in the possession of the father of lies. Why not feed the natural or carnal heart of your little ones on other things besides novels of a carnal nature, earthly, sensual, devilish? When the mind is empty, swept and garnished, what do you do? fill it with truth, the food of heaven, the bread of eternal life, as God requires? Nay, 'but with lies, the food of

Satan, and these lies enter in and dwell there, and the last state of your children is worse than the first.' (See Math. xii. 34, 44, 45.) Feed your offspring on good lies, and how long ere the carnal appetite hankers after the bad ones? Feed them on white lies, and how long ere they crave the black ones? Novels are lies, Webster says so, 'fictitious tales,' 'counterfeits,' 'false,' 'not genuine.'

"You know, or ought to know, Mr. Whiffler, that the thirst for novel-reading is cultivated by novel-reading; or that reading fiction, with a little sprinkling of religion, prepares children to love to read fiction, though it may have a sprinkling of irreligion.

"There is that in the character of fictitious writings, properly called novels, whether the subject be secular or religious, which forms a taste different from historical, didactic, or any of the other classes of writing, and this taste is as readily formed by holding the child upon religious novels in his younger years, as if he were supplied with secular novels.

"Thus the child is piously trained to seek his gratifications of mind amid elements of grossest corruption. If the enemy of all good should set himself to devise a scheme to take children out of religious families, and from them to rear a supply of victims of this form of ruin, he could, with all his cunning, hardly contrive a better way to avoid giving alarm and to secure the result. 'Stolen waters are sweet, and bread eaten in secret is pleasant. But he knoweth not the dead are there; and that her guests are in the depths of hell.'—*Prov.* ix. 17, 18.

"In the Sabbath-school library, and in the books purchased for children, we furnish them with the means of cultivating a taste for novel-reading, and so prepare them greedily to devour whatever fictitious trash may fall in their way, and then waste our breath in deploring their exposure to a corrupt literature.

"Are your children liars, fond of reading lies, fictitious writings, silly tales or stories—'The Little Corporal,' 'Our Young Folks,' and the like? Not if you have obeyed God in training them 'in the way they should go.' Whenever and wherever you see any one, old or young, eager after sickly, simpering, tickle, fancy publications, soulless and Christless as the barren fig tree, take it for granted there has been sad omission in family duty. Grace in the soul, heaven-born, is the safeguard, the cureall! Plant grace, then, deep down—water it with prayer constantly, as the dew of heaven, and Satan is cast out, finds no lodgment, no disposition or relish remaining for lying, reading lies, or telling lies.

> ''Tis truth that binds, and truth makes free,
> And sets the soul at liberty
> From sin and Satan's heavy chain,
> And then within the heart doth reign.

> 'They have a freedom then, indeed,
> That doth all freedom else exceed.'

"The truth of God—

> 'Where'er it enters in,
>   Is sharper than a two-edged sword,
>   To slay the man of sin.'

'Thy word have I hid in my heart,' says the Psalmist, 'that I might not sin against thee.'

"When once the truths of the Bible have taken firm root in the heart, and become more precious than gold, sweeter also than honey and the honey-comb, these sugar-coated poisons, snakes in the grass, satanic transformations—the popular periodicals of the day, the fashion-plate magazines and comicals, the multitudinous mixed-up thing of the bitter and the sweet, God and Mammon, Christ and Belial appear disgusting and heart-sickening. 'If any man be in Christ, he is a new creature; old things are passed away: behold all things are become new.'—2 Cor. v. 17. What avails a religion that does not cast out Satan and let in Christ? To bring up children in the nurture and admonition of the Lord, is our blessed privilege. Besides, God commands it— Eph. vi. 4. See also Deut. vi. 6–9, Prov. xxii. 6.

"What a sad, lamentable, soul-ruinous error do parents and teachers, having the charge of children and youth, fall into, when, to make home attractive, happy and joyful, they introduce trifling amusements—nonsensical, doll-baby publications, heart-sickening! *What!* is there not truth enough in all the world, aside from holy revelation, on which to nourish your little ones, mentally and spiritually, without feeding them on lies, the food of Satan?

> 'Fill first the bushel with the wheat,
>   With wisdom—food for souls to eat;
> Then chaff, the fiction of the day,
>   Will find no place, and blow away.'

"You see now what you are doing, Mr. Whiffler? Instead of obeying God in family discipline, taking your little ones to Christ forthwith, placing them in the arms of redeeming, sanctifying mercy, you take an opposite course, and place them *directly* on the lap of Satan, dandle them on his knees! Wicked man!"

It's Spring-time here, bright and smiling.

HERE's a farmer resting in the shade. Country folks are the happiest of the happy, or should be. Spring prefigures childhood, and youth betokens mercy, love and salvation. Childhood is, indeed, the spring-time of the year, the time for the singing of birds, the lambs to skip, the mountains and the hills to break forth in joyful praise, and the trees of the forest to clap their hands. "Out of the mouths of babes and sucklings thou hast ordained strength."

GATHERING NUTS.

SEE that little girl holding her hat for the nuts as her brother gathers them? Is she not beautiful? Does not her whole countenance indicate modesty and purity.

GATHERING FLOWERS.

"O sweet soul'd flowers with robes so bright,
  Fair guests of Eden's birth,
In cheerful characters of light,
What lines of love divine ye write,
  Upon the troubled earth."

Young friends, whenever you want fruits or flowers, be *sure* to ask permission of the owner. Never enter an orchard or flower garden unless you are first invited to do so.

These sprightly little folks represented in the engraving are innocent, harmless as doves—their every look indicates this.

Yet there are some boys and girls, we regret to say, who take great liberties, do things they ought not. Others, who have no fear of God before their eyes, go so far as to pluck fruits and flowers secretly, and do other very wicked things. Stealing is stealing, theft is theft, robbery is robbery, in little things and great things. A boy or girl who will steal an apple, a pear, or bouquet, will, doubtless, by-and-by, steal other things and greater things. Beware, little folks and great folks. "Thou shalt not steal," saith the holy one. "Be sure your sin will find you out."

> "On the goods that are not thine,
>   Do not dare to lay thy finger:
> On thy neighbor's better things
>   Let no wistful glances linger.
>
> "Pilfer not the smallest thing,
>   Touch it not, howe'er thou need it;
> Though the owner have enough,
>   Though he know it not nor heed it."

It is with health as with property; we rarely value it or know how best to use or to take care of it till it is gone.

THE GARDENERS RESTING IN THE SHADE.

"Out-door employment gives pleasure and gain,
And makes us our troubles forget;
For those who work hard have no time to complain,
And it's better to labor than fret."

BIRDY, BIRDY, PRETTY BIRDY—AIN'T IT BEAUTIFUL!

"Little birds sleep sweetly
In their soft round nests,
Crouching in the cover
Of their mother's breast."

Don't hurt the sweet, beautiful songsters, little folks, not a hair of their heads, nor their nests or little ones; it would be cruelly wicked to do so. Hark! how sweetly they sing! Sing praises? Yes, they do. Turn to the one hundred and forty-eighth Psalm and see how everything above and everything below, animate and inanimate, praise the Lord, and the birds among the rest.

Learn a lesson from these merry, melodious songsters? Certainly we can.

"We learn a lesson from the birds
Of life from day to day—
The things we set our hearts upon,
Oft quickly pass away!"

DON'T SHOOT THE BIRDS.

"Don't shoot the birds, the warbling birds,
   That cheer you with their song,
That fill the air with melodies,
   A bright and happy throng;
That carol forth their native lays
   From shrub and lofty limb,
And gaily sing their tuneful strains
   From morn till evening dim.
Don't shoot the birds, the joyous birds,
   That charm the traveler's way."

How thankful should we be that God has given us the dear birds to be our fellow-laborers and comforters, and the laborer is surely worthy of his hire. Why grudge him his pay? Why cheat him of his spring and summer work? Soon we shall see them very busy. Many have already begun.

LYING AND MAKING LIARS.

Conversation between Mr. STANDFAST *and* Mr. WHIFFLER.
(No. 3.)

"I will be a lying spirit in the mouth of all his prophets."—1 Kings xxii. 22.

S. "THESE arguments you offer for publishing—white lies to keep out the black ones—or to serve the devil a little to keep from serving him *a great deal*—are borrowed from that popularity seeking, novel sheet, 'The Hearth and Home!'"

W. "It's puffed and puffed by religious editors throughout the land, say what you will, Mr. Standfast."

S. "Of course. The time was when the earth helped the woman; but the tables are turned; now the woman helps the earth."—Rev. xii. 17.

W. "You place in the same category these puffers of lies, as you call them, with the writers of these lies—is this your logic?"

S. "The partaker is as bad as the thief. One writes lies for money, the other puffs lies for money."

W. "Money, you say, is the ultimatum?"

S. "Whoever penned a novel, romance, or silly tale, religious or otherwise, save on the idea of gain—filthy lucre, Achan's 'accursed thing'—Balaam's 'accursed thing'—Simon, the Sorcerer's 'accursed thing!' Would Beecher have stuck his nose in the dirt, lighted and snuffed Satan's candle, save for the $30,000—Achan's gold-wedge, and the cash incomes ever since from the same source and from the same motives? 'There is an accursed thing in the midst of thee, O Israel: thou canst not stand before thine enemies, until ye take away the accursed thing from among you.'—Josh. vii. 13."

W. "You link Beecher with the whole *batch* of religious novel-writers—the white-lying folks?"

S. "And *you* among the rest, Mr. Whiffler, save you stop lying and whiffling!"

W. "Did not our Saviour resort to fiction in illustrating truths? the good John Bunyan also, and many others?"

S. "The cloven foot sticking out again—another apology for clasping the old serpent to your bosom for the accursed lust of 'ill-gotten gain.' It's devilish, as devilish can be! Dr. W. H. Vandoren, a good Presbyterian brother in the ministry, calls this blasphemy! Hear him :—'We need not add,' says he, 'that when persons attempt to sustain religious novels by the quoting of Parables and Pilgrim's Progress, it seems to us simple blasphemy. Who ever was led by Pilgrim's Progress to dramatize it for the stage like Norwood or Uncle Tom's Cabin? It is a fact that religious novels excite a taste for the theatre, and soon the gate is opened wide which leads to ruin here, and ruin eternal!' Because the godly Bunyan and other devoted servants of Christ wrote allegorically the most blessed, spiritual, heavenly things, for the soul's salvation—and because our blessed Lord and Saviour illustrated, by parables, truths most glowing, sacred, solemn, and heavenly—you and other writers and puffers of religious lies excuse yourselves for taking the very Satan himself into your laps, and dandling him upon your knees!

'Torture the pages of the hallowed Bible
To sanction crime, and robbery, and blood.'

LYING AND MAKING LIARS. 57

"'The N. Y. Daily Witness' makes this silly apology for filling up a large portion of his sheet with tales, and stories insipid, frothy, puerile, heart-sickening! Thus occupying space with things light, trifling and profitless, that should be filled with golden gems—'apples of gold'—things beautiful, heavenly, divine! Shameful! The editor tells us 'that nothing offensive to purity and religion shall find a place in his paper.' *False!* diametrically. Nearly one-fourth of his regular issues had better be consigned to the flames! Very many of the Lord's people would thank him heartily for so doing. A beloved, intelligent, influential, godly woman said to us over and over, week in, week out: 'Do, for heaven's sake, write to the editor of the "N. Y. Daily Witness," to stop his silly tales, and fill the space thereof with something good, useful, edifying, solid and pure, that will minister grace, life, salvation! Say to him: "We are heart-sick of this religious nonsense. If the Lord be God, serve him; if Baal or the devil, take him."'

"'The Christian World,' published at No. 47 Bible House, I suppose makes the same plea for setting the whole community in a blaze, pergatorial! This Monthly, that should be pure as heaven can make it, occupies frequently some two or three pages in puffing, not only white lies, but of what the godly bishop, Littlejohn, of the Episcopalian order, says: 'The writers and publishers of such stuff are the enemies of public peace and morals, and the sacred ties of society and the purity of home plead against them.'

"Who first originated falsehood or fiction? And what the cost to our first parents for believing a lie from the father of lies? The devil deceived our mother Eve. How? By a tale, a story, a lie—just what you are doing! You're doing the devil's work! You're a liar, and a liar maker! And how many, think you, of these liars made by you will accompany you down to the lowest depths of hell? Why not as soon manufacture and sell grog and tobacco? Which do you suppose are taking more souls to the regions of death and damnation, intoxicating drink, and the vile, poisonous 'Indian weed,' or novels, romances, and fictitious tales?*

"Now to calm or hush a guilty, disturbed conscience, you have the impudent assurance to tell me that Bunyan, that holy man of God, bowed the knee to this Baal! Shameful! blasphemy! When and where did Bunyan's allegory, or the allegorical writings of any holy man of God, ever make fools, simpletons and dunces—liars and thieves—of little folks and great folks? When did they ever lead to frivolity, lightness of speech, senseless gabble, foolish talking and jesting—the fool's laughter, 'like the crackling of thorns under a pot,' as we see and hear in most novel writers, puffers and readers, in the pulpit and out of it?

"When did the writings of Bunyan, and other holy writers allegorical, ever lead to pride, worldly conformity in dress, folly-fashion, the pleasures of sense, carnality, games of chance, billiards, the card-table, the theatre, the opera, to elopements, abductions, seduction, and 'Free-

---

* It is still a question unsolved which of the two will land more souls in perdition rum and tobacco, or novels and romances, written and sent forth by persons calling themselves disciples of the Lord Jesus!

Mrs. Swisshelm, in her *Saturday Visitor*, declared unhesitatingly that the whole *batch* of fashion-plate Magazines, and other fictitious writings, spread more domestic misery and destruction over the human race than all the rum-sellers in the nation. "Yes," says she, "they instigate more murders than the tyranical bloody Nero!" The beloved Junson, and sister Vinton, Missionaries to Burmah, expressed similar sentiments, when on a visit to America.

loveism?' And last of all, the house of her whose steps take hold on hell?"

We see from the foregoing whence comes lies and lying, who are liars. Satan, as we have seen, is the author and instigator of all lying or falsehood, as he was a liar from the beginning, and the father of liars.

We see who are his most active helpers, chief agents indefatigable in the business of lying and making liars. These emissaries of his are doing what their "Father"—the "Father" of all liars—cannot do, if devilish enough to do it. Satan pen lies, set type for lies, publish and puff lies, mail and send them forth to curse the rising age—little folks and big! When? where? Not he. Who then is wicked enough to do this wicked thing if not Satan? Guess, friends. We speak advisedly what we know, see, and hear.

We see why children of religious parents grow up unconverted, hardened in sin, wreckless, disobedient, vagabonds! a curse to themselves, to their parents—to the world! How otherwise, if nourished up on lies? Dr. Arnold says:—"Childishness in boys even of good ability, seems to be a growing fault, and I do not know what to ascribe it to, except to the great number of exciting books of amusement. The habit is to the mind what indulgence in intoxicating drink is to the body. In both cases there is a constant craving for excitement, and for an excitement which unfits the faculties and draws away the affections from duty, from heaven and from God."

Address.... "**THE SWORD THAT CUTS,**"
303 West Twentieth St., New York.

The Baby Jesus, No. 1

"Jesus! the name to sinners dear,
The name to sinners given;
It scatters all our guilty fear,
And turns our hell to heaven."

A WORD to little Mary about this dear child, born of the Virgin Mary, holy, harmless, undefiled, separate from sin and sinners even while a babe. Was there ever such a child, so sweet, so innocent, so beautiful, so heavenly? Never; and there never will be.

When a little baby he was worshiped by men and angels. Turn, if you please, dear little niece, to the second chapter of Matthew, and you will see how the wise men from the east followed the star of Bethlehem till it came and stood over where the young child was. And where, think you, this precious little one from heaven was, when born? In a manger? Yes, he, who made all worlds, took his first lodgings in a manger.

The Wheat not Chaff—Truth not Fiction—Gold not Dross:
OR,
Education in Families and Schools on Bible Truths, and not on Fiction or Novels.

> " The Bible! the Bible! blest volume of truth,
> How sweetly it smiles on the season of youth!
> It bids us seek early the pearl of great price,
> Ere the heart is enslaved in the bondage of vice."

1. BECAUSE it is God's book—the Book of Books—the book above all books, the best of all books.

> " The Bible! in this book alone,
> We find God's holy will made known;
> And here his love to man is shown."

2. Because it is a fountain of purity, and all the streams issuing from this pure fountain must be pure. "The words of the Lord are pure words: as silver tried in the furnace of earth, purified seven times."—Psa. xii. 6. Every thing from a pure and holy God must be pure and holy.

> " Men's books with heaps of chaff are stored;
> God's book doth golden grains afford.
> Then leave the chaff, and spend thy pains
> In gathering up the golden grains."

3. The word of God is life, it is spirit, it is power; it convicts, converts, sanctifies, purifies—makes meet for heaven, for glory eternal.

4. The Bible should be made the text-book in all families and schools, because God has left us recorded examples of

the saving power of his word, in saving the rising age, even from infancy.

5. Another reason for taking the Bible for the text-book in the impartation of light and life to children and youth— it is a most beautiful, sublime, and perfect specimen of composition.

6. Again, the Bible should be the text-book or foundation of all intellectual and religious training, for wherever its blessed doctrines and precepts are embraced, treasured in the heart, and carried out practically in every-day life, there true grace prevails, true wisdom shines, and what things soever are true, honest, just, pure, lovely, and of good report.

7. The Bible should be made the text-book in our schools and families from the fact, the Bible, just now, is assailed by a most remarkable multiplicity and diversity of enemies.

8. Again, the Bible should be the first, midst, last, *always*, in educating the rising age ; for God Himself indicates the fact, gives line upon line, precept upon precept, here a little and there a little, from Genesis to Revelation.

9. Finally, the Bible should be the text-book, the first thing, and the last thing, in the cultivation of the youthful mind and heart, for by it we are to be judged at the final day. " He that rejecteth me, and receiveth not my words, hath one that judgeth him : the word that I have spoken, the same shall judge him in the last day."—John xii. 48.

The Bible is, beyond all controversy, the best book of education in the world. It is the best book for the formation of children's minds ; the best book for the acquisition and preservation of a pure idiomatic style in their native language ; the best book to promote and secure the purposes of family government ; the best book to make our children enlightened and good citizens of the Republic; the best book, in fine, to preserve them from all evil, and train them up in all good.

Our education needs a religious element; for it is not education alone that will save us; it will merely train a skilful race of gladiators for the arena of political strife. The only source of that element of safety is the word of God. And if you take the word of God from your common and public schools, you are teaching infidelity and practical atheism to the whole nation. You are filling the mind with elements that, without the safeguard of divine truth, are sure to become fiery, bitter, and poisonous.

In its general influence over the minds of our children and over the whole business of education, the Bible in our families and schools is invaluable.

> "The Bible! the Bible! we hail it with joy,
> Its truths and its glories our tongues shall employ:
> We'll sing of its triumphs, we'll tell of its worth,
> And send its glad tidings afar o'er the earth."

This is the word of everlasting life; this is the fountain from whence all thy comforts flow; this is the bread of life; this is the fortress of thy faith, the sword of the Spirit, thy buckler and defence.

Oh, meditate well herein; search, read, hear, mark, learn; so shalt thou find it heavenly manna to the soul.

This is the word of God; canst thou enough reverence it? canst thou enough esteem and delight in it?

Every line droppeth peace as the honey-comb; every page aboundeth with gladness and with good tidings, as the ocean is filled with water.

Little Mary reading with Mother.

WHAT book is this sweet little girl reading—a novel or story book? No. "The Bible?" Yes. She loves the Bible—it's her soul's delight! She can say, "O how I love thy law! it is my meditation all the day... How sweet are thy words to my taste! Yea, sweeter than honey to my mouth!"—Psa. cxix. 103. She feasts daily on this bread of heaven—angels' food! It's the first thing in the morning and the last in the evening. Retire to rest or wake in the morning without a lesson from this blessed Book of books? Sooner dispense with the food that nourishes her physical system—sooner lay aside her breakfast, dinner and supper! The Bible is first in the morning, the last in the evening. The first of all and the last of all is soul-food, spiritual, heavenly.

> "How pure the sacred word of truth,
> The blessed book to guide our youth,
> Given by our Father and our God,
> To guide to heaven through Jesus' blood!"

This lovely little Mary, you see in the picture, pouring

over the Word of life, was taught from early childhood to love and fear God from the sacred Scriptures, and like little Timothy, she became wise unto salvation when a *tiny* one! Blessed child! happy child!

Her godly parents would sooner place a biting serpent, a stinging adder in her hand, than a novel, romance, a tale—a silly, simpering catch-penny—godless, Christless, "Little Corporal," "Our Young Folks," or any one of the whole *batch* of Satan's *imps*, lauded to the skies by the religious press! These sugared pills, instead of leading children *to* God and *to* Christ, lead them *from* God and *from* Christ! While the Bible is a savor of life unto life, these "coiled serpents" are a savor of death unto death!

"There is a path that leads to God,
All others go astray."

The words of Christ are spirit—they are life—in the closet, in the family, in the hearts of parents and children! The Bible in the heart kills novels or lies, and novels or lies kill the Bible. Darkness and light, sin and holiness cannot coalesce: one is life, the other death; one is salvation, the other damnation!

Our fervent prayers, our concentrated efforts, are to lead parents and children to the Bible—to lay aside the chaff for the wheat!

"Bread of our souls! whereon we feed,
True manna from on high;
Our guide and chart, wherein we read
Of realms beyond the sky."

Parents, in educating your little ones, please keep your

eye fixed on little Mary.* See what Gospel training *can* do, *will* do, *should* do in every household. Begin with the Bible, continue with the Bible, and end with the Bible! Then will the morning stars again sing, and the sons of God again shout for joy over the earth, as they did when she rolled from the hands of her Maker, and man went forth formed in the Divine image.

The Bible is the grand guide-board to eternity. It tells you which way to travel; it warns you against by-paths and wrong roads, against false guides, pits, traps, slippery places and every other danger. If you follow its advice, it will conduct you safely along the narrow way, across the dark river of death, and up the shining path into the celestial city.

"O blessed Volume Divine,
Let everlasting thanks be thine,
For such a bright display
As makes the world of darkness shine
With beams of heavenly day."

---

* Little Mary is now almost five years of age. She reads a great deal, is fond of her books, especially the Bible. She is a lovely child. For the last two years we have not had occasion to reprove her. She seems to be constantly influenced by the Holy Spirit. She delights in family worship, and always takes the Bible and reads over the portions of Scripture read in worship, that she may understand it better. Nothing interests her as much as the story of the death and sufferings of the Saviour. We are obliged to be careful in dwelling upon that subject, as it affects her very deeply. She wonders greatly that all children in the civilized land do not love the Lord Jesus. We have no doubt but she is one of those little ones whom Jesus calls His lambs.

"Happy the child whose early years
Receive instruction well,
Who hates the sinner's path, and fears
The road which leads to hell."

Address.....*Author of "Apples of Gold,"*
No. 303 West Twentieth Street, N. Y.

"OF SUCH IS THE KINGDOM OF HEAVEN."

HAPPY? THE LITTLEST AND THE BIGGEST?

Who doubts it? Look at them, little readers, is there a single jar of discord here, the least frown of discontent exhibited on the face of one of these children? Does not each one wear a glowing smile of cheerfulness? What makes them happy—the love of Jesus in the soul, ruling and reigning?

> " Love is the little golden clasp
> That bindeth up the trust;
> Oh, break it not; lest all the leaves
> Shall scatter and be lost."

SATAN IN—SATAN OUT.—In the Pulpit—In the Press.

"Know ye not that the friendship of the world is enmity with God? whosoever therefore will be a friend of the world is the enemy of God."—*James* iv. 4.

Conversation between Mr. Timewell *and* Mr. Servility.
(No. 1.)

Timewell. "Good morning, Mr. Servility, beautiful day."
Servility. "Delightful."

T. "You are recently from the National Council, Congregational, held at Oberlin, O., Nov. 15, 1871. What for a meeting did you have?"

S. "Splendid! It was love from first to last—love, love, love!"

T. "Is this love you speak of Bible? If not it is false—spurious! Did it lead you or the 'Council' to rise up against evil-doers—stand up against the workers of iniquity? If not, there's no God in it—no Christ. What kind of love is that, that lets wolves into God's enclosures, to carry off and devour the sheep and dear lambs of the flock without a single warning—uplifted voice—'Wolf, wolf!' 'First pure then peaceable.' 'What peace?' said Jehu to Joram.—2 *Kings* ix. 18.

"Had you the love of Nathan the prophet, when he said to David, '*Thou art the man?*' Had you Samuel's love when he hewed Agag to pieces? How much did Eli love his sons, while permitting them to serve the devil as much as they pleased? God calls this hatred—'He that spareth the rod hateth his son, but he that loveth him chasteneth him betimes." 'Your glorying is not good,' Mr. Servility."

S. " Explain yourself, Mr. Timewell."

T. " Read the following from your printed reports :

' 'Had Henry Ward Beecher been present to preach the opening sermon, as was expected, and as he would have been, but for an unfortunate blunder as to the time appointed, it seems probable that he would have been elected Moderator.'

"On glancing my eye on this eulogy, I stood aghast! trembled! shook from head to foot! exclaimed aloud, 'What are we coming to ; what will the devil do next ?'

"' Hear, O heavens, and give ear, O earth : for the Lord hath spoken : I have nourished and brought up children, and they have rebelled against me.'

"'The ox knoweth his owner, and the ass his master's crib, *but* Israel doth not know, my people doth not consider.'

"' Why should ye be stricken any more? ye will revolt more and more : the whole head is sick, and the whole heart is faint.'

"' From the sole of the foot even unto the head, there is no soundness in it.'

"' Except the LORD of hosts had left unto us a very small remnant, we should have been as Sodom, *and* we should have been like unto Gomorrah.' "—*Isa.* i. 2, 9.

S. " What has Beecher done so terribly wicked ?"

T. " What has he not done to lower the Gospel standard —bring into disrepute the blessedness of the blessed, and raise Satan's flag sky-high?"

S. " Facts are called for, Mr. Timewell, in Courts of Justice—mere assertions without proof are ropes of sand, go for naught."

T. " 'This witness is true; wherefore rebuke them sharply, that they may be sound in the faith.'—*Tit.* i. 13.

"Again: 'their sorrows shall be multiplied that hasten after another god.'—*Psa.* xvi. 4. 'There be gods many, and lords many.'—1 *Cor.* viii. 5. Pride is a god, gold is a god. 'Covetousness is idolatry.' 'The love of money is the root of all evil.'

"What proved the ruin of Achan? 'The wedge of gold? Why was Balaam, the false prophet, rebuked by the dumb ass, and perished finally in the gainsaying of Core?—*Jude* 11. Was it not for reward, the wages of unrighteousness?

"What induced Judas to betray his Master? Was it not the love of gain? Would he have done this dark and damning deed, had it not been for reward—thirty pieces of silver?

"Was it not covetousness or love of gain that led Ananias and Sapphira to lie against the Holy Spirit, and for which lies they were struck dead instantly?

"Why did Simon the sorcerer, crave the miraculous power of healing, to whom Peter said: 'Thy money perish with thee, because thou hast thought that the gift of God may be purchased with money. Thou hast neither part nor lot in this matter: for thy heart is not right in the sight of God. Repent therefore of this thy wickedness, and pray God, if perhaps the thought of thine heart may be forgiven thee.' —*Acts* ix. 20, 21, 22.

"Would Henry Ward Beecher have written 'Norwood' for that wretched sheet, the *N. Y. Ledger?* and also for the theater, the hot-bed of lewdness; had it not been for the '*accursed lust*' of gain, $30,000? the wages of unrighteousness? Furthermore, would he continue his contributions regularly to this vile Weekly, were it not for this same damning sin of Achan, Balaam, Judas Iscariot, and of Simon the sorcerer?"

> "Gold banished honor from the mind,
> And only left the name behind!
> Gold sowed the world with every ill;
> Gold taught the murderer's sword to kill!
>
> 'Twas Gold instructed coward hearts
> In treachery's most pernicious arts:
> Who can recount the mischiefs o'er?
> Virtue resides on earth no more!"

S. "You place 'Henry Ward' in the same category with Achan, Balaam, Judas and Simon the sorcerer—am I correct?"

> *T.* "When a weak Judas tortured by the rack
> Of conscience, till his life was made a hell,
> Rushed madly to the temple and flung back
> The bribe which tempted him his Lord to sell.'

"You remember well, Mr. Servility, when placards were posted conspicuously in blazing capitals, in New York and Brooklyn, signifying that Beecher was to be in the theater such a night."

S. "Beecher in the theater! Not in person!"

T. "His novel—the same thing. 'As a man thinketh so is he.'"

S. "Well, what of it?"

T. "What of it? Such a rush to the theaters, devils' dens, as never before. And this rush impetuous has been continued from that night to this, increasingly!

"Novel writing, puffing and reading, also have increased fourfold. Souls go down to the sides of the pit of woe everlasting, through the instrumentality of this one novel writer and money lover! How many, think you, friend Servility, of once virtuous, innocent, precious youth, will date their downward course to perdition and final damnation from this one sugared pill—or 'coiled Serpent,' entitled 'Norwood,' advertised and puffed by religious editors and teachers clad in garments sacerdotal? Truly and emphatically, 'One sinner destroys much good.' All right, its Henry Ward Beecher!

" 'Great gifts may please the worldly-wise—
 They show the 'pride of life ;'
But oft they waken evil thoughts—
 Stir up a storm of strife.'

" 'Wo to the world because of offences,' * 'but wo to that man by whom the offence cometh.' It costs something to serve the old Serpent, the devil, the father of lies. If the reward is not dealt out here in full toll, the balance by-and-by! 'Some men's sins are open beforehand, going to judgment; and some men, they follow after.'—*Tim.* v. 24.

" 'Be not deceived, God is not mocked ; for whatsoever a man soweth that shall he also reap.'

" 'Every tree that bringeth not forth good fruit is hewn down and cast into the fire.' 'The wicked shall be turned into hell, and all the nations that forget God.' 'Let God be true, but every man a liar.' "—*Rom.* iii. 4.

" No more the sovereign eye of God
 O'erlooks the crimes of men ;
His heralds now are sent abroad
 To warn the world of sin."

---

* " The wicked," says David, " walk on every side when the vilest men are exalted."—*Psa.* xii. 8.

Look out for the dogs—Beware of them.

There are good dogs and bad dogs, as there are good men and bad men—good children and bad children. Wicked men, in Scripture, are compared to dogs; and they are the worst kind of dogs, the most dangerous. "They return at evening: they make a noise like a dog, and go round about the city. Behold, they belch out with their mouth: swords are in their lips; for who, say they, doth hear?"—*Psa.* lix. 6, 7.

"Give not that which is holy unto the dogs, neither cast ye your pearls before swine: lest they trample them under their feet, and turn again and rend you."—*Math.* vii. 6.

False prophets that refuse to speak out against popular sins, shun to declare God's full council, are called "dumb dogs, that *cannot* bark."—*Isa.* lvi. 9, 10, 11. From these *run!*—escape for your life!—*Run!*

The lovely Susan—beautiful!

"O what tender thoughts beneath
Those silent flowers are lying."

WHAT makes Susan beautiful or lovely? The blessed Bible she reads daily! Grace in her heart, the fruits of the Holy Spirit, love, joy, peace, long-suffering, gentleness, goodness, faith, meekness, temperance—against which there is no law!

There is nothing so very beautiful or prepossessing in her external appearance. Susan is not beautiful in what a fashionable world calls handsome or beautiful. She is not decorated in glittering costume, tipped off gaily in fine things—gewgaws, flowers and artificials—like many little girls, inflated with pride and self-importance, that remind us of the peacock or butterfly. These vain ones seem to think more of a pretty face, a new dress, a new bonnet, a new coat, or a new hat, than they do of the improvement of their minds and hearts—of the Bible and the Lord Jesus Christ!

Show us a girl that spends her leisure moments looking in the glass, or making some useless finery, and we will show you a girl with a head as symmetrical as a balloon, and as light or vain as the peacock.

> "Some poor little ignorant children delight
> In wearing fine ribbons and caps;
> But this is a very ridiculous sight,
> Though they do not know it perhaps."

Do you not know, little folks, that the poor sheep and silk-worms wore that very clothing long before? "The tulip and the butterfly appear in far gayer coats than you. Dress fine as you will, flies, worms and flowers exceed you still."

Does God take delight in fine clothes, that tend to vanity and pride? "My son, give me thy heart." Why not say—

> "Then will I set my heart to find,
> Inward adorning of the mind?
> Knowledge and virtue, truth and grace,
> These are the robes of richest dress."

Susan always appears neatly and modestly dressed, and in good taste; and when once attired, she seems not even to think of her personal appearance, as many others do. Her costume is plain, neat, simple, modest, economical.

Little girls should always be neat and clean in person and dress, because this is an evidence of respectability and the fear of God. No lady, who has any regard for herself or any respect for the society in which she moves, will be slovenly in her appearance or careless in her attire. To dress simply and without ostentation is not only a mark of modesty, but of gospel simplicity and purity.

Susan's adorning is not "that outward adorning of plaiting

the hair, and of wearing gold, or of putting on apparel; but the hidden man of the heart, in that which is not corruptible. Even the ornament of a meek and quiet spirit, which is in the sight of God of great price."

Here's the secret of secrets of Susan's loveliness, the sweet, heavenly smile playing upon her lips. Female piety lovely? It's the gem of all others which enriches the coronet of a lady's character.

What robe so rich, so white, so beautiful, as the robe of righteousness?

> "It never fades, it ne'er grows old,
> Nor fears the rain, nor moth, nor cold;
> It takes no spot, but still refines,
> The more 'tis worn, the more it shines."

Never yet was the female character perfect without the steady faith of piety. Beauty, intellect, and wealth are like pitfalls in the brightest day, unless the divine light, unless religion throws her soft beams around them, to purify and exalt, making twice glorious that which seemed all loveliness before.

> "And what, O what is good?
> 'Tis first to seek the favor of thy God;
> Let thy will blend with his, and honor him
> By walking in the way thy Saviour trod."

Behold the daughter of innocence! How beautiful is the mildness of her countenance; how lovely is the diffidence of her looks!

Her cheek is dyed with the deep crimson of the rose; her eye is placid and serene, and the gentleness of her speech is as the melting softness of the flute.

Her smiles are the enlivening rays of the sun; the beauty of her presence, as the silver light of the moon.

Her attire is simple: her feet tread with caution, and she feareth to give offence.

> "A bud of moral beauty. Let the dews
> Of knowledge and the light of virtue wake it
> In richest fragrance and in purest hues."

A well established character for morality and virtue, of purity of thought and action, is of great importance to people of every class and in all circumstances. But to a young lady, a good name is a priceless jewel. It is everything to her; in some sense it will clothe her with an attraction, a value, an importance in the estimation of others, which nothing else can impart. Possessed of a spotless character, she may reasonably hope for peace and happiness. But without such a character, she is nothing.

Youth, beauty, dress, accomplishments, all gifts and qualities will be looked upon as naught when tainted by a suspicious reputation! Nothing can atone for this, nothing can be allowed to take its place, nothing can give charm and attraction where it exists not. When the character of a young woman is gone, all is gone! Thenceforward she can look for nothing but degradation and wretchedness.

Many are the instances of a single word, spoken at random, in the giddy thoughtlessness of youthful vivacity, without the slightest thought of wrong, casting a shadow upon the character of a young woman which it required years to efface.

> "Modesty, like diamonds, shines most fair,
> More worth than pearls or rubies are."

Tall Trees of the forest.

God compares trees to men, men to trees. When the wicked, time-serving, hypocritical Scribes and Pharisees came to John as he was preaching in the wilderness, what did he tell them? "Now also the axe is laid unto the root of the trees: therefore every tree which bringeth not forth good fruit is hewn down, and cast into the fire."—*Math.* iii. 10.

Christ, in his sermon on the mount, says, "Ye shall know them by their fruits: Do men gather grapes of thorns, or figs of thistles? Even so every good tree bringeth forth good fruit; but a corrupt tree bringeth forth evil fruit. A good tree cannot bring forth evil fruit, neither can a corrupt tree bring forth good fruit. Every tree that bringeth not forth good fruit is hewn down and cast into the fire. Wherefore, by their fruits ye shall know them."—*Math.* vii. 16–20.

SATAN IN—SATAN OUT.—In the Pulpit—In the Press.

Conversation between Mr. Timewell *and* Mr. Servility.
(No. 2.)

'Speak thou the truth. Let others fence
And trim their words for pay;
In pleasant sunshine or pretence
Let others bask their day."

"Them that sin rebuke before all, that others also may fear."—
1 *Tim.* v. 20.

S. "You spoke reprovingly, Mr. Timewell, if I mistake not, of friend Beecher's placing Shakespeare next to the Bible in value, and also for his inviting Dickens, the prince of novelists, into his pulpit cordially?"

T. "These facts show which way the wind blows—in what direction his sympathies and kindlier feelings lie, what company is most pleasant and congenial. 'Chips of the same block,' 'jolly fellows well met' and well mated, of one heart and of one soul.

"'As in water, face answereth to face, so the heart of man to man.'—*Prov.* xxvii. 19.

"'That which is highly esteemed among men is abomination in the sight of God."—*Luke* xvi. 15.

"Shakespeare was libidinous. The lovely Charlotte Elizabeth tottered on the verge of everlasting death by poring over the pages of this licentious and bewitching author. [See her 'Recollections.' Pages 50 and 52.]

"Dickens was sensual—a slave to his carnal appetites, an open foe to temperance—a caricaturist of God's faithful ministers, and who fell at last a victim to loathsome gluttony! 'He dug his grave with his own teeth.'*

"Intemperance is a crime heaven-daring! It's a crime against ourselves—against others—against God!

"'Be not amongst wine-bibbers; amongst riotous eaters of flesh.

"'For the drunkard and the glutton shall come to poverty, and drowsiness shall clothe a man with rags.'"— Prov. xxiii. 20-22. (See also 1 Cor. vi. 10.)

S. "Both Shakespeare and Dickens, you know, Mr. Timewell, are held in high repute by very many theologians."

T. "Respect ministers esteem them highly for their work's sake? How can we, unless they respect themselves? the cause of God? walk worthy of their high vocation?

"Mark the ridiculous pow-wowings in the Plymouth house of worship, year in and year out, when the seats are knocked off under the auctioneer's hammer to the highest bidder? Pandemonium broken loose, and all the evil spirits therein, gabbling and cackling nonsense, and Beecher in the midst, taking the lead? What else?

"Therefore, avaunt! all sober looks,
All prayers and hymns, and godly books;

---

* Friends of love and of Gospel truth, do any of you question the facts that sensuality was the god of Charles Dickens? carnal pleasure, fleshly lusts? read, if you please, the account of his "amateur theatricals"—"dramatic revels"—now spread before us—written by one of his intimate friends.

"If the Lord be God, follow him; but if Baal, then follow him."—1 *Kings* xviii. 21.

Make God's own house a place of trade!
Its lecture-room, a mere arcade
For vanity—a Fair!"*

"'A whip of small cords' suffice for these buyers and sellers in a place previously dedicated to prayer, praise and holiness to the Lord? Nay, the lash of scorpions!

"What said our blessed Lord to a class, or money-loving, popular-seeking clique like these : 'It is written, My house shall be called the house of prayer ; but ye have made it a den of thieves.'

"All right, '*hush!* it's Beecher's house! *Hush*, don't say anything!'—Satan rule the day? No matter, *hush!* Beecher is king in the Ring!

"Look furthermore at the McFarland case, the marrying of a dead man to another man's wife!"

S. "Marrying a dead man to another man's wife! When? Where?"

T. "What else? Was not Richardson breathing his last when these nuptials were celebrated? No marvel holy indignation rose to the highest pitch, when this outrage on society and the Bible was committed! If a minister in humble life, or one of little note had done this wicked thing, would he not have been deposed and hissed from the community forthwith? But it was Beecher that did it, and how soon hushed by his party! Popularity is killing us! We are dying the death!"

---

* Similar religious pow-wowings we hear and see at the "Congregational Union Festivals," during May day meetings! Shameful! Surely

"If Lucifer, flying from Hades,
Could gaze at this crowd with its paniers and paints,
He would say, looking round at the lords and the ladies,
Oh, where is All Sinners if this is All Saints?'"

> "What if cowards fear and tremble,
> Or dishonest men dissemble;
> If *you* know your duty, *do it*,—
> Choose the right and then pursue it."

S. "You lay mighty stress on light reading, novels, tales and stories."

T. "It's the letting out of waters; it kindles hell fire here, it kindles hell fire there! But thanks be to God some few eyes are opening. That speech of De Witt Talmage cut to the quick, did it not? Sharp as a two-edged sword."

S. "What speech, Mr. Timewell, the one on white-lying or the coiled serpents you speak of?"

T. "The very same."

S. "Was this intended as a rebuke for Henry Ward?"

T. "Who questions it? It was delivered in the very shadow of the Plymouth house, quite under the *droppings* of high-handed *iniquity*."

S. "Give a specimen or an outline, if you please?"

T. "The question had been put to him—touching the '*N. Y. Ledger*,' '*The Weekly*,' and other works of similar tendency. He speaks thus:

"'This question asked me by letter is vital, and in this Friday evening's talk I shall answer it. In every family where the children have come to nine or ten years of age, it has been discussed. The family altar is nothing; catechisms are nothing; religious instruction is nothing, so long as there is an unhealthy periodical in the house. From the two leprous lips of that one sheet there will be a poison breathed on the family Bible, on the piano, on the arm-chair, on the cradle, on the dining-table, and the whole house will be plague-smitten. The question amounts to this: 'Shall my family be blessed or blasted?'

"'I give an infallible rule. Seek some one who has been reading a paper for several years, and find out if her character is growing more symmetrical, is she a better daughter, a holier mother, a more consistent church member. If, on the contrary, her talk is groveling, her imagination debased, her ideas of life twisted and sprung, then better decree that such a paper shall not come into your house by postman or messenger, or as wrapping paper around a dry-goods bundle.' 'Every tree is known by its fruits.'

" 'If there be one gulf in hell deeper than another, it shall be the doom of those newspaper men whose pen is stabbing to death the purity of American society. The newspaper stands are blotched with accursed pictorials, and I pray God that if these polluters of public morals may not be arrested by the voice of conscience, or silenced by the indignation of our sorrow-struck communities, that then they may be hurled out of this life speedily, that the plague may be staid. God redeem our country from the damning influence of a corrupt newspaper literature.' "

S. "Is this the kind of literature Beecher has been sending forth?"

T. "With lightning speed. Year in, year out, for ten, fifteen or twenty years, to curse nations yet unborn; and is still rushing the same Satan's cars! And who rebukes this wickedness? Who is on the Lord's side, who?"

S. "Is it true as reported, that Mr. Beecher said in a sermon recently, 'God bless the theaters?"

T. "This assertion he denies, but why should he not bless theaters, operas and other sink-holes of moral pollution, when time after time he has put his shoulder to these same wheels of Satan? It's merely following the train of his other carnal amusements. It is only saying 'Go on, Mr. Devil, you have my best wishes, hearty co-operation!' I speak not unadvisedly. I have just clipped this from a religious weekly:

" 'Bay City is trying to induce Henry Ward Beecher to open the new Opera House. Having recently consecrated places of amusement, in general, it is believed that he will not refuse to dedicate this particular one.'

"'By whom shall Jacob arise?' 'Who will rise up for me against the evil-doers? or who shall stand up for me against the workers of iniquity?'

"'Cry aloud, ye sons of men,
   Like a trumpet lift your voice;
To my people show their sin,
   And the guilt of Jacob's house.

"Novel-selling and novel-reading could not long exist, were it not upheld and patronized by those having a name to live, and are dead, lovers of pleasure, more than lovers of God. Idolatry in dress and equipage could not long exist were it not sustained by an idolatrous church and ministry. So with every evil.

"It is in the power of the church, filled with the love of Christ, clad in the full armor of God's righteousness, to cause the earth to blossom as the rose, salvation to go forth as the light of the morning, and angels to rejoice anew— 'glory to God in the highest, peace on earth and good-will to man.'

"O what guilt, mountain-weight, rests upon the church! Will not God visit for this?

"What iniquity is there that is not upheld, sustained, perpetuated by the professed followers of the Lord Jesus Christ?"

Family Bible Readings.

Do not angels behold a picture like this, complacently, joyfully? Could they if this same lovely family were seated around a chess board, billiard table, or pouring over a novel, a tale of fiction—with lightness of speech, senseless gabble—the fool's laughter? "Wisdom is justified of her children."

THE HAPPY MOTHER TRAINING LITTLE FOLKS.

"Of all the spots that heaven has blest,
    The dearest place is home:
'Tis there the fond heart loves to rest,
    And never loves to roam:
While love plays round the smiling hearth,
'Tis heaven's own bliss enjoyed on earth."

SATAN IN—SATAN OUT.—In the Pulpit—In the Press.

Conversation between Mr. TIMEWELL *and* Mr. SERVILITY.
(No. 3.)

"Some will hate thee, some will love thee,
Some will flatter, some will slight;
Cease from man, and look above thee,
Trust in God, and do the right."

S. "MR. TIMEWELL, you alluded to a 'Ring.' What Ring—the 'Tammany?'"

T. "Worse, ten-fold! Indeed, there would have been no Tammany 'Ring' dreamed of had the church done her duty and not succumbed to popular iniquity. This doctrine of expediency—compromising with sin and Satan—is a curse to both church and State. The guilt, crimson-colored, lies at our door. The 'Tammany,' devilish as it is, is a mere offshoot of the theological 'Ring,' or of the Sanhedrim!

"Look at the majority of the sermonizings, the religious editorials. What are they? life, soul, power Holy Spirit teachings? Are popular sins exposed? Cross the popular 'Ring?' deviate a hair's breadth from the Sanhedrim? Not for the world!

"The 'Ring' is often approached, even to its edge, and we begin to pray and to hope a stepping outside, and a little Gospel. But alas! 'hope deferred maketh the heart sick.' These 'Ring' folks turn back, whiffle about, keep within the circle.

"'The children of Ephraim, being armed, and carrying bows, turned back in the day of battle.'—Psal. xxxvii. 9.

"Ephraim is a cake not turned.

"Strangers have devoured his strength, and he knoweth it not; yea, gray hairs are here and there upon him, yet he knoweth not.

"And the pride of Israel testifieth to his face, and they do not return to the Lord their God, nor seek him for all this.

> "'The veriest coward upon earth
> Is he who fears the world's opinion;
> Who acts with reference to its will,
> His conscience swayed by its dominion.'

"Sin is winked at, covered, passed over. What now? Prosper? God says not, and we believe God what He says.

"Prosper? and cover sin, the vilest, the most devilish? Who says so? God? Not a word of it. Israel prosper and let Achan alone with his golden wedge? Prosper and not hew Agag to pieces? The very vitals of salvation are eaten out. The half told? Not a fiftieth part! Angels weep—heaven is veiled in sackcloth! The devils rejoice—hell is in jubilee!

"The doctrine of worldly expediency and compromise is, of all sins, the most destructive, soul-ruinous, to both church and State. And at no sin does God thunder anathemas more terribly!

"We are making infidels by scores and thousands—causing the enemies of truth to rejoice and blaspheme! Look out for thunderbolts from high heaven, causing every ear to tingle!

"'Ephraim feedeth on wind, . . . his iniquity is bound up; his sin is hid.'

"'I hate, I despise your feast-days, and I will not smell in your solemn assemblies. Though ye offer me your burnt offerings and your meat offerings, I will not accept them; neither will I regard the peace offerings of your fat beasts. Take thou away from me the noise of thy songs; for I will not hear the melody of thy viols.'—Amos v. 21, 22, 23.

"The Papacy, bad as it is, murderous as it is, idolatrous, superstitious and soul-ruinous as it is, is a myth, a shadow, compared to what we, called Protestants, are coming to, except we mend our ways."

S. "How is this?"

T. "We are sinning against superior light—holding the truth in unrighteousness. 'The wrath of God is revealed from heaven against us.'—Rom. i. 18. Turn also to Math. xiii. 12; Acts xvii. 30.

"'Thou therefore which teachest another, teachest thou not thyself?—thou that preachest a man should not steal, dost thou steal? Thou that sayest a man should not commit adultery, dost thou commit adultery?—thou that abhorrest idols, dost thou commit sacrilege? Thou that makest thy boast of the law, through breaking the law dishonorest thou God? For the name of God is blasphemed among the Gentiles through you.'"

S. "Do you make it out that the Scribes and Pharisees were in this same 'Ring' you speak of?"

T. "Truly and emphatically! And 'darkness was on the face of the deep;' and 'gross darkness covered the people.' It's so now!—worse!"

S. "What say you of Christ and his apostles?"

T. "Christ was born out of the 'Ring,' lived out of it, died out of it, went to glory out of it! But his pathway was sprinkled with blood, every step, till nailed to the cross!"

SATAN IN—SATAN OUT.

S. "How with the apostles—Paul, Peter, James and John?"

S. "After the baptismal power given, the tongue of fire, they were out of the 'Ring' completely—kept out of it, died out of it, went to glory out of it!—and like the Master, the Lord of glory, they resisted unto blood, striving against sin all the way."

S. "Have there not been those outside this 'Ring,' more or less walking in white from time to time immemorial?"

T. "Even during the days of bloody Popery.

"Luther, blessed man, stepped outside the 'Ring.' What now? Tie him to the stake!—burn him up!

"Wesley, blessed man, ventured outside the 'Ring. What now!—confiscation!

"Bunyan, blessed man, stepped outside the 'Ring.' What now? Shut him up!—incarcerate him twelve years!

"Take brother Geo. B. Cheever's case, of modern date—blessed man. Scarcely had he stepped one foot outside this 'Ring' of the Sanhedrim, ere, seemingly, all the bull-dogs of the infernal regions were let loose upon him!"

S. "By whom?—outsiders?"

T. "Not a dog would have moved his tongue had not the yelping began inside the 'Ring,' and that too by the leaders of his own denomination!"

S. "Is Cheever dead?—have the 'Ring' folks killed him?"

T. "Dead! Kill one of God's chosen ones in the battle-field till the work is finished assigned to him? When? where? Did Paul die? When? Before he fought the good fight, or after? Look and see. A true man of God die, standing in front of battle, loading and firing in quick succession—storming the fort of Satan—causing him to fall as lightning! Where? Such a soldier of the cross never dies! Though dead he lives—and lives for evermore!"*

"Truth is earnest, truth is fearless,
Ever dwelling in the light;
Still by error's frowns undaunted,
Striving only for the right."

"If God be for us, who can be against us?" "Fear not them which kill the body, but are not able to kill the soul; but rather fear him who is able to destroy both soul and body in hell."—Math. x. 28.

"I am not come to send peace on earth," saith the Lord, "but a sword."—Math. x. 34.

"Thy saints in all this glorious war
Shall conquer, though they die;
They view the triumph from afar,
By faith they bring it nigh."

"God has a work for brother Cheever when his enemies 'shall lick the dust' and his persecutors are dead and buried. Some of them are already dead—'twice dead, plucked up by the roots.'

---

*"God sends some teachers unto every age,
To every clime, and every race of men,
With revelations fitted to their growth
And shape of mind, nor gives the realm of Truth
Into the selfish rule of the whole race;
Therefore each form of worship that has swayed
The life of man, and given it to grasp
The master-key of knowledge—reverence,
Enfolds some gems of goodness and of right,
Else never hath the eager soul which loathes
The slothful down of pampered ignorance,
Found in it even a moment's fitful rest."

303 West Twentieth Street, New York.

Poverty in death, but glorious!

This aged saint died as she lived—lived as she died. She lived in poverty—died in poverty. And yet, rich *all the time!* her income was unbounded! "There is that maketh himself rich, yet hath nothing: there is that maketh himself poor, yet hath great riches."

"Hearken, my beloved brethren, hath not God chosen the poor of this world rich in faith, and heirs of the kingdom which he hath promised to them that love him?"—James ii. 5.

Blessed are the dead that die in the Lord.

SEE THIS WOMAN ON A BED OF LANGUISHMENT NIGH UNTO DEATH.

WHAT for? What the first cause—sin? Had not sin entered, there would have been no sickness, no pain, no death.

SATAN IN—SATAN OUT.—In the Pulpit—In the Press.

Conversation between MR. TIMEWELL *and* MR. SERVILITY.
(No. 4.)

"This life is a battle with Satan and sin,
And we are the soldiers the victory to win,
And Christ is the Captain of our little band,
Whatever opposes, for Him we shall stand."

T. "ALLOW me, Mr. Servility, to repeat, what I have more than hinted at, once, twice, three times, that this man expediency doctrine, is death, double death, it's damnation in church and State. It's the leprosy of the age, a cancer on the body politic. It kills life, spiritual, in the church, the ministry, the editorship, in seminaries of learning. It's a curse to this nation, every nation, to every benevolent institution. The false prophets of old compromised, and it killed them dead! King Saul compromised, and it killed him dead. The Scribes and Pharisees compromised, and it killed them dead! Judas compromised, and he went to his own place. Ananias and Sapphira compromised, and it killed them dead! Peter compromised once or twice, and he wept bitterly! This same compromising has been going on and on till the whole world is filled with compromisings and compromisers, and where are we now? dead—dead and damned, in the church and out of it!"

S. "You place our friend Beecher, I perceive, among the popular seekers, time servers, or among those who compromise sin and Satan, and yet, how question his usefulness?

He says of himself, again and again, 'People will go where they are fed, and will not go where they are not fed.'"

T. "What is the food alluded to by this distinguished divine? Gospel food, that nourishes the soul? What does he preach? The doctrines of the Bible, 'holiness to the Lord,' entire consecratedness to God's service? Does he tell his audience to 'come out from the world and be separate, and touch not the unclean thing'—abstain from all appearance of evil? When? Where?

"People judge differently as to what is worth hearing, as preachers differ as to what is worth saying. Very many are delighted with nonsense, trifling witticisms in the pulpit, foolish talking and jesting, and 'heap to themselves teachers having itching ears,' who would find no pleasure in hearing the sermon on the mount. This popular preacher, boasting of the multitudes that flock to hear him, should bear in mind that there are many kinds of 'fodder, and a correspondingly great variety in the feeders of the fodder. The crow, that would turn up his nose at the manna that fell in the wilderness, would riot in the carrion that made the dove fly away in disgust. The common supposition, that a man 'feeds' multitudes because they go to hear him, or that another man has nothing 'worth hearing' because his audiences are not so large, is the sheerest nonsense. The man is puffed up, the love of applause has killed him.

"'That which is highly esteemed among men, is abomination in the sight of God.'"—*Luke* xvi. 15.

ELOQUENCE IN SPEAKING AND WRITING.

S. "Beecher is eloquent, you must acknowledge, from the fact that so many flock to hear him—hang upon his lips."

T. "What makes him eloquent? by the prayerful study of the Holy Scriptures, copying after the holy prophets and apostles? or by writing, puffing and reading novels? pouring over the writings of corrupt authors, a libidinous Shakespeare whom he places side by side with the Bible? From his pulpit delineations, I infer that he is more enamored with Shakespeare and similar authors than he is with the pure word of life! Who, among public speakers, have a greater gift of the gab than Unitarians, who deny the Lord that bought them, or the deluded Mormons, Spiritualists, and Freelovers?

"'Having eyes full of adultery, and that cannot cease from sin; beguiling unstable souls: an heart they have exercised with covetous practices; cursed children.'—2 *Pet.* ii. 14.'

"Tilton has become marvelously eloquent since taking Apolyon into his fond embrace, and Mrs. Woodhull as a special help meet!

"Who more eloquent than Satan himself, on certain occasions? who can preach a more eloquent, glowing sermon, make a more fervent, or orthodox prayer, quote Scripture more fluently? And does not his satanic majesty give special aid to his faithful servants? The 'old Serpent' may not employ a stenographer for the purpose of having these beautiful, eloquent prayers and sermons of his inserted in some religious weekly or monthly, with his 'Lecture-room talks.'

"Very many pulpit orators have a remarkable flow of language, speak with the tongues of men and of angels, while living in lust, the pleasures of sense, full of pride, folly and fashion as they can button up, serve the devil upliftedly aside, from your admired friend, the Plymouth pulpit orator! 'Help Lord, for the godly man ceaseth.'"

S. "How do you define true eloquence, Mr. Timewell?"

T. Using the Bible term, there is no eloquence worthy the name, save soul eloquence, the fire of heaven, salvation fire, emanating directly from God himself, the third heavens. It's fire, *fire*! FIRE! It begins with fire, soul-kindling, soul-subduing, soul-elevating, and keeps on with the same glowing, sparkling, heavenly fire to the end. It's the Holy Spirit's dictations, inspirations. A speaker in God's stead must not only *profess* Gospel, but *possess* Gospel in his inmost soul, deep down, and this same Gospel of God in the soul must be *lived* out, seen, felt, known and read of all men. 'Be ye doers of the word, and not hearers only, deceiving your own selves.'—*James* i. 22.

"The more holy the servant of God is, the more deeply and frequently he drinks at the 'Fountain of Living Waters'—the more earnestly, fervently and constantly he is at the mercy-seat—'lifting up holy hands without wrath and doubting,' the more eloquent of course: heavenly sparks fly here, fly there—fires pentecostal blaze out here, blaze out there. It's fire, fire! *fire!* Lord, send these fire brands of heavenly fire."

S. "Please give a few specimens."

T. "Moses, though he told the Lord he was not eloquent, but 'slow of speech, slow of tongue,' yet, who more eloquent? Look at his pen, what seest thou? Fire from first to last, fire on *fire!* He began with fire at the burning bush, and kept on with fire increasingly till God kissed him away. The same fires he kindled while here, are still burning and will continue to burn forever! Though dead he speaks—kindles fires. Blessed man!"

S. "Who next?"

T. "It is fire! fire! fire! all the way from Genesis to

Revelation. The fire of beauty, of sublimity. The Psalms are full of it; Jeremiah is full of it; Ezekiel is full of it; Daniel is full of it; Hosea, Micbah, Habakkuk, Zechariah, and Malachi are full of it. 'The blessed Jesus spake as never man spake: with authority and not as the Scribes.' The word of God was in his soul, rooted and grounded, burningly, everlastingly.

> " 'The Bible—book of wondrous love,
> Borne from God's eternal throne
> In mercy's arms to fallen man,
> To tell the mission of the Son.'

"Paul is full of this Bible eloquence or holy fire pentecostal; Peter, James, and John—fire on fire! Every thought is condensed, brought to a burning focus! *

"The Bible is the book of holy eloquence. In comparison, Byron loses his fire, Milton his soarings, Gray his beauties, and Homer his grandeur and figures. No eye like rapt Isaiah's ever pierced the veil of the future; no tongue ever reasoned like sainted Job's; no poet ever sang like Israel's Shepherd King, and God never made a wiser man than Solomon. The words of the Bible are pictures of Immortality, dews from the tree of Knowledge, pearls from the river of Life, and gems of celestial thought. As the moaning shell whispers of the sea, so the Bible breathes of love in heaven, the home of angels, and joys too pure to die.

---

* How did Jeremiah exhibit his eloquence? Turn to his Lamentations: "They that sow in tears shall reap in joy. He that goeth forth and weepeth, bearing precious seed, shall doubtless come again with rejoicing, bringing his sheaves *with him*."—*Psa.* cxxvi. 5, 6.

How did Paul display his eloquence? By writing novels for the ready cash? Deliver popular lectures at opera houses, write and speak funny things, foolish and vain, to excite the fool's laughter? Turn to Paul's Epistles. Read especially the 12th of Romans.

> "What glory gilds the sacred page,
>   Majestic, like the sun!
> It gives a light to every age,
>   It gives, but borrows none.'

"Parents and children, pastors and teachers, religious editors and book makers, little folks and great folks, are you desirous to improve your style in writing and speaking? to possess this glowing eloquence, beautiful, majestic, glorious, sparkling, bright as the noonday sun; full of fire; pure, virtuous, heavenly? Go to the Bible, the Book of books; read it, search it, pray over it, meditate in it, drink into its spirit, hide it in your heart, commit it to memory. Go over it and over it till you can say: 'O how love I thy law; it is my meditation all the day.' 'How sweet are thy words to my taste; yea, sweeter than honey to my mouth.

> "'This precious food our heart revives:
>   What strength, what nourishment it gives!
> Oh, let us evermore be fed
>   With this divine, celestial bread.'

"Here lies the secret of pulpit eloquence, editorial eloquence, eloquence that burns, flashes out, cuts like a razor, or a two-edged sword, slays on the right hand and on the left, causes Satan to tremble, fall as lightning from heaven! Then, every word from your pen and your lips will be fire, fire! tell on the conscience, the heart, the life; be a barbed arrow to the guilty one, in the church or out of it. Oh for this Bible-fire, the fire of the Bible! The Lord send it.

> "'One fragment of his blessed word
>   Into the spirit burned,
> Is better than the whole, half heard,
>   And by thy interests turned."

THE LITTLE THIEF CAUGHT IN THE ACT.

"Theft will not be always hidden,
  Though we fancy none can spy;
When we take a thing forbidden,
  God beholds it with his eye."

IMPERIAL PROCESSION OF THE GRAND MOGUL.

"Thus, unlamented, pass the proud away,
The gaze of fools, and pageant of a day."—(*See next page.*)

ELIJAH FED BY THE RAVENS. 1 Kings, xvii. 5-6.

Elijah was a good man, perfect in his generation; and, like Enoch and Noah, he "walked with God," and "God took him."

Young folks, what think you—do you suppose the Lord would have sent Elijah food, night and morning, by these ravenous birds, if he had been wicked, a false prophet, man-fearing or time-serving—a wolf in sheep's clothing? one that bowed to conservative, popular views, connived at sin, prophesied smooth things, healed slightly, cried, "Peace, peace," when there was no peace? Never, never.

Nor would He have translated him, taken him to glory in a "chariot of fire." See 2 Kings, ii.

"God, give us men. A time like this demands
 Strong minds, great hearts, true faith, and ready hands·
  Men whom the lust of office does not kill;
 Men whom the spoils of office cannot buy;
  Men who possess opinions and a will;
 Men who have honor—men who will not lie."

SATAN IN—SATAN OUT.—In the Pulpit—In the Press.

Conversation between Mr. Timewell *and* Mr. Servility.
(No. 5.)

"How fond is man,
Dressed in a little brief authority,
To play fantastic tricks before high heaven."

S. "Beecher has his admirers after all, Mr. Timewell.

T. "So had the false prophets in the time of Jezebel—those who listened to their false teachings.

"No matter how wicked a teacher or professed minister of the Gospel may be, how foolish, vain, selfish, sensual, money-loving, he will not lack for admirers and followers—those who embrace his pernicious errors, drink into his devilish spirit.

"He may sip the wine-cup, sit around the card-table, the checker-board, engage in idle, frothy chit-chat, attend the theater, the circus, the ball-room, write novels, romances, sickly, sentimental, foolish love-stories. Teachers of this class will be admired. 'They are of the world, therefore speak they of the world, and the world heareth them.'— 1 *John* iii. 5.

"To these, the religion of the Bible is not a satisfying portion. 'Give us pleasure else we die.'"

S. "You have expatiated largely on the dark side of our friend's theology; why not dwell a little on the bright side of it? His 'Life of Christ,' for instance, have you not for this a word of commendation? It has been extolled by distinguished D.D.'s—J. P. Thompson, Cuyler, Abbott, the editors of 'The Religious Herald,' the 'N. Y. Evangelist,' 'Independent,' the 'Congregationalist,' 'The Baptist Union,' and how many others I know not."

T. "What the ruling motive of friend Beecher in issuing this new work?—the same as that of writing 'Norwood' for the 'N. Y. Ledger' and the theater! Who questions it? When the thirst for gold, or 'ill-gotten gain,' has taken full possession of the soul, there is no quenching it—it burns to the lowest hell!

> 'The craving, burning wish that will not rest,
> The vulture passion of the human breast."

"It's the horse-leache's two daughters crying: 'Give, give!'—Prov. xxx. 15. Taking this view of the subject, what but sacrilege, or blasphemy, high-handed, God-defying, can it be in penning it? This, then, is the capping climax of all his former misdeeds. It's adding sin to sin. And his publishers—puffers—are more or less involved in the same guilt and condemnation! Suppose, by way of illustration, the lying, hypocritical, time-serving Scribes and Pharisees had presumed to write a 'Life of Christ' for speculation at the very time they were denying him by wicked works, would not the heavens have gathered blackness, the thunders have rolled, the lightnings have flashed, in token of vengeance of high heaven? What sin could be greater, more aggravating? The sin of Judas appears trifling in comparison! It's shocking! It's taking heaven's livery to serve the devil in!"

S. "You link together the whole batch, I perceive—the author, his publishers, puffers, sellers and readers!"

T. "From first to last. The partaker is as bad as the thief. 'Neither be ye partakers of other men's sins.' Take another step still lower downwards, if possible. The fraternizing Universalism, Unitarianism, Parkerism, Spiritisms, Freeloveisms—are these from above or from beneath? from heaven or from hell? This fellowshipping the unfruitful works of darkness—intermingling Christ and Belial—is death to Gospel purity and salvation!

> 'The church and world amalgamate,
> A union worse than that of State.'

"If the foundations be destroyed, what can the righteous do?"

S. "Don't Christ say in his parables, 'let both the tares and the wheat grow together till the harvest?'"

T. "That is, let Satan's children remain in the church till the end of the world (or age)! Christ tells us that 'the tares are the children of the wicked one—the enemy that sowed them is the devil.'—*Math.* xiii. 38, 39.

"Carry out this doctrinal preaching which is now extant, and instead of a pure church, 'without spot or wrinkle, an holy priesthood, to offer up spiritual sacrifices, acceptable to God by Jesus Christ,' how soon would it be 'a cage of unclean birds,' made up of black-legs, liars, thieves and robbers—'the world, the flesh and the devil!'"

S. "Friend Timewell, allowing as I do and must, that our friend H. W. Beecher fellowships what is termed 'Liberal Christianity' (semi-infidel), yet can you say authoritatively, he embraces Spiritualists and Freelovers?"

T. "Actions speak louder than words. Why accept the presidency of the women's suffrage movement? did he not know at the very time he accepted the office, that not a few of the members of that society were rank free-lovers and spiritualists of the Theodore Tilton and Woodhull stamp?* 'We are known by the company we keep.' 'Can two walk together except they be agreed?' 'Birds of a feather flock together.' 'Can a man take fire in his bosom and his clothes not be burned?'—*Prov.* vi. 27.

"Look at this subject of Free-loveism; was there ever a heresy more abominable or satanic? Mormonism, as bad as it is, does not compare with it. It is simply a demand for irresponsible licentiousness, and if generally practiced, it will utterly destroy all domestic happiness, and uproot the entire foundations of society.

"'And what concord hath Christ with Belial? or what part hath he that believeth with an infidel?'—2 *Cor.* vi. 15.

"'Though we, or an angel from heaven, preach any other Gospel than that which we have preached to you, let him be accursed.'—*Gal.* i. 8.

"'If there come any unto you and bring not this doctrine, receive him not into your house, neither bid him God speed: For he that biddeth him God speed, is partaker of his evil deeds.'—2 *John* i. 10, 11.

"'There is a conspiracy of her prophets in the midst thereof. . . . Her priests have violated my law, and have profaned mine holy things: they have put no difference between the holy and profane, neither have they shewed *difference* between the unclean and the clean.'—*Ezek.* xxii. 26."

---

* This same Tilton, I am informed, is a member in full communion with the saints of Mr. Beecher's society! And how many more of the same faith and order unite with the pastor at their regular communion seasons? "Like priest like people."

Cain and Abel offering Sacrifices.

The Origin of Unitarianism or Liberal Christianity.

GOD accepted Abel's sacrifice, but would not accept Cain's—Cain was a Unitarian!

Abel, out of love to God, brought what he knew would please God. Cain brought what God did not like, and not from love to God. This was no sacrifice at all, and so God would not have it. This, instead of making Cain sorry, and causing him to bring something like Abel's, that God did like, made him very angry with God, and so hate his brother Abel, that afterwards he killed him; which shows plainly that it was pride, and not love, that made him bring his offering to God.

THE END OF SCOFFERS AND BLASPHEMERS OF THE BIBLE.

Hear the Apostle Peter (chap. ii. 3, 4): "Knowing this first, that in the last days scoffers will come, walking after their own lust, saying: Where is the promise of his coming?"

The scoffing and blaspheming Voltaire said to his physician: "I will give you the half of my property, if you secure me my life for six months longer." But when the answer came that he could not survive so many weeks, he exclaimed: "Then I must go to hell!" Afterwards he alternately called upon Christ, and blasphemed God. Mirabeau cried, in the agonies of death: "Give me more laudanum, that I need not think of eternity, and of what is to come." Hobbes fared no better. His atheism, also, left him without a foundation in that trying hour. He exclaimed: "I am about to take a leap in the dark." It is true, the truthfulness of these citations, which might be multiplied, is denied by the Infidels of our day; but it must be remembered that it is to their interest to deny statements, however truthful, which might work detrimental to a cause to the support of which they are pledged. It is a tacit confession, on their part, that a cause which forsakes its adherents in the most perilous hour is a bad one.

Says an eminent divine: "I have seen Universalists and Infidels die, and during a ministry of fifty-five years I have not found a single instance of peace and joy in their views of eternity.

STEAL, LITTLE FOLKS OR GREAT FOLKS?

Not a pin, a pear, a peach, a plum.

> "On the goods that are not thine,
> Do not dare to lay thy finger;
> On thy neighbor's better things,
> Let no wistful glances linger."

A boy or girl who will steal an apple, a pear, or bouquet, will doubtless, by and by, steal other things and greater things.

SATAN IN—SATAN OUT.—In the Pulpit—In the Press.

Conversation between Mr. TIMEWELL *and* Mr. SERVILITY. (No. 6.)

> " Woe, woe to him on safety bent,
> Who creeps to age from youth ;
> Failing to grasp his life's intent,
> Because he fears the truth."

S. " BEECHER's history, I perceive, is before your mind's eye vividly."

T. " Familiar with it as *a, b, c,* from first to last. I know his twistings, turnings, popular seekings, time servings—how much of the Lord is here and there—how much of Satan, the old serpent, is intermingled here, intermingled there. Conceal our iniquity, seal it up or tie it up in a bag, put it under a bushel, when it is on a candlestick, blazing out? 'Murder will out!' 'Be sure your sins will find you out.'"

S. "Did our friend Henry Ward jump at once into that slow—this mud and mire of moral impurity? Was there not a period in his public ministrations when he, measurably, repudiated these works of the flesh and spirit to which you allude so graphically?"

T. "'*Measurably!*' Well put in. True, there was a time when he said, very softly, 'Get thee behind me, Satan!' But oh! how soon after this began he in good earnest to bow the knee to Baal—sip the muddy streams of sensuality!

Where now? Sitting around the flesh pots of Egypt? Alas! for broken bones! and broken cisterns that hold no water!

"'Alas! how the mighty are fallen, and the weapons of war perished! Tell it not, publish it not! "Lest the daughters of the Philistines rejoice, lest the daughters of the uncircumcised triumph."'—2 *Sam.* i. 20.

"'O foolish man, what hath bewitched you, that you should not obey the truth?'—*Gal.* iii. 1, 2, 3.

"'Satan's ways are moveable.' Sin is gradual—it creeps in little by little—'But a continual dropping weareth away stones.' No man or woman leaps at once into the very arms of Beelzebub! 'Give Satan an inch, he takes an ell.'

"When Jericho was sacked, levelled to the ground, Achan hadn't a distant thought of secreting the golden wedge, to his own destruction. It never entered the noddle of Balaam, in the outset, that he would be, by-and-by, rebuked by the dumb ass for loving the wages of unrighteousness! The four hundred and fifty false prophets that sat at Jezebel's table were not false or dumb dogs all at once. The first step to their low estate might have been receiving honor one of another, and not seeking the honor that cometh from God only. Healing slightly, conferring with flesh and blood, followed of course. What next? bowing to popular expediency! So it was then—so it is now. Had it been suggested to King Saul, when Samuel poured the anointing oil on his head, elevating him to the kingly office, that he would ever have spared Agag and the best of the sheep and oxen, in positive disobedience to heaven's high mandate, or that he would consult the witch of Endor, he would doubtless have been exasperated! Did the Scribes and Pharisees become whited sepulchres all at once?

Very likely they began with tithing mint, anise and cumin, and omitting the weightier matters of the law—judgment, mercy and faith! Had any one told Henry Ward Beecher at the time he penned his 'Lectures to Young Men,' that he would eventually fall into Satan's trap, accept a bribe, write a foolish novel for $30,000 for the 'N. Y. Ledger' and the theatre, take Old Nick into his lap and dandle him on his knees, would he not have exclaimed, as Hazael did to Elisha: 'But what, *is* thy servant a dog, that he should do this great thing? And Elisha answered, The Lord hath showed me that thou *shalt be* king over Syria.'—2 *Kings* viii. 13.

"'When the unclean spirit is gone out of a man, he walketh through dry places seeking rest,' etc. Please turn to Math. xii. 43, 44; also to 2d Peter ii. 20, 21, 22.

> "'First, Appetite enlists him Truth's sworn foe,
> Then obstinate Self-Will confirms him so.
> Tell him he wanders—that his error leads
> To fatal ills—that, though the path he treads
> Be flowery, and he sees no cause of fear,
> Death and the pains of hell attend him there:
> In vain! the slave of arrogance and pride,
> He has no hearing on the prudent side.'

"Friend Servility, did you ever read the tract by the lovely and ever blessed Hannah More, entitled: 'Parley the Porter?'"

S. "Published by what Society?"

T. "'The American,' No. 150 Nassau street."

S. "Why, what of it?"

T. "Henry Ward's picture is drawn to life by this angel of a woman!"

S. "Do you look upon Beecher's case as hopeless?"

T. "What saith the Lord?—'Unto every one that hath shall be given, and he shall have abundance: but from him that hath not, shall be taken away, even that which he hath. And cast ye the unprofitable servant into outer darkness, there shall be weeping and gnashing of teeth.'—*Math.* xxv. 28, 29, 30.

"Look at those whited sepulchres—while the heavens were veiled in thick darkness three hours, the earth quaked, and the rocks rent, the dying agonies of Jesus on the cross rung in their ears, 'Eli, Eli, lama, sabachthani.' Any relentings or heart-softenings bursting forth from these seared consciences? But when 'The centurion, and they that were with him, watching Jesus, saw the earthquake, and those things that were done, they feared greatly, saying, Truly this was the Son of God.'—*Math.* xxvii. 54.

"Even the publicans and harlots enter the kingdom sooner than many who say 'Lord, Lord.' 'There is a sin unto death: I do not say he shall pray for it.'—1st *John* v. 16.

S. "And yet, Mr. Timewell, the good Dr. Watts tells us,

'That while the lamp holds out to burn,
The vilest sinner may return.'"

T. "It's a fearful thing, Mr. Servility, to grieve the Holy Spirit by sinning against light. If the light that is in us become darkness, how great that darkness!

"Hear what Christ says to the man who digged in the earth and 'hid his Lord's money,' or the talent given—'Take therefore the talent from him, and give it unto him which hath ten talents. For unto every one that hath shall be given, and he shall have abundance: but from him that hath not, shall be taken away even that which he hath. And cast ye the unprofitable servant into outer darkness: there shall be weeping and gnashing of teeth.'—*Math.* xxv. 28, 29, 30.

More Dogs—Worse and Worse! Terrible!

RUN, *run!* escape, flee! Here is a boy in the very jaws of a cruel mastiff. Horrible! In a former article we compared wicked men and boys to dogs as God does. But all the dogs in creation that run mad, biting this one and that one, little and big, are not half so much to be deprecated and shunned as "wolves in sheeps' clothing," or even the greedy, dumb dogs who cannot or will not bark.

"Beware of dogs, beware of evil workers: beware of the concision. For we are the circumcision, which worship God in the spirit, and rejoice in Christ Jesus, and have no confidence in the flesh. For without *are* dogs, and sorcerers, and whoremongers, and murderers, and idolaters, and whosoever loveth and maketh a lie. 'I, Jesus, have sent mine Angel, to testify unto you these things in the Churches. I am the root and the offspring of David, and the bright and morning star."

WICKED BOYS.

WICKED? who doubts it? Look at them. A wicked boy or girl can not be wicked long without being known. "Be sure your sin will find you out." Guilt shows itself in every thought, word, and deed, and is sure to bring disgrace, shame, and misery.

Boys and girls are known by their looks and the company they keep.

SATAN IN—SATAN OUT.—In the Pulpit—In the Press.

Conversation between Mr. Timewell *and* Mr. Servility.
(No. 7.)

"Let the righteous smite me ; it shall be a kindness : and let him reprove me ; it shall be an excellent oil, that shall not break my head."—*Psa.* cxli. 5.

S. "You call names I perceive, Mr. Timewell."

T. "This habit I acquired of the old prophets. Elijah, Elisha, Isaiah, Jeremiah, Ezekiel, Daniel, not only called names but declared the fearful consequences of holding our peace :

"'Son of man, I have made thee a watchman unto the house of Israel : therefore hear the word at my mouth, and give them warning from me.

"'When I say unto the wicked, Thou shalt surely die ; and thou givest him not warning, nor speakest to warn the wicked from his wicked way, to save his life ; the same wicked *man* shall die in his iniquity ; but his blood will I require at thine hand.

"'Yet if thou warn the wicked, and he turn not from his wickedness, nor from his wicked way, he shall die in his iniquity ; but thou hast delivered thy soul.

"'Again, When a righteous *man* doth turn from his righteousness, and commit iniquity, and I lay a stumbling-block before him, he shall die : because thou hast not given him warning, he shall die in his sin, and his righteousness which he hath done shall not be remembered; but his blood will I require at thine hand.

"'Nevertheless, if thou warn the righteous *man*, that the righteous sin not, and he doth not sin, he shall surely live, because he is warned; also thou hast delivered thy soul.'—*Ezk.* iii. 17–21.

"This proxy sinning is one of the commonest, widespreading, awful, soul-damning in this 19th century. It's the curse of the land, in church and State. The devil is in it. Look at the publishers of Beecher's books, sermons and periodicals, and the ministers and religious editors of every name, that are holding on to his skirts, puffing the man and and his works, inserting his 'Lecture-room Talks.' Don't they sin by proxy? His sins are not under a bushel, but 'on a candle-stick,' seen and known afar off, spreading the land over, North, South, East and West—across the big waters—from the rising to the setting sun, with lightning speed! And yet they are winked at, dark and damning as they are! Where's Bacon, Thompson, Storrs, Buddington, Cuyler, and a host of other eye-witnesses, sitting under the very *droppings* of this blood guiltiness, we have already alluded to; why hold their peace?

"Why do they not sound the alarm, cry 'Wolf! wolf! look out for the wolf!' Why do they not thunder and *thunder*, and keep on thundering, louder than seven thunders, when they see and hear 'the iniquity which God knoweth?' When they see and know that God is dishonored and truth is bleeding at every pore! Is not the love of popularity at the bottom of this covering sin, or this sinning by proxy? Beecher is popular, carrying a wide row, to rebuke him would be unpopular, he is in the 'Ring,' moves in the same circle with us. Besides, there's capital at stake.

"Call names? How help it? The very stones would cry out. Call names? Louder and still louder, thunder them from pole to pole, thunder on thunder—peal on peal. Every one in public life, in the church, professing discipleship and still on the side of Satan, upliftedly, should be held up sky-high in all his naked, devilish deformity, in characters of blood! as a beacon of warning to young and old, little and big. *What*, kill folks body and soul, murder in open sunshine deliberately, and no one to *scream* out, 'murder! *murder!* MURDER!' stop the murderer, hang him! *Quick!*

"Pilate, Judas Iscariot, Ananias, Simon Magus, Porphyry, Celsus, Galevis, Voltaire, David Hume, and Thomas Paine, are united witnesses that 'the way of the transgressor *is hard.*' The shocking fate of all these men should teach modern opposers of religion the end to which they are hastening. What cause have Christians to fear when another madman raises his puny arm against the Creator and Ruler of all things? Do we fear that God cannot govern the world?"

S. "You dwell on proxy sinning or sinning by proxy, friend Timewell, that is, one man's sin becomes another's by substitution?"

T. "Clear as the noon-day sun. Paul didn't throw any stones at Stephen, he merely looked on, and took good care of the clothes of them that were stoning Stephen to death! *Acts* vii. 58.

"By holding our peace, suffering sin to rest on our mutual friend, H. W. Beecher, his sins, scarlet-colored as they are, become ours by proxy. When he writes novels and other silly things for '*N. Y. Ledgers*' and theaters, 'for so much gold,' do we not the very same?

"When he goes to the Grand Opera house, to deliver a

popular lecture for ready pay, do we not accompany him—take a seat by his side in this sink-hole, or hot-bed of lewdness?

"'A feast is made for laughter, and wine maketh merry: but money answereth all things.'—*Ecc.* x. 19.

"When he gives loose to a flippant, nonsensical tonge, is not this same wicked tongue ours?

"'The tongue *is* a fire, a world of iniquity: so is the tongue among our members, that it defileth the whole body, and setteth on fire the course of nature; and it is set on fire of hell.'—*James* iii. 6.

"When he engages in carnal pleasures and amusements, goes to the nine-pin alley, or takes his seat around the chess or checker board, or the billiard table, are we not there with him in high glee, having a jolly time—cracking jokes, saying, 'Let us eat, drink and be merry, for to-morrow we die?'

"'Will ye play, then, will ye dally
With your music and your wine?
Up! it is Jehovah's rally!
God's own arm hath need of thine!'

"'It is better to hear the rebuke of the wise than for a man to hear the song of fools. For, as the crackling of thorns under a pot, so is the laughter of the fool.'—*Eccles.* vii. 6. 'The heart of the wise is in the house of mourning; but the heart of fools is in the house of mirth.'—*Eccles.* vii. 4.

"When he says:—

"'On with the dance! Let mirth be unconfined;
No sleep till morn, when youth and pleasure meet,
To chase the glowing hours with flying feet,'

are we not, meanwhile, in the same merry company skipping the fantastic toe?

"'Ye adulterers and adulteresses, know ye not that the friendship of the world is enmity with God? whosoever, therefore, will be a friend of the world is the enemy of God.'—*James* iv. 4.

"'If any man love the world, the love of the Father is not in him.'

"A dancing minister soon finds his estimation of all. The celebrated Adam Clark, the commentator, says: 'I consider dancing a branch of that worldly education which leads from heaven to earth, from things spiritual to things sensual, and from God to Satan. Let them plead for it who will, I know it to be an evil, and only evil. "No man in his senses would dance," said Cicero, a heathen. Shame, then, on those Christians who advocate a cause by which many sons have become profligate, and many daughters have been ruined.

> "'Oh, world! how deeply fallen from thy sphere!
> Oh, mind! how lost thy noblest wing of thought!
> Oh, soul, how base thy form—how lost art thou
> To God's similitude—how deep thy stain!'

"When he, from the pulpit, intermingles things, solemn as heaven, fearful as eternity, with facetiousness, jests and trifling witticisms, exciting the fool's laughter, are we not present, meanwhile, cackling nonsense, or offering strange fire! And have we not cause to fear that God, in anger, will send fire from heaven and burn us up, as he did Nadab and Abihu?'—*Levit.* x. 1, 2, 3.*

"Again, false doctrines lead to wicked practices. Do we

---

* "And if ye offer the blind for sacrifice, is it not evil? and if ye offer the lame and the sick, is it not evil? Offer it now unto thy governor; will he be pleased with thee, or accept thy person? saith the Lord of hosts."—*Mal.* i. 7-8.

declaim against these? or hold our peace, wipe our mouth and say we have done no wickedness?

"When he meets those around the communion table, whose garments are spotted all over with the flesh, denying the Lord that bought them, spots in our feasts of charity, sporting themselves with their own deceivings, 'feeling themselves without fear,' are we not present eating and drinking with them damnation to ourselves?

"'For he that eateth and drinketh unworthily, eateth and drinketh damnation to himself, not discerning the Lord's body.'—1 *Cor.* xii. 29.

"'Ye cannot drink the cup of the Lord, and the cup of devils : ye cannot be partakers of the Lord's table and of the table of devils.'—1 *Cor.* x. 21.

"Mr. Servility, you get the idea by this time, I trust, what I mean by proxy sinning? Isaiah, however, makes the subject still plainer. Chapter lvi. 9, 10, 11 :

"'All ye beasts of the field, come to devour, *yea*, all ye beasts in the forest.

"'His watchmen *are* blind : they are all ignorant, they *are* all dumb dogs, they cannot bark ; sleeping, lying down, loving to slumber.

"'Yea, *they are* greedy dogs *which* can never have enough, and they *are* shepherds *that* cannot understand ; they all look to their own way, every one for his gain, from his quarter.'

George Washington and his Mother.

WHAT is this lovely mother doing? imparting instruction to little George? From what, the Bible?—or a novel, a book of lies? Had he been nourished on lies or fictions, would he have been honored as the father of his country? Lying makes cowards, in the church and out of it! Who ever knew a writer, puffer or reader of lies or novels that was a true Bible reformer—a bold soldier of the cross? or one that possessed any good degree of spiritual fire, gospel vim or backbone? Such a thing was never dreamed of!

Little Mary and her Mother.

A word to Mothers on keeping Good Company!

> "At first, the pages of the book
> Are blank and purely fair,
> But time soon writeth memories,
> And painteth pictures there."

CAREFUL of little Mary's associations! None more so—

> "That no stain of sin may settle,
> Like the dust on wayside daisies,
> On their souls, to soil their sweetness."

Where can we hope for virtuous modesty, gospel purity and simplicity, except in Christian mothers?

> "How can ye hope that she will live,
> If ye, for flesh, a serpent give?"

When you attire Mary in a beautiful white dress, and after a little you see it all smutted up, dark with greasy spots here and there on it, how speedily you *off* with it, and put on something in its place, nice, plain, neat, and comely. You can't endure to see her go slip-shod, or with dirty, or spotted garments, a single moment. Are you equally cautious, beloved, in keeping her soul unspotted by the flesh?

"Sophronius, a wise teacher of the people, did not allow his sons and daughters, when they were grown up, to associate with persons whose lives were not moral and pure.

"'Father,' said the gentle Eulalia, one day, when he had refused to permit her to go in company with her brother to visit the frivolous Lucinda, 'father, you must think that we are very weak and childish, since you are afraid that it would be dangerous to us in visiting Lucinda.'

"Without saying a word, the father took a coal from the hearth and handed it to his daughter. 'It will not burn you, my child,' said he; 'only take it.'

"Eulalia took the coal, and behold, her tender, white hand was black, and, without thinking, she touched her white dress, and it was blackened.

"'See,' said Eulalia, somewhat displeased, as she looked at her hands and dress, 'one cannot be careful enough when handling coals.'

"'Yes, truly,' said her father. 'You see, my child, that the coal, even though it *did not burn you*, has, nevertheless, *blackened you*. So is the company of immoral persons.'"

Of all the snares to which children are exposed, we know of none more fatal, more ruinous than those which spring from *improper companions*. The Word of God expressly forbids associating with evil companions. "Enter not into the path of the wicked, and go not in the way of evil men.

Avoid it, pass not by it, turn from it, and pass away." "If sinners entice thee, consent thou not. My son, walk not thou in the way with them; refrain thy foot from their path." "Be not equally yoked together with unbelievers; for what fellowship hath righteousness with unrighteousness? and what communion hath light with darkness?" "Blessed is the man that walketh not in the counsel of the ungodly, nor standeth in the way of sinners, nor sitteth in the seat of the scornful." "A companion of fools shall be destroyed."

The very atmosphere of the unchaste or vicious is infectious, malaria, more to be feared than the deadly sirocco, or a "bear robbed of her whelps."

> "Far off the road which leads to death
> Looks beautiful and fair!"

You are, we venture to say, beloved parent, guarding this precious little jewel, as the apple of the eye, against the first approach of evil—the least particle of contaminating influence, folding her in the very bosom of the Saviour's love.

> "If he lay His hand on the children,
> My heart will be lighter, I know
> For a blessing forever and ever
> Will follow them as they go."

Nothing short of continued, steadfast, Bible discipline will meet the emergencies of the case. This unwavering, ceaseless diligence in the path of duty and holy living is what God indicates in the precept, "Train up a child in the way it should go, and when it is old it will not depart from it."

> "Happy the soul that reads the page
> That guides our youth and cheers our age;
> Yea, blessed evermore is he,
> O Lord, who learns to come to thee."

SATAN IN—SATAN OUT —In the Pulpit—In the Press.

Conversation between MR. TIMEWELL *and* MR. SERVILITY.
(No. 8.)

> " Art thou faithful? then oppose
> Sin and wrong with all thy might;
> Care not how the tempest blows,
> Only care to do the right."

S. "WHY pounce thus upon Beecher, aim your forty-pounders at his head, load and fire in quick succession? Are there not others equally deserving castigation? You tell us 'the partaker is as bad as the thief.'"

T. "Beecher is king in the 'Ring'—the great high priest in the Sanhedrim. He stands at the head of this papacy—he is the Diana whom all 'the world worshippeth.'—*Acts* xix. 27. 'Sirs, ye know that by this craft we have our wealth.'"

S. "Friend Timewell, I appreciate your motives highly; but is not the picture drawn here too highly colored?"

T. "The dearest, sweetest, the most exalted, heavenly, gospel truths are trailed in the dust. Exaggerate? the half is not told! We speak that we do know, testify that we see.

"If our leaders are corrupt, blind leaders of the blind, what can we expect of the people? Is it a marvel the whole world is tottering on the very brink of dark damnation?

> ' 'Tis when the cross is preached, and only then,
> That from the pulpit a mysterious power
> Goes forth to renovate the moral man.
> He that without it wields
> The sacred sword, at best in mock display,
> A useless weapon flourishes in its sheath;
> None feel its edge—none fear it.'

"Friend Servility, I have merely glanced at a few items touching the awful, superabounding, soul-ruinous state of things, theologically, from writing lies, puffing lies, selling lies, reading lies—little lies and big lies, white lies and black lies—lies of first, second and third rate, malignity. Also from love of popularity, the receiving honor one of another, and seeking not 'the honor which cometh from God only.' I have uttered the words of truth and soberness. I believe, therefore I speak, speak what I know and what multitudes of God's dear people know and weep over when their sons and daughters are decoyed into the traps of Satan through the instrumentality of this one man in sacerdotals!

"I ask, in the name of our Lord and Saviour Jesus Christ, how can you help forward these works of the flesh, fellowship the unfruitful works of darkness, at a time when iniquity of every kind abounds, and the love of many wax cold?

"With soul-melting love we can thunder, thunder, lighten, lighten—cut here, cut there, on the right and on the left—use the two-edged sword of God's truth with ample execution! Formalists, dead professors, novel writers, time servers, will kick at this, kick at that, cry 'Censoriousness, persecution, bitter spirit,' etc., when determined to hold on to their lusts, though words of reproof used are gentle as grace can make them—in language, too, sweeter than angels use! So it was, so it is. 'For every one that doeth evil, hateth the light, neither cometh to the light, lest his deeds should be reproved.'—*John* iii. 20.

"What now? hush reproof—let Satan do his worst? What saith the Lord to Ezekiel?

"'And they, whether they will hear or whether they will

forbear, (for they are a rebellious house,) yet shall know that there hath been a Prophet among them.

"'And thou son of man, be not afraid of them, neither be afraid of their words, though briers and thorns be with thee, and thou dost dwell among scorpions: be not afraid of their words, nor be dismayed at their looks, though they be a rebellious house.

"'And thou shalt speak my words unto them, whether they will hear or whether they will forbear, for they are most rebellious.'—*Ezek.* iii. 5, 6, 7.

"'A reproof entereth more into a wise man, than a hundred stripes into a fool.

"'And now, O ye Priests, this commandment is for you.

"'If ye will not hear, and if ye will not lay it to heart, to give glory unto my name, saith the Lord of hosts; I will even send a curse upon you, and will curse your blessings: yea, I have cursed them already, because ye do not lay it to heart.'—*Mal.* ii. 1, 2.

"My words are ended—speak if thou hast anything to say. 'Speak, open thy lips wide, else forever hold thy peace!'

"'Let me not, I pray you, accept any man's person: neither let me give flattering titles unto man.

"'For I know not to give flattering titles: in so doing my Maker would soon take me away.'—*Job* xxxiii. 21, 27."

S. "Thus saying, thou reproachest me also!"

T. "If the coat fits, Mr. Servility, put it on. 'To him that knoweth to do good and doeth it not, to him it is sin.' 'How long halt ye between two opinions? if the Lord be God, follow him; but if Baal, then follow him.'—1 *Kings* xviii. 21.

"Your name is 'Servility'—significant, representing a

class to which you belong! Are you not tired, sick, ashamed of these galling chains, when it is your blessed privilege to be free in Christ Jesus!

> "'Break every yoke,' the Gospel cries,
> 'And let the oppressed go free,
> Let every burdened captive rise,
> And taste sweet liberty!'"

S. "What council give you in Beecher's case, friend Timewell?"

T. "Jesus Christ's of course. To the law and the testimony: if we abide not by these, it's because there's no light in us. What saith the inspired Paul, in a case not dissimilar? Turn to 1 Cor. v. 5, 6: 'Deliver such an one unto Satan for the destruction of the flesh, that the spirit may be saved in the day of the Lord Jesus. Your glorying is not good. Know ye not that a little leaven leaveneth the whole lump?'

"Mark also what follows, verses 9, 11: 'I wrote unto you in an epistle not to keep company with fornicators. . . . or covetous, or an idolater, or a railer, or a drunkard, or an extortioner; with such an one do not eat.'

"'Therefore put away from among yourselves that wicked person.' '(For many walk, of whom I have told you often, and now tell you even weeping, that they are the enemies of the cross of Christ: Whose end is destruction, whose God is their belly, and whose glory is in their shame, who mind earthly things.)'

"Peter likewise, in his 2d epistle, chap. ii. 1, 2, says: 'There were false prophets also among the people, even as there shall be false teachers among you, who privily shall bring in damnable heresies, even denying the Lord that bought them, and bring upon themselves swift destruction. And many shall follow their pernicious ways; by reason of whom the way of truth shall be evil spoken of. And through covetousness shall they with feigned words make merchandize of you: whose judgment now of a long time lingereth not, and their damnation slumbereth not.'

"I could fill up, and keep filling up, page after page, similar passages from heaven's inspiration, showing what your duty is, and the duty of every one naming the name of Christ, 'to be careful to depart from all iniquity.'"

S. "Are these quotations from the inspired volume peculiarly applicable to the present time?"

T. "To all time. What killed the seven churches of Asia dead, *dead!* twice dead? Just what you and your National Councils are doing. Wherefore did these churches, once flourishing, dwindle and dwindle, become more and more corrupt, till not fit for the land, nor yet for the dunghill, and God spued them out? Blind! who more? While they vainly and proudly imagined they were rich, increased in goods, and had need of nothing, at that very time God told them they were 'wretched and miserable, and poor and blind, and naked.'—*Rev.* iii. 17. See your picture drawn to life and that of your 'Council'—two hundred and fifty in number! And what doth the Holy Spirit tell you to do? Read verse 18th in this same 3d chapter of Revelation."

S. "It is said of these same Laodiceans to whom you allude, 'they were neither cold nor hot!' Was this wretched state of things brought about by healing slightly, embracing in full fellowship 'garments spotted with the flesh?'"

T. "The fraternizing also, meanwhile, errorists, false teachers and false prophets? The same you are doing. 'Behold, how great a matter a little fire kindleth.'

"Hark! 'But I have a few things against thee, because thou hast there them that hold the doctrine of Balaam, who taught Balak to cast a stumbling-block before the children of Israel, to eat things sacrificed unto idols, and to commit fornication.

"'So hast thou also them that hold the doctrine of the Nicolaitanes, which thing I hate.

"'Repent, or else I will come unto thee quickly, and will fight against them with the sword of my mouth.'—*Rev.* ii. 14, 15, 16.

"Likewise, hear what the Spirit saith to the church of Thyatira.

"'I have a few things against thee, because thou sufferest that woman Jezebel, which calleth herself a prophetess, to teach and to seduce my servants to commit fornication, and to eat things sacrificed unto idols.

"'And I gave her space to repent of her fornication, and she repented not.

"'Behold, I will cast her into a bed, and them that commit adultery with her into great tribulation, except they repent of their deeds.

"'And I will kill her children with death; and all the churches shall know that I am he which searcheth the reins and hearts: and I will give unto every one of you according to your works.'—*Rev.* ii. 20, 21, 22, 23.

"'He that is unjust, let him be unjust still: and he which is filthy, let him be filthy still.'"

Address....Author of "THE SWORD THAT CUTS,"
303 West Twentieth St., New York.

THE SLOUGH OF DESPOND. (See Bunyan's Pilgrim.)

The Mother and the Little Ones.

ASKING a blessing, giving thanks for the bounties of heaven spread before them? Beautiful! *What*, sit down, eat and drink to the full, and not a single out-bursting thought of humble gratulations! Shameful! Even the animals express tokens of gratitude for favors conferred. We know a little boy, not bigger than our sweet Mary, who never puts a bit of food to his mouth, without opening his lips wide in thanksgivings to God, the giver of all good. Christ is our example in this and in everything good and beautiful.

When he fed multitudes on a few loaves and fishes— what the first thing? Give thanks? *always*. See Matthew xiv. 19.

"WIDE-AWAKE AND POPULAR!"

Indeed, Mr. Editor of the "*Examiner and Chronicle*," what makes your weekly so very popular? On account of the novels you insert, advertise and puff? Among what class of readers is your sheet popular? The Godly, those whose souls are alive in God? or with the giddy multitude, the gay, pleasure-seeking, and frolicsome, that pour over the religious novels you send forth weekly—fictitious tales—inlets to reading, the most corrupting, soul-revolting! By filling your sheet thus, do you not pander to the already corrupt tates of the ungodly? Is this the way you honor the Master? Is this the food you place before ministers and people—newly born souls? Sunday School children? Mean *you?* Yes, we mean *you*, friend editor, you are the guilty one whose skirts are dripping with the blood of souls?

How many dear, young disciples of the Lord Jesus, have already lost their first love, returned to beggarly elements, "the flesh-pots of Egypt," pride, folly, fashion, carnal pleasures, the ball room, theater; then down, down! to the steps of hell! through you? What a fearful harvest you are reaping! Sow to the wind? What now? reap the whirlwind? Kill piety? eat out the life and essence of Gospel salvation? Nothing surer than what you are doing?

Do you tell us, friend, that you do not insert black lies, but religious? Worse still. Stop your wicked religious white lying, and we have no black lying.*

---

* We tell the "*Christian Intelligencer*," "*The American Tract Society*," "*Sunday School Union*," "*The Religious Herald*," "*The Congregationalist*" of Boston, the very same. Satan is here, Satan is there! Where is he not?

Stop tippling, and we have no drunken sots, no deaths by delirium tremens, no drunkards' graves, no drunkards' hells!

We may keep our children from the theater, and so train them that they shall never desire to frequent it; but there is now an educator presented within their reach which soon may undermine all the home lessons of purity, and, by easy steps, lead them to perdition.

The teachings of our schools and our churches must be to a great extent in vain, while these wretched panderers to depravity are undoing the work of the school and the church. One such periodical may do more evil than many pulpits can correct. If this raid of license remains unchecked, preaching, teaching, and warning will be alike in vain. "Help, Lord."

Mean *you*? Who else? "THOU ART THE MAN." We mean you, and every one thus helping the devil out-stretchedly!

Satan was the first author of novels, and his followers have been quite successful in carrying out the principles of his school. It was he who first addressed the imagination and passions of Eve in the garden of Paradise, and was it not a deceptive and unfounded tale, that "brought death into the world, and all our woe?"

> "How shall I speak thee, or thy power addresss,
> Thou god of our idolatry, the Press."

> "Life's hours are short and few,
> As transitory as the morning dew.
> 'Tis meet that they should be
> Well spent; for, oh! if wasted, they but bring
> A present cloy, and, for their closing time,
> Treasure remorse, the spirit's deathless sting."

TOYS FOR CHILDREN.

*"There is a path that leads to God,
All others go astray."*

VICE and infidelity assail even childhood and in fancy, and by means so insidious and infamous, so seemingly innocent, that the child is not only captivated, but even the watchful and pious parent is likely to be deceived and beguiled, until the secret poison, thus artfully disguised, has been injected into the unsuspecting victim.

Such are the toy cards, toy dominos, and other games, artfully prepared with flowers and cuts, to catch the fancy of children, for the purpose of inducting them into the habit and love of the gambler's art, and imbuing them with the gambler's fiendish heart and hellish guilt.

We warn all parents against subjecting their children to the influence of these demoralizing and corrupting toys. They differ nothing from other gambling apparatus, but in their adaptation to the capacities of children; and on that account are the more dangerous, and therefore the more to be dreaded. They prompt the same feelings, fire the same unhallowed passions, are susceptible of the same uses, and work out the same results as any other, even the most fraudulent and corrupting gambling apparatus.

Take another view of this prevailing evil, considered by many as laudable or harmless—the toys and playthings of every description, with which all our fancy stores are filled during Christmas holidays.

The amount expended on these articles, of little or no value, is *immense.* Is this in accordance with Bible stewardship? Were children trained in the way they should go, nurtured from early infancy in the fear of the Lord, on gospel principles, would they delight, as they now do, in these trifling toys?

> "With such poor *trifles* playing,
> Moments make the year and *trifles* life."

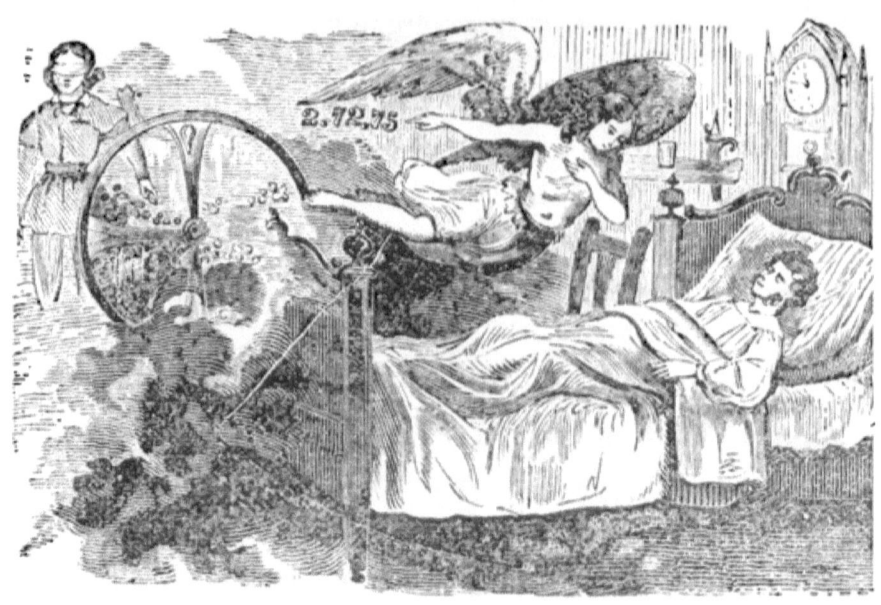

The Lottery Dreamer—Satan Helping!

If church folks gamble, sell tickets, have their feasts, festivals, sociables, fancy fairs, tea-parties, oyster suppers, post offices, grab-boxes, ring-cakes, scenes of mirthfulness and levity, sit down, eat, drink and rise up to play for money—why not Satan's children follow suit? The church helps the world. Novels, fictitious writings and readings are more or less inlets to this wickedness—gambling in the church and out of it.

No one can deny that the mental passion of gambling is as terrible and destructive as the physical appetite for strong drink; and they are, to a great extent, concomitant, supplementary, one of the other.

"THE BEST FOOD FOR THE MIND."

What do you mean by this, Mr. Editor of the "*Hearth and Home?*" Do you tell parents and children that novels or religious lies are the best food on which to feed precious immortals? How large a portion of your weekly is made of fiction, or religious lying? silly things to excite the fool's laughter? Look and see? Do you publish these to please the Master? or to fill your coffers?

By doing what you are doing, is it what the blessed Redeemer would do? Could you possibly put your hand and heart *to any thing* more pleasing to the old Serpent, the devil? You call yourself a Christian? What is a Christian? To be like Christ. When about to send forth these religious or white lies to hundreds of thousands of families, do you bow the knee to the mercy-seat and implore the Lord to bless these silly tales or white lies to the conviction, conversion and sanctification of parents and children?

If you feed little folks and great folks on lies, will they not be converted to lies? Will it add to your comfort, consolation or joyfulness at the final day, to see and know you have been instrumental in leading multitudes to perdition? What avail then your "ill-gotten gains?" the love of filthy lucre? Hear James, from the mouth of inspiration:

"Your riches are corrupted, and your garments are moth-eaten. Your gold and silver is cankered; and the rust of them shall be a witness against you, and shall eat your flesh as it were fire. Ye have heaped treasure together for the last days."—*James* v. 2-3.

You are the Christian man that tells us we must have good stories, good tales, good novels, to counteract the bad ones—that is, you give your readers good, or white lies, to keep out the bad or black lies. How long, friend, think you, after feeding on your silly, nonsensical white lies, ere the little folks swallow greedily the black lies—the blackest of the black, the most devilish? Do you tell us, religious editors advertise and puff your novel sheet that caters to a corrupt taste? *

How is this to better the matter? this putting shoulder to Satan's wheels unitedly? Stop this wickedness? No, you won't, friend. It's popular to serve the devil, money is made by it, and you go it with your compeers. What we say to you, we say to the editor of the "*Christian Union*," and others, not a few, treading in your steps! and who doubtless will receive the same reward: "Beware! your sins will find you out."

---

* The taste for strong drink, the cup that intoxicates, the poisonous, degrading, "Indian weed," you are aware is unnatural, vicious, obstinate, deeply rooted, and nothing will effectually destroy the relish for these poisons but superabounding grace—God's infinite mercy. So it is with the reading or mental taste—a taste formed for the light, frivolous, fictitious and vicious! The forming of this unnatural and vicious taste, in both these cases, is the work of Satan, the old Serpent, the devil, to decoy, entrap, and ruin both soul and body. It is a question, yet unsolved, whether the enemy of all good succeeds in taking more souls to perdition through the instrumentality of rum and tobacco, or that of the light, frothy, popular literature—novels and romances. Both are intoxicating, dissipating, soul ruinous!

"NO TIME TO PRAY?"

INDEED! What is time? Whose is it? Who made time? Is time yours, or God's? Has God given you time to live, breathe, walk, talk, pray? Why not pray, then—mind what God says? God commands you to pray, pray always with all prayer and supplication in the Spirit.

"But I have so much business."*

"Business" indeed! What business? Yours, or God's?"

---

* It is said of Martin Luther, that the more he had to do the more frequently and fervently he prayed. On one occasion he remarked to a friend, "I have so much to do to-day that I shall have to pray three hours." May not this custom of the great Reformer contain a valuable suggestion to us, who, in the midst of a continual pressure of duties, are in danger of being " overcharged," and forgetting to seek that relief and strength which alone can be obtained in prayer, in earnest supplication to God?

THE HOUSE-TOP: OR, THE ANCIENT MODE OF HOUSE-BUILDING.

The roof is flat, often covered over with solid earth, or a kind of plaster made of coals, ashes, stones, and other substances pounded together. On these roofs a little grass grows and shrubbery; but these soon wither under the heat of the sun. *Psalm* cxxix. 6–8.

The roofs of these houses have always been much used as places of pleasant retirement, where any one, little folks or great folks, can, if they choose, retire to read, meditate, and pray—pour out their souls in prayer to God for themselves and for others. On the tops of these houses it is common to walk in the evening, enjoy its cool breezes, and there, in summer, persons often sleep under the broad arch of heaven. On such a roof, Rahab concealed the spies with stalks of flax. *Josh.* ii. 6. Samuel talked with Saul.

Teaching Little Mary the Way of Life!

Or Early Piety—"Apples of Gold."

"When Jesus was here among men,
 He called little children as lambs to his fold."

A SWEET and lovely spirit of piety in a little child's heart, is like the sunlight shining on the dew-drops of the morning.

Our Father is good and kind to his little ones; he listens to their earliest prayers, and rejoices in the first faint fragrance of the opening bud, which, if tenderly shielded and prayerfully nursed, will even now yield the ripened fruit of a holy life.

"Suffer little children to come unto me, and forbid them not, for of such is the kingdom of heaven."

Jesus was once a child, a holy child; and here is the great plea for childhood. He who was once a child perfectly understands and sympathizes with the heart of childhood. And how dare we limit the Holy One, and say that a child may not be a true Christian? However early we begin our teachings, we will find that the Holy Spirit has been before us. Isaiah speaks of teaching those just weaned—here a little, there a little, precept upon precept, line upon line—which is the proper manner of teaching children.

Children apprehend religious truths more readily than almost anything else. It has even been maintained by some, that the children that cried in the temple, "Hosanna to the Son of David!" had discovered, with their nicer apprehensions, the Christ whom the rulers ignored. Early childhood is certainly the favored time for the inculcation of religious truth. Then there are no doubts. You never meet a child-atheist. The very credulity of childhood is a great advantage. Truth is allied to innocency, and the child believes implicitly until deception has induced distrust. Not that religious faith is the gift of nature. But the very aptitude to believe is favorable to the reception of religious truth. The child has not formed the habit of questioning and doubting that troubles so many adults. The old athiest can testify to the truth of this.

Every child knows what it is to love his mother, but can he tell you anything more about it than that he feels it? Can any man say more?

Every child can take hold of his father's hand and go with him in the dark, and that is having faith in his father; but he cannot tell what faith is.

The child Samuel could say, "Speak, Lord, for thy servant heareth," though he could not know the voice of the Lord from the voice of Eli.

So the little child can believe in Christ, and love Christ, though he cannot know all the deep things in religion. He can live upon the sincere milk of the word, and grow thereby, and that is all that is necessary for his being gathered to Christ.

So the little one does not know how he believes in Christ, and how he lives by faith, but he does. And the tall trees of the forest, and the giant oak on the hill, can no more tell how they are nourished by the rain and the sunshine, than the violets that grow in the crack of a rock; and the lofty tree in the garden and the frail lily are alike fed, they know not how. When the child has said that he feels love to Christ in his heart, could a Newton, with all his great mind, say more?

On one occasion, a little child sat quietly upon its mother's lap. Its soft blue eyes were looking earnestly into her face, which was beaming with love and tenderness. The maternal lips were busy with the story of the Cross. The tones of her voice were low and serious, for the tale was one of mingled sadness and joy. The listening babe caught every sound. The crimson deepened on its little cheek as the story went on increasing in interest. Tears gathered in its eyes, and a low sob broke the stillness. The child inquired,

"Did he die for *me*, mamma—and may I love him always, and dearly, too?"

"Yes, my darling; it was to win your love that he left his bright and beautiful home."

> "Scatter ye seeds in the garden of heart—
>   Seeds of affection, of truth, and of love;
>   Cultivate carefully each hidden part,
>   And the flowers will be seen by angels above."

Address ... *Author of* "*Apples of Gold,*"
203 West Twentieth Street, New York.

HERE THEY ARE, FATHER, AND MOTHER, AND THE SWEET LITTLE ONES.

These parents united in family discipline harmoniously? Unquestionably; else, how clock-work, heaven in the domestic circle? What father says, mother says; what mother says, father says. When father corrects the little ones for disobedience, the mother coincides heartily, joyfully—says, "So let it be." And when mother applies the rod of chastisement when it ought to be applied, does father interfere, say, "Spare the rod?" Not for a thousand worlds! He knows it would cause friction, and may-be the ruin of the child. Here lies one grand secret of success in household training. Without this united, harmonious union, where is hope of good family government, salvation?

LOOK HERE, LITTLE FOLKS—WHAT DO YOU SEE?

BABIES, BABIES—LITTLE FOLKS AND LITTLE FOLKS?

Babies here, babies there, little folks here, little folks there, heaps on heaps; and oh! what a blessing these sweet little godsends, trained in heavenly wisdom! Little folks make the world better and happier? Children trained for Jesus are the salt of the earth, lighthouses. The lambs, trained up lambs, mild, gentle, loving, in the bosom of redeeming, sanctifying grace, are polished stones, olive-plants, roses that bloom all the year, send forth a delicious fragrance sweeter than the perfumes of Arabia.

TABLES TURNED—THE WOMAN HELPING THE EARTH.

The World Converting the Church!

"The church and world amalgamate,
A union worse than with the State."

"While men slept the enemy came and sowed tares among the wheat and went his way."—*Matt.* xiii. 25.

Conversation between Mr. TIMEWELL *and* Mr. SERVILITY. (No. 9.)

S. "What! still at it, Mr. Timewell?"

T. "Is it you, friend Servility, or have you changed your name?"

S. "Not exactly changed it, but since our last interview I've been thinking, thinking, thinking!"

T. "The Lord help you, not only to think and keep on thinking, but to think right, speak right, act right, stand for truth, obey God, though the heavens fall to rise no more.

"'How long will ye judge unjustly: and accept the persons of the wicked?'—*Psa.* lxxxii. 2.

"'Dare to be right! Dare to be true!
Other men's failures will not excuse you.'

"A man, to be a man of God, must *dare* to be in the minority, dare to be despised of men, dare maintain his rightful position, though it cost him his *life!*

"Look at the 'Congregationalist,' one of your denominationals, on which side is it the most actively engaged? the Lord's or the devil's?"

S. "You have eyes behind, eyes before, and on either

side. What ship now has sprung a leak? what new fires are kindled?"

T. "On February 22d, this linsey-woolsey sheet says: 'I've no objection to light reading, the reading of fiction, if you take in ballast with it.' That is, tell families, parents and children, first of all, take a dose of lies or fictions, as many as you choose, can swallow, cram down, then top off with truth enough to balance or equipoise. In addition to this shaking hands with Diabolus, what do you see nearly every week in this same sickly periodical of yours, under the heading, 'FICTION?' a whole column or more eulogizing—Satan here, Satan there—snakes here, snakes there—white lies and black lies, to feed the already visciated taste of parents and children! Could Beelzebub, the prince of devils, desire an agent more efficient or competent to people his dark domains, of weepings, wailings and gnashings of teeth?

"If there ever is such a thing as a jubilee in hell, among the hosts at the bottom of the pit bottomless, surely deeds like these call forth one of the most jubilant of all jubilees! the vaults of the infernal regions ring! And this is merely a specimen of what the devil is doing through his active and persevering agents in pulpits and editorial chairs, throughout the land! Curse on curse, damnation on damnation follow rapidly in the train of this writing, advertising and puffing, these religious novels—tales of romance!

"And, Mr. Servility, you behold with open eyes this blackness of darkness, this hugging the old Serpent, and not a syllable of reproof or cry of warning is heard from your lips; wherefore? It's popular to serve the devil. Furthermore, 'Sirs, ye know that by this craft we have our wealth.'—*Acts* xix. 25.

"Your name is Servility, and Servility it will be. 'Though thou shouldest bray a fool in a mortar among wheat with a pestle, *yet* will not his foolishness depart from him.' "—*Pro.* xxvii. 22.

S. "You make everything of lying, of writing and telling of lies, Mr. Timewell. Are there not other sins equally reprehensible and mischievous, coming under your notice for rebuke? Why make a hobby of this one?"

T. "Name a single sin, Mr. Servility, in church or State, in high places or in low, that springs not forth sooner or later from this 'Pandora box,' this accursed lust of gain, filthy lucre! Millions on millions, twice told, are poured into the coffers of these agents of the devil through this traffic in lying, writing, puffing and selling lies. The whole atmosphere is impregnated with falsehoods.

"Look into editors' sanctums, what do you see? lies, heaps on heaps. Take a peep into religious book stores everywhere, what do you see? lies? heaps on heaps, shelves *groaning* under the weight of lies—black lies, and white lies? Go into reading rooms, public and private: any lies—snakes here, snakes there? View center-tables of Christian families, any lies to be seen? Cast your eyes on the paper and book stands through our cities, anything *but* lies? Ask these panderers to vice, why they thus help the devil to do his devilish work? The reply is: 'We must live, come life come death.' Like the traffickers in strong drink and tobacco, the motto is, 'If we don't kill, poison to death body and soul, some one else will.'

"Into what Sunday-school book store or Sunday-school library are not found fiction, heaps on heaps, that should be consigned to the pit bottomless, where it originated! Our mail-bags are loaded with fiction, groaning, being burdened!

From day to day cart loads upon cart loads are sent forth from our General Post-office, of cursed fiction, to curse the rising age—the whole world!

"Religious novels, silly tales, fashion plates, comicals, etc., are flooding the land, darkening the heavens like the flies, frogs, lice and locusts of Egypt, but far more dangerous. They 'go up and come into thine house, and into thy bed-chamber, and upon thy bed, and into the house of thy servants, and upon thy people, and into thine ovens, and into thy kneading-troughs.'

"Rev. T. Dewitt Talmage says: 'There are enough bad newspapers weekly poured out into the houses of our country, to poison a vast population. In addition to the home manufacture of iniquitous sheets, the mail-bags come in from other cities, gorged with abominations. New York scoops up from the sewers of other cities, and adds to its own newspaper filth.'"

S. "You talk about white lies and white lying, where is your Scripture for this?"

T. "I use the term by way of accommodation, speaking after the manner of men. In reality there is no such thing as a little or white lie; the littlest lie, and the whitest lie ever told is black enough and devilish enough to send every one concocting it to 'the lake that burneth with fire and brimstone—this is the second death.'

"This fearful doom denounced upon '*all liars*,' ought to stop the mad career of these religious writers and puffers of lies, who are 'treasuring up wrath against the day of wrath.'* Friend Talmage, in his new book, tells us truly:

---

* "A wonderful and horrible thing is committed in the land. The prophets prophesy falsely, and the priests bear rule by their means, and my people love *to have it* so; and what will ye do in the end thereof?"—*Jer.* v. 30-31.

'The most stupendous of all lies is a newspaper lie. If an individual make a false statement, one or twenty may be damaged; but a newspaper of large circulation, that wilfully makes a misstatement in one day, tells fifty thousand falsehoods. An unscrupulous man in the editorial chair may smite as with the wing of the destroying angel.'

" 'The getting of treasures by a lying tongue, is a vanity tossed to-and-fro of them that seek death. A righteous man hateth lying; but a wicked man is loathsome, and cometh to shame.'

" 'I have not sent these prophets, yet they ran; I have not spoken to them, yet they prophesied. But if they had stood in my counsel, and had caused my people to hear my words, then they should have turned them from their evil ways, and from the evil of their doings.' "—*Jer.* xxiii. 21–22.

" How far may we go in sin—
How long will God forbear?
Where does hope end, and where begin
The confines of despair?

" An answer from the skies is sent:
Ye that from God depart,
While it is called to-day repent,
And harden not your heart."

Address ...*Author of " Apples of Gold,"*
203 West Twentieth Street, New York.

SEE THIS MOTHER, LITTLE FOLKS AND GREAT FOLKS

What is she doing? Imparting light heavenly to this child of hers—telling him about Jesus, who shed his precious blood on Calvary to save sinners, little sinners and great sinners—"the way, the truth, the life?" Beautiful, ain't it? Too soon? No, it ain't, mother. You should have commenced this blessed work at the earliest intellectual dawning, even before this little one of yours could utter a single syllable audibly. Begin where God begins. Let your smiles preach, your eyes, your inward thought, every muscle.

We say, and keep on saying, the Holy Spirit is waiting to be gracious, ready always to apply the truth, take the things that belong to Christ and show them even to the littlest of the little ones. The Spirit and the Bride say to the little folks, "Come." And let every one that heareth say to them, "Come."

The true ideal of Christian culture is—the salvation of childhood.

Little Mary at her Bible Lesson.

Love the Bible? She delights in it, feeds upon it. It's her meat and her drink, "a lamp to her feet, a light to her path." She reads the Bible more than any other book twice told.

From this blessed volume she receives wisdom, pure, peaceable, gentle, heavenly light, hope, joy, "the sword that cuts, the fire that burns." Not all the treasures of the world are worth half so much to this sweet little Mary, as the word of life. Part with it? What for? Gold, heaped mountain high?

> "No treasures so enrich the mind;
> Nor shall thy word be sold
> For loads of silver well refined,
> Nor heaps of choicest gold."

The gold and the crystal cannot equal it, and the exchange of it shall not be for jewels of fine gold. No mention shall be made of coral or pearls; for the price of this heavenly treasure is above rubies.

> ' 'Tis handed down from parents fond
> To children's children dear—
> A loom, a trust, a heavenly bond,
> Commingling love and fear."

Children trained from early infancy in the way they should go, in strict obedience to the holy precept, are sweet-tempered, mild, gentle, patient, meek, loving, lamb-like, God-fearing. They hate sin in every form, pride, folly, self-will, and wicked companions. They love the truth, the word of life, prayer and praise, the society of the blessed.

> ' Plant blessings and blessings will bloom;
> Plant hate and hate will grow;
> You can sow to-day—to-morrow shall bring
> The blossom that proves what sort of a thing
> Is the seed—the seed that you sow."

"Sow to the Spirit, you reap life everlasting." "Sow to the flesh, you reap corruption." "Whatsoever a man soweth that shall he also reap."—*Gal.* vi. 7.

Let those parents who excuse themselves by observing: "We cannot give grace to our children," lay their hands on their heart and say whether they ever knew an instance where God withheld his grace while they were in humble subserviency to him, fulfilling their duty. The real state of the case is this: parents cannot do God's work, and God will not do theirs; but if they use the means, he will never withhold his blessing.

> Parent, watch o'er thy child,
> Keep back no goodly thing.

Mother giving Lessons from the Bees.

"How doth the little busy bee,
 Improve each shining hour;
And gather honey all the day,
 From every opening flower."

WE learn important lessons from the busy bee, and the ant. "Go to the ant, thou sluggard, consider her ways, and be wise. Which having no guide, overseer, or ruler, provideth her meat in the summer, *and* gathereth her food in the harvest."—*Prov.* vi. 6, 7, 8.

"Live for something; be not idle,
 Look about thee for employ;
Sit not down to useless dreaming,
 Labor is the sweetest joy."

THE BABY JESUS.

"Then lift your little hands in prayer;
   The Saviour bids you come;
Safe in His bosom He will bear
   The lambs to His bright home
Then lay your little hand in His;
   He'll lead you gently on,
Through trials of a world like this,
   To scenes of bliss beyond."

How lovingly the dear Saviour—the Lamb of God—welcomes little children to His happy fold! He numbers the lambs among His flock. "Suffer little children to come unto me, and forbid them not, for of such is the kingdom of God."—Luke xviii. 16. When you hear the Saviour saying to you in the tenderest accents of His love, "Child, give me thy heart," will you not listen to His voice? If you come to Jesus now, He will take you in His arms and bless you, and make you happy while you live, and, when you die, will take you to dwell with Him forever.

"Dear Mary, Jesus loves you:
   Once He left His home on high,
Suffer'd on the cross to save you,
   Died that you might never die.

Little Mary, Jesus loves you;
   From His arms no longer stay;
He is waiting to receive you;
   Mary, come without delay.

Dear Mary, Jesus loves you;
   And when life with you is o'er,
To His heavenly home He'll take you,
   There to dwell forevermore."

"O LORD, MY STRENGTH, AND MY REDEEMER."

LYING—MEDITATED, CALCULATED, PERPETUATED!

Lies succeeding lies, week in, week out.

"He that worketh deceit shall not dwell in my house; he that telleth lies shall not tarry in my sight."—*Psalm* ci. 7. "Wherefore, putting away lying, speak every man truth with his neighbor."—*Eph.* iv. 25.

Conversation between Mr. Timewell *and* Mr. Servility.
(No. 10.)

T. "Allow me, Mr. Servility, to call your attention to the 'Serials,' or the continuation of fictions or falsehoods—stories and tales, tales and stories—continued week in, week out, in every paper, in every crevice, crack, and corner of the house. Stories fall from the pen faster than leaves of autumn, and of as many shades and colorings. Stories blow over here in whirlwinds from England. Stories are translated from the French, from the Danish, from the Swedish, from the German, from the Russian. There are serial stories for adults in 'The Atlantic,' in the 'Overland,' in the 'Galaxy,' in 'Harper's,' in 'Scribner's,' 'The N. Y. Daily Witness'—in Baptist, Methodist, Presbyterian, and Congregational Weeklies and Monthlies. There are serial stories for youthful pilgrims in 'Our Young Folks,' the 'Little Corporal,' the 'Riverside,' the 'Youth's Companion,' and very soon we anticipate newspapers with serial stories for the nursery. We shall have illustrated magazines, the Cradle, the Rocking-Chair, the First Rattle, and the First

LYING—MEDITATED, CALCULATED, PERPETUATED. 161

Tooth, with successive chapters of 'Goosy, Goosy Gander, and 'Hickory, Dickory, Dock,' and 'Old Mother Hubbard,' extending through twelve, or twenty-four, or forty-eight numbers.

"You perceive, Mr. Servility, from the foregoing, that Satan and his active coadjutors are not content with telling a few lies now and then or occasionally, but they look forward, calculate on weeks, months and years of lying—devise means, turn and twist every way, like a serpent in the grass, for so doing. And these periodicals alluded to are only a few of the lying ones—mixed publications, partly good, partly evil, partly Lord, partly devil, partly Christ, partly Belial—Satan's sugared pills—tools of the Old Serpent to carry on his work of soul-destruction."

S. "Your friend, Talmage, observes, if I mistake not, 'the more unscrupulous an editor is in conducting a periodical, the greater the likelihood of success!'"

T. "He remarked, furthermore, that 'one of the proprietors of a great paper in this country gave his advice to a young man then about to start a paper: "If you want to succeed,' said he, "make your paper trashy—*intensely* trashy—make it *all trash!*"'

"Brilliant advice to a young man just entering business!"

S. "You opine, then, I take it, Mr. Timewell, that as a paper purifies itself, its circulation decreases, and sometimes when a paper becomes positively religious, it becomes bankrupt—am I right?"

T. "You hit the nail exactly for once, Mr. Servility—the Lord open your blind eyes still more. Individuals, male or female, nourished upon lies—tales of fiction—have very little relish for Bible truth, the sweets of redeeming, sanctifying grace, the bread of heaven. When Satan is in, God is out!

"Let these popular works of fiction, that are flying over the face of the earth like leaves in autumn, conceiving mischief and bringing forth iniquity, hatching cocatrices eggs, weaving the spider's webb—cease fellowshipping the unfruitful works of darkness—repudiate the devil and all his works—assume the prophetical and apostolical—take Jesus Christ and him crucified, come life, come death. What now? Any shaking among the dry bones? Where now the boastings of these panderers to a corrupt taste of their one hundred thousand subscribers! Not one in a thousand would hold on to these linsey-woolsey, sickly sentimentals. 'Wheresoever the carcas is, there will the eagles be gathered together.'

"You see from this how awfully, fearfully, extensively the devil has done his devilish work in vitiating the public taste in church and State—how and by whom! What say you, Mr. Servility, any of this witchcraft laid at your door? Ask, if you please, those religious novel-writers and puffers in pulpits and in chairs editorial whom you endorse, what fingers they have had in this pie—how much stock they have taken in this fire and brimstone business! How many once beloved, virtuously pure and lovely, *they* have led on to the burning pit instrumentally! Moreover, ask your *special* friend in the Plymouth pulpit, what he says to pushing these cars of Satan? Point him to what Solomon says— 'Such is the way of an adulterous woman : she eateth, and wipeth her mouth, and saith, I have done no wickedness.'— *Prov.* xxx. 20.

"All this and still more for the accursed lust of gain— the love of filthy lucre! Talmage says, in the love and fear of his Master, 'Where is the Church of God that she allows in her membership such gigantic abominations? Were the thirty pieces of silver that Judas received denounced as unfit, and shall the Church of God have nothing to say about this price of blood? Is sin to be excused because it is as high as heaven, or deep as hell?

"'If he who steals a dollar from a money-drawer is a thief, then he who by dishonesty gets five hundred thousand dollars, is five hundred times more a thief. And so the last day will declare him.'*

"'As the partridge sitteth on eggs, and hatcheth them not: so he that getteth riches and not by right, shall leave them in the midst of his days, and at his end shall be a fool.'—*Isa.* xvii. 11.

"'Because ye have said, We have made a covenant with death, and with hell are we at agreement, when the overflowing scourge shall pass through, it shall not come unto us: for we have made lies our refuge, and under falsehood have we hid ourselves.'—*Isa.* xxviii. 15.

"No one is any better than the paper he reads or the company he keeps."

S. "What now? Shut down the gate—stop publishing because the general acceptation is only for the light and frivolous?"

T. "Stop sinning, stop telling lies, stop bowing the knee to Baal—stop poisoning body, soul and spirit!

"What do you tell the rum and tobacco trafficer—the man who sells the degrading, poisonous 'Indian weed'—

---

* A strong love to the world, and to the things of the world, may be called the basest and most sordid of passions. The minister, or even the man, in whom you discover it, you may safely mark down as one who loves neither God nor man. Neither devotion nor humanity can reside in the same breast with avarice.

164 LYING—MEDITATED, CALCULATED, PERPETUATED.

deals out the intoxicating cup, liquid death, and distilled damnation? What you say to this faithful servant of the devil, 'stop your awful wickedness,' so we say to you, 'stop, *stop!*' 'Your hands are full of blood!' 'If ye refuse and rebel, ye shall be devoured with the sword, for the mouth of the Lord hath spoken it.'—*Isa.* i. 20.

"'So speak ye, and so do, as they that shall be judged by the law of liberty. For he shall have judgment without mercy, that hath showed no mercy; and mercy rejoiceth against judgment.'—*James* ii. 12, 13.

"'Resist the devil and he will flee from you.'

"'Provide things honest in the sight of all men.'

"'Abstain from all appearance of evil.'"

S. "Why expend all your ammunition on sacerdotals—those clad in priestly vestments? Why not draw your two-edged sword on outsiders—the openly obscene, libidinous, who concoct and send forth leprosy, the froth and scum of the pit?"

T. "Mr. Servility, my work is not now nor has it been in time past outside the camp, but *inside*—in the 'Ring!'

"'Thou blind Pharisee, cleanse first that which is within the cup and platter, that the outside of them may be clean also.'—*Math.* xxiii. 26.

"Purify a corrupt fountain, and the streams will be pure. My course has been hitherto and ever will be apostolical. I begin where God begins. 'Awake thou that sleepest, and arise from the dead, and Christ shall give thee light!' The purport of Paul's whole life, by pen and word of mouth, after the scales fell from his eyes, was to purge out the old leaven, that the entire lump or body might be unleavened, pure, 'without spot, and blameless.'

"For this Christ died, shed his precious blood, that he

might sanctify and cleanse the church—'that he might present it to himself a glorious church, not having spot, or wrinkle, or any such thing; but that it should be holy and without blemish.'

'"For what have I to do,' says Paul, 'to judge them also that are without?—do not ye judge them that are within? But them that are without God judgeth. Therefore put away from among yourselves that wicked person.'— 1 *Cor.* v. 12, 13.

"'Salt is good: but if the salt have lost his savor, wherewith shall it be seasoned? It is neither fit for the land, nor yet for the dunghill: but men cast it out. He that hath ears to hear, let him hear.'—*Luke* xiv. 34, 35.

"We rejoice to see political editors opening their eyes to this rascality in high places and in low! Very many of these speculators in froth and fiction and the souls of men, are not satisfied with destroying the very life of virtuous purity in adults, but are stretching every nerve to demoralize the little folks—the first buddings of immortality! Mr. Greeley, in the 'Tribune' of March 15th, speaks thus: 'While we are prosecuting the purveyors of obscene literature for adults, may it not be worth while to look at the character of some of the popular periodicals for children? In a recent number of "Frank Leslie's Boy's and Girl's Weekly" we find a story of such a grossly improper tendency, that it is hard to understand how any respectable editor should have accepted it. . . . There is nothing to redeem this wretched story, for its style is unpardonable, and some of its suggestions are prurient.'"

THE SHEPHERD AND HIS FLOCK.

"How many sheep are straying,
　　Lost from the Saviour's fold!
Upon the lonely mountains
　　They shiver with the cold;
Within the tangled thickets,
　　Where poison vines do creep,
And over rocky ledges,
　　Wander the poor lost sheep.

"Oh! who will go to find them?
　　Who, for the Saviour's sake,
Will search with tireless patience
　　Through brier and through brake?

From what book is this mother teaching her little ones?

A NOVEL—a book of fictions? or from the Bible, the book of life?

> "Bread of our souls! whereon we feed;
> True manna from on high!"

How came little Timothy wise unto salvation? Through the instrumentality of his pious mother, grandmother, and the Holy Scriptures, he became wise in heavenly things, even from his childhood—"through faith which is in Christ Jesus."

Do we make the salvation of our children the first and supreme object? A knowledge of the Bible is indispensable.

> " 'Tis a mine of richest treasure,
> Laden with the purest ore;
> And its contents, without measure,
> You can never well explore."

Parents beloved, take this Book of books, open it in the presence of your little ones, and let God speak and declare what he requires of both parents and children. God's authority is supreme, infinitely above all human authority or enactments.

Would we train up the children aright, we must train them in accordance with the divine requirements. The man of our counsel must be the unerring Word of Truth. If we are Christ's, we shall seek to measure our conduct by His word, and equally anxious should we be to measure or to have measured the conduct of our children by His word. Whatever parents may require, or whatever they may forbid, should be in conformity with the instructions given them by their great teacher—God. Let this be done, and let children see it, and feel it; and then how infinitely more easy it will be to induce them to walk in the right way!

Here the authority is stamped with the broad seal of heaven, and is as much higher than that of parents merely as heaven is higher than earth, as the authority of the Infinite, the Uncreated, the Eternal, is higher than that of finite, created beings of yesterday.

Among the first lessons taught children from the Bible, those relating to parental obedience seem especially to claim attention. When the fact that God requires children to obey their parents is well established in their minds, a very important object is gained. Will they not listen with fearful attention, with filial confidence, when told that God says, "Hearken unto thy father that has begotten thee, and despise not thy mother when she is old;" "Children, obey your patents in the Lord, for this is right;" "Honor thy father and mother (which is the first commandment with promise), that it may be well with thee, and that thou mayest live long on the earth;" "Children, obey your parents in all things; for this is well pleasing unto the Lord!"

Then, when reminded that obeying their parents is not only right, but well pleasing unto the Lord—that with it is connected the promise of long life and well-being!

> " Promises of life eternal, of a crown that never fades,
> Of a kingdom full of glory, which no sorrow e'er invades,"

And that disobedience is connected with fearful denunciations—when told these things, will they not feel that, with all the heart, they will seek to render cheerful and ready obedience?

Parents, if you do not begin with God, Christ, and the Gospel—Satan begins with his creed and his practice, the first article of which is Atheism. The child's mind is given to you to furnish, not to keep unfurnished, and you are bound to furnish it with such principles and pictures of faith, such articles of truth from God, that by and by it can be trusted safely to make its own selection. You are bound to educate the habits, tastes, feelings, judgment of the opening mind aright, and you cannot do it in the neglect of God's word.

"Our Blessed Lord laid down the grand rule of a child's education, when He said: 'Suffer little children to come unto me.' And there is no period so early in which they may not come; but at that early period to which our Lord more particularly referred they must be brought, to come at all; they must be carried in the arms of others' faith, borne by others' instructions, drawn from the word of God. If they come at all, it is the Christ of the Scriptures to whom they must come, the Christ of that faith taught by the Scriptures, and not an imaginary Christ. And for this especially the Bible is a child's book, because it is so full of Christ, and because its grand requisite of character is a childlike faith in Him; a thing which, as it is taught only in the Scriptures, can be produced only by their instrumentality. If you undertake to keep your child's mind empty, swept, and garnished, till an intelligent choice, the child's own will, shall arrange its religious furniture, you are certainly retaining it for a habitation of the wicked one. But the child's mind is given to you to fill it with wheat, not with chaff. The way to exclude darkness from a room, is to fill it with light. Occupy the mind with good things, and there will be no room for bad ones. The truth once established, possession is not only nine-tenths of the law, but error cannot get a foothold.

>"O blessed Volume Divine,
> Let everlasting thanks be thine,
>   For such a bright display
>   As makes the world of darkness shine
>   With beams of heavenly day."

Look at the influence on the mere *education* of a family. The Bible is the greatest of all classics. There is more in it to form the mind, to fire the imagination, to fill the thoughts— nay, even to fashion the style and furnish the tongue with all the resources of strong and beautiful speech, than in any other book.

>"Great book of heaven! I bind thee to my heart;
> Treasure of truth, so varied, rich, and rare!
> Let friends forsake, and cherished ones depart—
>   Thy hopes still point me to that country fair,
> Where blight comes not, where change and death are o'er,
> And eyes that wept on earth shall weep no more!"

"Apples of Gold," 303 West Twentieth Street, New York.

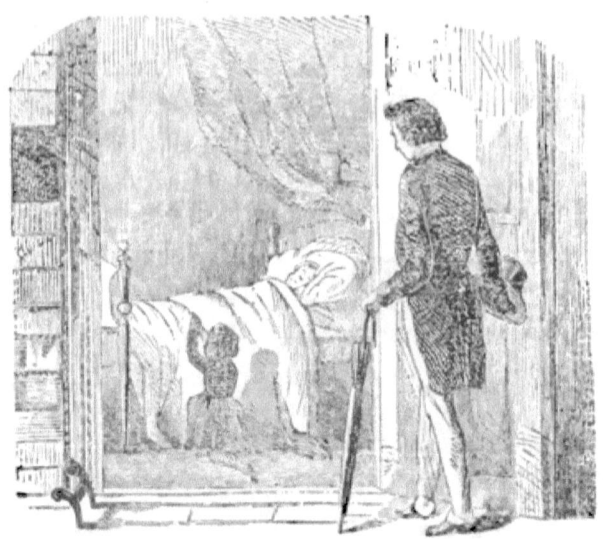

THE MOTHER'S DEATH-BED.

"We watched her breathing through the night,
   Her breathing soft and low,
  And in her breast the wave of life
   Kept heaving to and fro.

"So silently we seem'd to speak,
   So slowly moved about,
  As we had lent her half our powers
   To eke her being out.

"Our very hopes belied our fears,
   Our fears our hopes belied,
  We thought her dying when she slept,
   And sleeping when she died.

"For when the morn came dim and sad,
   And chill with early showers,
  Her quiet eyelids closed—she had
   Another morn than ours."

WHITE LYING TO PREVENT BLACK LYING,
—OR—
The Writing White Lies to keep out Black Lies!

"Treasures of wickedness profit nothing: but righteousness delivereth from death."—*Prov.* x. 2.

Conversation between Mr. TIMEWELL *and* Mr. SERVILITY. (No. 11.)

S. "You remarked, Mr. Timewell, in a previous conversation, that all sin originated from thought: can this idea be substantiated?"

T. "Think truly, and thy thoughts shall be a fruitful seed. Live truly, and thy life shall be a great and noble creed. 'As he thinketh in his heart, so is he.'—*Prov.* xxiii. 7.

"Thoughts are words, words are deeds. Sin begins in the heart. If you keep your thoughts pure, your life will be blessedness and blameless. The indulgence of sinful thoughts and desires, produce sinful actions. When lust hath conceived, it bringeth forth sin. The pleasurable contemplation of a sinful deed is usually followed by its commission. Never allow yourself to pause and consider the pleasures or profit you might derive from this or that sin. Close your mind against the suggestion at once, as you would lock and bolt your doors against a robber. If Eve had not stood parleying with the devil, and admiring the beautiful fruit, the earth might have yet been a paradise. No one becomes a thief, a fornicator, a murderer at once, nor a writer or publisher of lies, white or black, little or big. The heart is first corrupted by wicked thoughts. Wicked suggestions from the father of liars are indulged, revolved in the thoughts until the sin of lying, or the love of filthy lucre loses its hideous deformity, and the anticipated gain or pleasure comes to outweigh the evils of the transgression.

"Your imagination paints forbidden pleasure in gay and dazzling colors. It is the serpent's charm. Gaze not upon the picture. Suffer not the intruder to get a lodgement. Meet the enemy at the threshhold and drive it from your heart. As a rule, the more familiar you become with sin, the least hateful it appears; so that the more completely you preserve your mind from unholy and wicked thoughts, the better.

> " 'Vice is a monster of such frightful mien,
> That, to be hated, needs but to be seen ;
> But seen too oft, familiar with its face,
> We first endure, then pity, then embrace.'

"Avoid evil associations and communications, the society of the obscene or unchaste, as you do the plague! Reading an author is keeping company with that author. Reading the works of a lying author is more dangerous than conversing with the same lying author face to face. A bad or lying book or periodical is more dangerous than a bad man or a bad woman. 'Touch not, taste not, handle not the unclean thing.'

> " 'Just as the broadest rivers run
> From small and distant springs,
> The greatest crimes that men have done
> Have grown from little things."

"Cultivate the society of the virtuous. Read nothing

that is unchaste or immoral. Make a covenant with your eyes. Familiarize not your mind with the loathsome details of crime. Never harbor malicious or envious thoughts. Direct your thoughts towards pure and holy subjects. Contemplate the character of the spotless and perfect Son of God. Keep your spirit untainted, your thoughts uncontaminated, so shall your life be virtuous. Take care of the thoughts, and the actions will take care of themselves. Lies are lies, whether spoken, written, put in type, bound or unbound."

S. "You spoke of a good Christian man sanctified wholly, who resolved to stop black lying, the publishing of obscene or perdition literature, by issuing religious novels, or what you term white lies."

T. "He told me the fact in the outset, and engaged some of the *best pious* gentlemen and lady novel writers, that could write the prettiest, finest and most delicate, genteel, religious lies, and on he went."

S. "What did you say to him?"

T. "Sir," said I to him kindly, lovingly, "Satan could not desire better help; these white lies or religious novels you send forth will surely lead to lies, black as jet!"

S. "Did he take your word for it?"

T. "After serving the prince of darkness faithfully, indefatigably some six or eight years, this 'blind-leader of the blind' began to open one eye a little, to see and know that he was kindling sparks that were setting the whole world on fire—the fires that burned to the lowest hell! One leak sinks a ship, one spark of fire sets a house, a whole city on fire! Look at Chicago!"

S. "Did he stop lying then, or quit his sending forth religious white lies?"

T. "Happy, thrice happy, had he committed his miserable sheets to the flames, and washed his hands clean from the filth. Instead of this, he sold his wretched white lying monthly to another liar of white lies less scrupulous, if possible, about lying; and now it is white and black, black and white lying, just as happens. If so be white lies bring in cash more plentifully, white lies take the lead—if black, black!"

S. "Do not the 'American Tract Societies,' the '*N. Y. Daily Witness,*' the '*Christian Union,*' the '*Christian World,*' the '*Hearth and Home,*' the '*Female Guardian,*' the '*Guide to Holiness,*' take nearly or quite the same views touching the writing, puffing, selling and reading religious novels or white lies?"

T. "By their fruits we know them, how else? If a man, religious or otherwise, writes lies, puffs lies, keeps lies for sale, tells the public the very same, unblushingly, what now? Take it for granted the man is a liar, notoriously, barefacedly?

"The whole batch of religious monthlies and weeklies seem tared with the same brush. The editors of the *Illustrated Weekly,*' at 150 Nassau St., tell us over and over their main purpose is to do away, kill out entirely and forever the devil of devils. the lion devils, the obscene issues, the sink-holes of moral pollution, by introducing angelic devils, neat, beautiful, refined, soft, silky white lies, religious novels, splendidly illustrated. Thus setting the wheels of Satan's whole machinery in perpetual motion!

"'A little theft, a small deceit,
Too often leads to more.'

"What cares the father of lies for Tom Paine, Voltaire,

the lewd, licentious, shameless Bulwer, the Mysteries of Paris, and the whole brotherhood of infernals, so long as he has the American Tract Societies, Sunday School Unions, writers on moral purity, holiness, entire sanctification, religious weeklies and monthlies completely under his thumb? saying, 'Go on, Mr. Clovenfoot, do your very best, we are at your service heartily, go on with your devilishness, peopling the regions of death and damnation—all we possibly can do by way of white lying, rest assured sir, we do with our might. As to black lies or lion devils, our minds are not fully made up, but as to religious novels, white lies or angel devils, you have our hearty, cordial and entire approval. These are popular, besides they yield a harvest, the ready cash! '*Amen*.' Here the confab ends, for a little space.

"Then on top of all this helping Satan to do his worst, you see and hear these same liars and publishers of lies, white and black, whining, whimpering and sniveling, shedding crockadile tears, over the ramparts of hell! the bubblings of the pit bottomless, the idolatry in dress, pride, folly, fashion, theatrical and opera house, diabolisms, the land of whoredoms and prostitutions, the numerous elopements and suicides, the entire smashdown of the marriage relation, domestic happiness, purity and love, and the perpetual rush to spiritualisms, free-loveisms, and all manner of devilisms! 'Such is the way of an adulterous woman; she cateth and wipeth her mouth, and saith, I have done no wickedness.'—*Prov.* xxx. 20.

" 'Stolen waters are sweet, and bread eaten in secret is pleasant: But he knoweth not that the dead are there, and that her guests are in the depths of hell!' "—*Prov.* ix. 17, 18.

WHITE LYING TO PREVENT BLACK LYING. **177**

S. "Are there no misgivings in the breasts of these footballs of Satan, as you call them, Mr. Timewell?"

T. "'Conscience!' a novel, writer, publisher, puffer and seller of white lies, angelic devils? have conscience? When? Where? These consciences you speak of have long since been coffined and laid in the grave! Nothing so surely and speedily hardens the heart and sears the conscience as lying, writing, reading and puffing lies. Our whole nation, through this medium, has become a nation of liars. We talk about Tammany lying, defrauding, stealing and robbing; but what are all these liars, thieves and cut-throats, put into one bag and shaken together, compared to what is going on all over the land, in church and State, through the instrumentality of these writers, puffers and sellers of religious novels, white lies, devils transformed, mixed publications, sugared pills, the bitter and the sweet intermingled, a little of Christ and a good deal of Belial!*

"This Tammany deviltry, bad as it is, devilish as it is, issuing from the pit bottomless as it does, is a mere drop to the ocean, speaking comparatively."

---

* "Behold, I will corrupt your seed, and spread dung upon your faces, *even* the dung of your solemn feasts, and one shall take you away with it. For the priest's lips should keep knowledge, and they should seek the law at his mouth: for he is the messenger of the LORD of hosts. But ye are departed out of the way: ye have caused many to stumble at the law: ye have corrupted the covenant of Levi, saith the LORD of hosts. Therefore have I also made you contemptible and base before all the people, according as ye have not kept my ways, but have been partial in the law."—*Mal.* ii. 3–9.

---

*Address....*Author of "**THE SWORD THAT CUTS,**"
303 West Twentieth St., New York.

GIVING ALMS? WHAT ELSE CAN IT BE?

BEAUTIFUL? WHAT MORE?

This little girl has, doubtless, been early taught "to remember the poor," "rejoice with them that do rejoice, and weep with them that weep;" "that it is more blessed to give than to receive." "Blessed is he that considereth the poor."

"Give, and it shall be given unto you: good measure, pressed down, and shaken together, and running over, shall men give into your bosom. For with the same measure that ye mete withal, it shall be measured to you again."

GIVING ALMS?

"Withhold not good from them to whom it is due, when it is in the power of thy hand to do it." *Prov.* iii. 27.

> " 'Twas the widow's mite which call'd
> Blessings from the Lord;
> Not the lavish treasures thrown
> From the rich man's hoard."

Little folks, are you on the giving order? First of all, have you given all to Jesus, presented your bodies living sacrifices to God, which is your reasonable service?

It is only by commencing early in life the consecration of ourselves, our substance to God, that we can establish the habit of benevolence. While we postpone the discharge of our duty until we have become wealthy, the love of gain is insensibly acquiring strength, we listen to the claims of benevolence with less and less sensibility, and at last become deaf to the voice of humanity. When we are able to give without the smallest self-denial, the disposition to give has perished, and we have been transformed into the very misers whom once we thoroughly despised.

CHARITY.

> "While thou hast a heart to feel
> Sympathy and love,
> And thy voice can lift a prayer
> To the Lord above:
>
> "Say not thou hast nought to give—
> Nought to call thine own:
> Life's best pleasures do not spring
> From one source alone."

SATANIC TRANSFORMATIONS,

—OR—

What the devil is doing through the agency of the professed followers of the Lord Jesus Christ.

Testimony of H. C. Dana, Esq.—(No. 1.)

IN a recent lecture of his, he says: "It is a sad sight to examine the display of sin, crime and moral corruption that is made in every news depot throughout the land. Children are made familiar with sin and crime before they even know what they mean. We are blind, and unless we get our eyes open soon we shall become sadly dead to shame. Marriage has been stripped of its sanctity, and above it has been raised the horrible temple of divorce. This great evil, this moral vampire, has sucked the life-blood of marriage, and left it under dark clouds, and it is fast sinking in its death-throes.* Men and women unite under its most sacred bonds with the thoughtlessness of trade. Divorce will cure all mistakes, they say, and so rush blindly along towards sin, crime and ruin. Those are some of the causes, and the Christian world has a mighty responsibility resting upon it, that it sees that those causes are corrected and removed."

Testimony No. 2.

In a recent number of the *Sunday School Times*, H. S. Osborn, LL. D., remarks: "We are living in *peculiarly dangerous times* from the reading which is now brought out.

---

* Alluding to fictitious publications.

SATANIC TRANSFORMATIONS.

At no former time in the history of our country has light reading been so much in demand as at the present day. All classes of persons—learned and ignorant—professional men, business men—educated ladies as well as the nurse and help, the cook and the chambermaid, demand light reading —tales, stories, novels, or something 'exciting.' I have heard it asserted that more works of this character have been sold in the past two years, than had been sold during the preceding sixty years!"

Testimony No. 3.

The godly bishop Littlejohn, an Episcopalian, has thrilled the public with his lectures on the evils of religious or sentimental fiction.* We have space for a single item only from his gifted pen :

"Our time is remarkable for the development of a new type of the human family, viz : the 'strong-minded woman.' A restless, busy, fragmatical thing is this modern Amazon, who divests herself of all those soft, sweet attributes that were wont to be considered the adornments of womanhood, that she might be the better prepared to engage in scenes of strife and turmoil more dear to her than an honest husband in his home. Our modern heroine of fiction is a slave to vanity, pleasure, ease and fashion. This lotus-eater of fiction is a frail reed that breaks in the day of need, and pierces the heart that leans on it for support.

---

* The reader perceives that in nearly every instance, these testimonials allude, not to the putrid or leprous publications, but to religious novels, sentimental fiction, (inlets or entering wedges to the rottenest of the rotten, the very scum and bubblings of the pit of hell !) written, sold and puffed by those whose garments ought to be unspotted, and whose characters ought to be above suspicion.

"The sentimental fiction defends itself by the shallow argument that it aims at making vice odious and virtue attractive. It professes the philosophy of Barnum, as put forth in his autobiography, where he says that the age insists on vast sensations and stupendous humbugs, and adopts his policy. Virtue needs no such auxiliaries as the reeking fumes of the bar-room or the pestiferous atmosphere of a gambling-hell to make her attractive. The writers and publishers of such stuff are the enemies of public peace and morals, and the sacred ties of society and the purity of home plead against them."

Testimony of the Rev. T. De Witt Talmage.—(No. 4.)

"Many papers that are most rapidly increasing to-day are unscrupulous. The facts are momentous and appalling. And I put young men and women and Christian parents on the look-out. This stuff cannot be handled without pollution.

"The only question is: 'Will it pay?' And there are scores of men who, day by day, bring into the newspaper offices manuscripts for publication which unite all that is pernicious; and, before the ink is fairly dry, tens of thousands are devouring with avidity the impure issue.

"O ye reckless souls! get money—though morality dies, and society is dishonored, and God defied, and the doom of the destroyed opens before you—get money! Though the melted gold be poured upon your naked, blistering, and consuming soul—get money! Get money! It will do you good when it begins to eat like a canker! It will solace the pillow of death, and soothe the pangs of an agonized eternity! Though in the game thou dost stake thy soul, and lose it forever—get money!"

SATANIC TRANSFORMATIONS.

Testimony of Dr. W. H.—(No. 5.)

Vandoren, of Chicago, a minister of the gospel, on religious novels or white lying in families and Sunday schools, pushed into favorable notice by *ministers and religious publishers*, says:—" Ours is verily a fast age. One writer dramatizes the Saviour's life in the 'House of David.' Another ventures to endorse and describe heaven in 'Gates Ajar.' Others, under the splendid drapery of romance, inculcate the doctrines of repentance, faith, new birth, etc.

"The question arises, why are these works of fiction tolerated? Why are responsible publishers and Christian associations found to print them? But above all, why are parents and pastors found to permit them on their tables or to their Sunday-school libraries? We can easily answer why the youth love to read them. Is it for the infinitessimal amount of religious element contained in them? We answer, No. The fascination of the multiform pious novels that now swarm into our Sunday-school libraries, is anything and everything but their religious instruction.

"It were a thousandth-fold better if nine out of ten Sunday-school libraries were taken from their shelves and committed to the flames.

"Five distinguished elders of the city of New York, told the writer, with tears, 'We are compelled to keep our children out of Sunday-school altogether, because of the swarms of pious novels which infests the shelves.'

"These pious novels may not only advocate any one bad practice or evil principle; but as punches and various drugged wine lead directly to form a taste for alcohol, so these books lead to novels. The fact that some professors of Christianity and so-called ministers write them, is no more an argument for their being harmless than our reverend forefathers' use of brandy made it a safe precedent for their children. It is a well-known fact that those bearing the office of ministers have proved among the bitterest curses with which our race has ever been visited."

[Is not this emphatically true of the author of "Norwood?"—Ed.]

"Novels, religious and secular, cause not only an immense sacrifice of mental power and of moral energy, but also of precious time. How many hours, days, and weeks are thus worse than murdered by the youths of both sexes in our land! Some children bring these miserable pious novels to church, and under the very sound of the Gospel, Sinai's thundering and Calvary's calls of mercy, pore over their exciting pages.

"We have known parents to neglect their offspring to gloat their imaginations over the scenes of passion glittering through the pages of novels.

"What is time? Ask death-beds; the queen of England, who cried in her expiring moments, 'millions! *millions!* for an inch of time!'

> "'I asked a spirit lost—but, oh! the shriek
> That pierced my soul! I shudder while I speak!
> It cried—" A particle! a speck! a mite
> Of endless years, duration infinite!"'

"The morbid desire for novelty destroys that sobriety of mind inculcated by the Holy Ghost upon the youth to be 'sober-minded.'

"The wine to an invalid imparts an unnatural glow. Young minds, depraved in all their energies, soon reach an *abnormal* state. They have a glow, not of health, but of the *hectic*.

"Novels are no proper food for an immortal soul. What would have been thought if young Samuel or Timothy had spent their days and nights sighing over fables—false scenes of sorrow, fictitious scenes of heroism, and falsehood everywhere? What a sad preparation for secret prayer is the flush of emotion and passion kindled in sensitive minds! We repeat, who can answer for the precious moments, hours and days *worse than wasted*, over these pious romances!

> "'Time is eternity;
> Pregnant with all eternity can give;
> Who murders time, he crushes in the birth
> A power ethereal, only not adored.'

"These religious romances lead our youth to the broad, gilded, flowery paths of modern novels. A novel is a *theatre in the mind!* All the gorgeous curtains, actors, actresses, enchantry, fascinating the depraved heart, kindling all its passions, fast prepare the road to the theatre.*

It makes one sick at heart to think of pleasure's siren voice, and the promises given of joyous days and years to come.

> "'Alas! the dead are in her house,
> Her guests in depths of hell;
> She weaves the winding-sheet of souls
> And lays them in the urn of everlasting death.'"

We might fill volumes of similar testimonials did our space permit.

---

* How true is this of Beecher and Dickens.

303 West Twentieth Street, New York.

TRUTH AND LYING.

Testimony of Elder H. Buckley.

"Wherefore putting away lying, speak every man truth with his neighbor."—*Eph.* iv. 25.

"WHEN a child I believed everything which was printed to be true, and when at length I learned the contrary, I was shocked and felt indignant. Until within a few years I supposed all Sunday-school books to be truthful, and I was greatly shocked and grieved on learning that a large portion of them were fictions. I very much fear that the professed servants of the Lord are now sowing seed in Sunday-school publications which will result in a very fruitful harvest for Satan.

"No matter how *good* the story, or correct the principles illustrated, if the facts are wanting, or if they are colored, the lawyer, lecturer, teacher or preacher thus illustrating his subject, is guilty of falsehood, and would be called a liar if exposed.

"Is it not sinful to fabricate stories or tales for children? Or to mix fact with fiction for the purpose of interesting them? Does not the youthful mind feel disgusted when informed that the highly interesting book is the offspring of somebody's imagination? Or, if not disgusted, does he not conclude that he may make a *good* story when it serves his purpose? Again, does not all fiction lose its interest when the mind does not appropriate it as truth—except it be with such as 'love a lie?' I apprehend that no work of fiction is read with interest unless it makes an impression of reality. Nearly, if not all, such works give a false coloring to real life. And such religious works virtually admit that truth in its sinful, native dress, is not sufficiently attractive. I am convinced that all such works, instead of making truth more attractive, so far as their influence goes, renders it less so. The Bible, the blessed Bible—that great fountain of truth—becomes *dry* to readers of fiction, and so does anything not highly sensational. Mrs. Harriet Beecher Stowe, I fear, with many others, are using their noble, God-given powers in the wrong direction."

Our beloved brother Buckley is not alone in fearing the sad downfall of this woman. Multitudes weep over her departure from gospel purity. Once she warmly advocated entire consecration to God's service. Where now? Alas, clasping hands with the prince of darkness!—contending earnestly for worldly pleasures, billiard-tables, nine-pin alleys—stages for getting up tableaux, dramatic performances, and other games of chance—utensils of Satan, leading to gambling dens and gambling hells!

These carnal implements of the evil one are commended to the church of Christ in preference to Sunday-schools! *

Did she ever dream of putting her hands to this iniquity, outstanding and heaven-daring, till she fell into the trap of Satan, viz., the reading novels and writing novels?

"Behold how great a matter a little fire kindleth!"

We see what Satan is doing through the medium of religious novels—or white-lying—how Christ is wounded in the house of his friends. One lie prepares the way for another —one spark from the pit kindles other sparks—one little fire kindles other fires, till the whole world is in a blaze.

---

* We quote from public records, but the half is not told.

SACRED MUSIC IN PUBLIC WORSHIP.

"Oh! reform it altogether!"

THOSE who are in the habit of attending the more popular and fashionable churches are aware of the fact that nearly all the singing is done by some half dozen voices in the organ gallery, while others are silent. Surely, this is not fulfilling the purpose of sacred music, as a part of public worship.

Objections to the Choir System.

1. Choir singing, as now practiced in our churches, is *unauthorized*; the inspired penman gives us no examples on record in the New Testament.

2. The most consistently and devotedly pious are grieved at this departure from gospel purity and simplicity.

3. Choir worship, as a general thing, is *not spiritual* worship—how can it be, when those composing them are not spiritual worshippers—but gay, thoughtless, worldly, fashionable! Is it meet to take the children's bread and cast it to dogs? See Math. xxv. 26.

Can the wicked sing—make melody in their hearts to the Lord?

"Let those refuse to sing
Who never knew our God;
But children of the heavenly King
May speak their joys abroad."

The artistic performance of a beautiful piece of music will produce feeling—is it therefore devotional feeling—the music or melody in the heart? The opera of a French troupe will excite feeling—but is this feeling a devotional feeling? "Be not deceived, God is not mocked." "My son, give me thy heart." "That which is highly esteemed among men, is abomination in the sight of God."

Hark! hear the voice of the Holy One: "Offer unto God thanksgiving, and pay thy vows to the Most High. But to the wicked God saith, What hast thou to do to declare my statutes, or that thou shouldest take my covenant in thy mouth; seeing that thou hatest instruction, and castest my words behind thee."—*Psa.* l. 16.

4. Choir singing *deprives God's people* and the audience of one of the most interesting, profitable, joyful, soul-kindling, soul-reviving exercises of God's house. Go into any church where the whole congregation join in singing God's praises, making melody in their hearts to the Lord, and who can doubt the desirableness of congregational singing? Except an entire congregation on their knees in prayer, we know not of a more beautiful sight than is presented when all the people rise to sing. Instead of gazing coldly and with a critic's eye at a choir, as at a company of musicians performing for their especial amusement, (for as far as the music is concerned, many churches are little better than divine opera houses), to mark whose voice excels, and how the parts are maintained: proud of their professional skill they exert their powers to please a fastidious audience!

How different this from mingling harmonious voices with grace in the heart—each with a book, intently earnest to do his part in singing the high praises of God! The sweet voices of childhood are mingled with those of riper years, all blending in one grand choral harmony; giving us a blessed foretaste of that praise which will be rendered to

God, when *all voices*, and not a *select* few, shall join around the throne, in singing the song "of Moses and the Lamb."

> "Oh! could I hear those good old songs—
> The songs my mother sung,
> As round the fire her lov'd ones sat,
> In days when I was young.
> But ah! those songs are out of date!
> I ne'er may hear them more."

5. The *indistinctness of enunciation* of many choirs renders it utterly impossible for those of the congregation who would otherwise unite, to do so! Why not as soon speak in an unknown tongue? "Things without life, giving sound, whether pipe or harp, except they give a distinction in the sounds, how shall it be known what is piped or harped?" Very often not a word or a syllable can be traced or understood; and this is especially the case when a large organ and other instruments of music are ringing in our ears.*

6. *Levity* in choirs is a prevailing evil, a matter of common notoriety and complaint. This besetting sin is a disgrace to the house of God and his holy worship. So great and glaring is this evil of levity and light-mindedness in choirs, that many pious persons have declined uniting with them: knowing they could not do so without great annoyance and spiritual loss. Others have left the choir to avoid backsliding.

---

* Reader, would you be thoroughly convinced that the introduction of instrumental music in public worship is evil and *only* evil? We refer you to a recent work of Rev. R. Johnson, of 80 pages, price 25 cents. Address Author of "Apples of Gold," 303 West Twentieth-street, New York.

We quote a single sentence of the author:—"Believing that any attempt to praise the Infinitely Holy One by the noise of sundry kinds of machinery in public worship is an unscriptural innovation, displeasing to God and unprofitable to man, I count it my duty to lift up my voice against it."

Will this levity, trifling, and solemn mockery in God's house ever cease, 'till a system of congregational singing is adopted?

7. Whence the *apples of discord* and *disunion?* the roots of bitterness springing up in the churches of God, by which many are troubled and many defiled? In nine cases out of ten, originate they not from the choir? God has spoken once, twice, *three times*, "beware of this unhallowed leaven!" "Be sure your sin will find you out."

Mark the testimony of the Rev. A. S. Robertson, who has traveled and preached for many years, and whose praise is in all the churches. After long experience and careful observation, what is the final conclusion? Touching the choir system he speaks thus:

"We shall never find language to utter one-half of our astonishment at the tame submission of so many pious minds, under the ruinous and evil workings of the *choir system* in our churches in the cities, and elsewhere. Never was so great an evil tolerated in Zion, sustained at so great a cost, and resulting in so little good. The mind can grasp no other thing in the church more prolific of unsought mischief! Envy, evil speaking, pride, ostentation, vanity, ambition, division, are almost invariably the result of choirs, sooner or later. Not unfrequently the leaven spreads like wild-fire through the congregation, and involves the minister and all the members in the difficulty. Nor is it strange that such should be the result, when we call to mind the class of persons of whom choirs are usually composed. Three words tell all—*young, thoughtless, irreligious*. But why, in view of so powerfully distracting results, is it still sustained? Is it because the goddess of fashion must be worshiped at all hazards?"

8. We object to choirs and instrumental music in the house of God, for the very important reason that, in our opinion, Christian union or primitive Christianity will never be fully restored so long as they are continued in use. They are clogs to the wheels of salvation!

9. They *retard growth in grace, hinder revivals*, the conviction and conversion of sinners.

Spiritual singing, or singing with grace in the heart, making melody to the Lord, is not only soul-cheering and soul-elevating to the Christian, but very often sends conviction to the heart of the sinner. Many a rebel against God has dated his first serious, abiding impressions from the heavenly praises flowing from sanctified hearts. Did choir music ever produce these happy and glorious results?

10. Choir singing *tends to backsliding* and *cold formality*. How can it be otherwise when Christians disobey God—refuse to open their mouths in praise!

" Whoso offereth praise, glorifieth me."—*Psa.* l. 23.

11. Choir singing in the house of God tends to banish singing in family worship. Does one family in ten ever think of tuning the heart in praise around the family altar? Why not? No singing of God's praise in the sanctuary, of course none in family devotions.

12. No Christian who fails to sing praises to God as an act of Christian worship, complies with *God's command*. The command of God to sing praises to him is equally positive with that in respect to prayer or supplication.

" Sing unto the Lord, all ye lands," " sing praises, sing unto him, sing psalms unto him." " Sing unto the Lord a new song, and his praise in the congregation of the saints." " Let everything that hath breath praise the Lord."

13. Have we any more right to sing *by proxy*, (by the

mouth of sinners,) than to pray by proxy! Why not employ some one of fluent speech, to do our praying—while we look on and gaze with wonder at the marvelous gifts! Will our souls be benefited? Is God well pleased?

How was singing attended to in the apostolical churches? Did Christians *then* sing by proxy? When the hymn of praise was sung, who were the *choir?* Knew they of praising God by proxy? No, no, indeed—*themselves* sang "with grace, making melody in their hearts unto the Lord." The choir were they—they each, they all—and like the church in heaven, the church on earth herself did sing, in strains so sweet and fervent, the praises of the Lamb. In every act of worship "they served the Lord" themselves. None asked to be excused, nor thought of delegation or proxy, but themselves prayed and praised, and that with fervency of spirit.

Such were the churches then. Are such the churches now?

Would the apostles, first preachers, and first Christians feel at home in the churches now? Would they admire the change that has come over them? Would they pronounce them improvements? We think not—but would be moved to tears at the sight of our silent, close-lipped professors, and our proxy worshipers, together with the cold, lifeless formalism which pervades the churches; and would exhort them to an immediate return to the spiritual simplicity and fervency of first Christians and first Christian churches.

No one need wonder that the churches grew and multiplied, under such preaching, and amid such living, practical Christianity as that which distinguished and was the glory of the first Christian churches. Nor need wonder exist that things now are as they are in the churches, when so much that is vital in itself, and life-inspiring, is found to be wanting.

That there should be a *leader* and *leaders* in public acts of prayer and praise, who can condemn? But proxyism in either, who would not? Do they in heaven by proxy worship? Did Christ by proxy die? Or does he now in heaven by proxy pray for us? Till this primitive, this personal,[*] this individual fervency of spirit in the worship and service of the Lord shall again distinguish the pulpits and the pews, the pastors and the churches, "Ichabod" shall stand written upon them in characters of DEATH!

Churches of Jesus Christ! come back; come back to first principles—first practices—"*your first love!*" "Remember how you [then] heard and received, and hold fast, and repent." Then you served the Lord—served him in fervency of spirit. Then you prayed, you sang his sounding praise, not by proxy, but you yourselves; and served, and sang, and prayed with a "*fervent spirit!*" Do again your "first works." Return to your first love, first simplicity, first humility, honesty, zeal and fervency in the service of God; and he, the Lord, will return and dwell among you, and bless you, and make you a blessing to untold multitudes!

Away, *away* with show and parade—with cold, stiff forms and formalism, in the service of God! Such were not to be found in the church in her first and best days, and such must disappear, before she be terrible to her enemies "as an army with banners."

In the day of conflict, what combatants think of the polish—but of the strength and keen edge of his sword? These, not the polish, do the work required—gain for him the victory.

---

[*] "If singing come not from the heart," says Calvin, "it is worth nothing, and can only awaken God's wrath."

CHARLEY RIDING OUT.

WHAT a noble animal the horse! Treat him kindly and gently, and he will treat you kindly and gently. See the sister of Charley placing her hand on this beautiful pony.

NURSING LITTLE FOLKS FOR THE LORD.

TRAINING THEM "IN THE WAY THEY SHOULD GO."

Blessed woman!

> "There, 'mid the sunshine and the flowers,
> No longer mayst thou lightly stray;
> The great trust of thy womanhood
> Is laid upon thy soul to-day."

WHEN God lays a new-born babe in the arms of a wedded pair, he says to them, "Take this child and nurse it for me, and I will give thee thy wages." God offers the only wages that can satisfy the claims of love. He pays the heart's claim in the heart's own coin. What wages could repay Hannah's prayerful care like the sight of Samuel's after-career as Israel's upright judge? Moses standing on the mount was the "wages" of the Hebrew mother who cradled him in her basket of rushes. St. Augustine's mighty service for the gospel was the best reward that God could give to Monica. John Wesley's mother was repaid for all her patient discipline. George Washington was God's reward to Washington's good mother; as Archibald Alexander and Brown of Haddington were to theirs.

The "wages of sin is death," and of no sin more surely than parental. It is death to peace of mind; death to domestic happiness; death to the neglected or misguided souls of their offspring.

"Take this child and nurse it for ME, and I will give thee thy wages," is the inscription which God's hand writes on every cradle. "When I dressed my child each morning, I prayed that Jesus would clothe it with purity," said a godly mother to one who inquired her secret of good training. "When I wash it, I pray that his blood will cleanse its young soul from evil; when I feed it, I pray that its heart may be nourished with truth, and may grow into likeness with the youthful Jesus of Nazareth." Here was religious training from the cradle. It began with the dawn, and its course was like the sun, growing more full-orbed in beauty until the "perfect day." That mother received her golden wages in the early conversion, usefulness, and honor of all her children. "Go thou and do likewise."

> "Lo, when our loving Saviour comes,
> And death yields up its prey,
> We'll meet those darling little ones
> In realms of endless day."

"THE fear of the Lord is the beginning of wisdom, and the knowledge of the holy is understanding." *Prov.* ix. 10.

MOULDING THE LITTLE FOLKS GOSPELLY.

Look, young readers, aint this beautiful? Here's *an angel mother moulding her little ones in the gospel mould. Blessed woman!*

Seest thou a family of obedient children, sweet-tempered, orderly, kind, affectionate, active, industrious, "olive-plants around the table," lamb-like, the *beau ideal* of loveliness, the model of perfection? How came they so? Through whose moulding? The mother's? Yes; the angelic mother. She wrought the fine needlework of gold, reared the tender thought, implanted the seeds of modest simplicity and purity, and watered them with her prayers as the dews of heaven.

SITTING DOWN TO EAT AND DRINK—AND RISING UP TO PLAY.

"The love of pleasure and of gold,
On some professors have such hold,
They oft forget their names."

Dialogue between Mrs. FICKLE *and* Mr. LOVEGOOD.

L. "Good morning, Mrs. Fickle, walk in, hope you are well, please take a seat."

F. "Thank you, Mr. Lovegood, I've come expressly to invite you, your dear wife and family to our 'Sociable.' It will be splendid! It's been weeks and weeks in preparation. The whole community is in a perfect blaze of excitement, little and big!"

L. "Where is it to be held, Mrs. Fickle?'

F. "In the basement of our church, and if that should be too small, a large public hall will be provided."

L. "Will it be similar to the 'Sociable' alluded to by David when he said: 'Come *and* hear all ye that fear God, and I will declare what he hath done for my soul?' Or like the one of which the prophet Malachi, speaks in chapter iii. verses 16 and 17?

"'Then they that feared the LORD, spake often one to another, and the LORD hearkened and heard *it*, and a book of remembrance was written before him, for them that feared the Lord, and that thought upon his name. And they shall be mine, saith the LORD of hosts, in that day when I make up my jewels, and I will spare them as a man spareth his own son that serveth him.' Or, will it be copied after the one in the 2d chapter of Acts?

"It must have been a very sociable time, blessedly so, in that upper room at Jerusalem, where the 120 disciples were assembled for prayer and praise, day in and day out, for ten days. And still more sociable it must have been on Pentacostal day, when the spirit was poured out, and tongues of fire sat upon each of them. 'And they were all filled with the Holy Ghost, and began to speak with other tongues, as the Spirit gave them utterance.'—*Acts* ii. 4.

"These disciples thus, very soon became familiarly and intimately acquainted with each other. Not only so, but they must have been happy, joyous, soul-kindlingly.

"'And they, continuing daily with one accord in the temple, and breaking bread from house to house, did eat their meat with gladness and singleness of heart; praising God, and having favor with all the people. And the Lord added to the church daily such as should be saved.'—*Acts* ii. 46, 47.

"'Bless'd be the tie that binds
Our hearts in Christian love;
The fellowship of kindred minds,
Is like to that above.'

"I know of no better or surer way to promote sociability, friendship, love, and Christian union. Nothing binds God's people so closely and firmly in the bonds of affection and love, as the baptism of the Holy Spirit—the tongue of fire. This spirit, too, will banish all trifling, levity, foolish talking, and jesting so common at many of these social parties or festivals.

"It will also heal all divisions, backslidings, heartburnings, roots of bitterness, all envyings and evil speakings.

SITTING DOWN TO EAT AND DRINK. 201

Besides it will qualify for active service, spiritual labor, holy zeal, self-sacrifice in the cause of God, in the salvation of souls.

"Is the sociable you have in view similar to the sociabilities I have alluded to? If so, I would like to be present.

> " 'Tis not high power that makes a place divine,
> But sacred thoughts in holy bosoms stored.' "

F. "Not exactly like these you speak of, but—"

L. "Stop, if you please, allow me to enquire the special object of your meeting or 'Sociable?'"

F. "It's to raise money for our pastor, first of all: he has a growing family, and his salary does not more than half meet his current expenses. Then, if there be an overplus resulting from our sales, it will go to cushion the pulpit. The carpet, moreover, on our church floor begins to look shabby, and our Sunday School library needs replenishing! You see the objects of our gathering are purely benevolent."

L. "If your minister's salary is too little, why not make it larger at once by laying aside on the first day of the week as God prospers you, and not set the world on fire with your fancy fairs, sprees and church gambling? If the church gamble, set Satan's ball in motion, what else expect of the world, sons of Belial? It's neither honest nor benevolent to obtain funds for God's cause by such means, when persons can just as well give directly for such purposes as the word of God directs.

"Is money to be raised for church debts, church building or repairing? A Sabbath-school or missionary enterprise? For the increase of the minister's salary? To relieve the poor or for any benevolent operation? What now? How is this money to be forthcoming? In a sober, rational Gospel way? Nay, a feast is prepared; a soiree introduced, a fancy fair, a pic-nic, a concert or exhibition of some kind, a donation, tea or strawberry party, a sleigh-ride, oyster-supper, a tin or gold wedding, something to inflame the appetite, produce a little fun, or vulgar merriment.

"Where is there a church or society, white or colored, Popish or Protestant, that does not resort to these unholy excitements, these stratagems of Satan to raise funds for some object of benevolence? It is money, money! Money we want, money we will have, Gospel or no Gospel, heaven or no heaven. Gospel and soul-saving are laid aside.

"The excitement for weeks is more or less dissipating, swallowing up every thought of the soul's welfare. Children and youth are on fire for a spree—and what else are very many of these festivals and pic-nic excursions but sprees or frolics?

"All false religions seek to attract interest by amusements and animal gratifications. The worshipers of the golden calf sat down to eat and drink the oblations to their new god, and then rose up to play. And a bait of sensuality in some form has always been the lure to heathen worship. Popery has always followed in the same line. Even Sabbath worship connects a dance with the mass. And throughout the whole structure of that 'mystery of iniquity,' the sensual and the comic are interwoven with the pomps and ritual of worship. And one of the most common methods by which decay advances upon sound churches is by pleas of amusements to give an attractive and hilarious character to religion—which usually are so many pleas for conformity to the world."

F. "Are we to renounce all mirth, be dull and melancholy, Mr. Lovegood?"

L. "Seriousness and solid happiness are inseparable."

F. "Does not Solomon say: 'To everything *there is* a season, and a time to every purpose under the heaven?'"

L. "Does Solomon tell us there is a time for sin and folly? I am not unaware of the value of a cheerful religion. I respond to the reasonableness of the command to 'rejoice evermore.' And yet we read that the 'joy *of the Lord* is your strength,' and that our rejoicing must be in God to make it a religious joy. It is not a religious joy, where professedly religious men indulge in gratifications that are worldly, sensual and frivolous.

"'There is a path that leads to God;
All others go astray.'

"Mrs. Fickle, you were familiar with the life and writings of that eminently godly minister of Christ, J. W. Alexander?"

F. "Pastor of the church on Fifth Avenue, corner of Nineteenth Street?"

L. "Precisely—for many years."

F. "Well, what of him?"

L. "In writing to a friend, he speaks thus: 'As I grow older as a parent, my views are changing fast as to the degree of conformity to the world which we should allow to our children. I am horror-struck to count up the profligate children of pious parents, and even ministers. The door at which those influences enter which countervail parental instruction and example, I am persuaded, is yielding to the ways of a pleasure-seeking world—"the lovers of pleasure more than the lovers of God." By dress, books and amusements, an atmosphere is formed which is not that of Christianity. More than ever do I feel that our families must stand in a kind but determined opposition to the fashions of the day.'"

F. "You give 'pic-nics' a slap—what harm of these, pray?"

L. "Object to amusements for little folks or great folks? When—on what occasion? Sooner hush the tuneful lark, tie the legs of the skipping squirrel, stop the flowers from blooming, or the woods and the fields from growing green, than deprive the buoyant youth of innocent recreation, excursions to the shady grove!

"The twinkling stars, the sun, the moon, all nature pours forth her sweet melodies. The little hills skip like lambs, the mountains break forth into singing, and all the trees of the forest clap their hands joyfully. But when Satan takes the lead, comes in for a large share of the spoils, I say hands off, stop the leakes, put out the fires!

"What are Sunday-schools for? To tickle the fancy? gather in 'little ones' for sport? This blessed institution, intended *exclusively* for soul-saving, is frequently a Gospel-hardening, conscience-searing process. The truths taught here, instead of being a savor of life unto life, are a savor of death unto death! Children grow up infidels, go out into the world infidels, reprobates under the mid-day sunlight of the Gospel, take seats with the scornful! How seldom do we hear of any special revivals in Sunday-schools at the present day! And when awakenings do occur, alas! how superficial, how short-lived! 'Like the morning cloud and early dew.' Is there not a cause for this dearth and spiritual death? Is it not this perpetual *rush* for the visionary? the lack of Gospel teaching? 'If the salt have lost its savor, wherewith shall it be salted?'—*Matt.* v. 13.

"To make schools, on the Lord's day or any day, scenes of

hilarity, merriment, fun, frolic, is to defeat the special object in view."

F. "I perceive where you stand, Mr. Lovegood; you contravene even our Sunday-school exhibitions or concerts, the delightful speechifyings of the juveniles!"

L. "The way they are usually conducted, ungospelized, I do. Children are naturally excitable, inclined to pride, folly, and self-complacency. And instead of fostering these reptiles, every *possible* means should be resorted to, to counteract and exterminate them, and lead them directly to the feet of Jesus. Very many of our common Sunday-school exhibitions tend to puff up or inflate juvenile minds."

F. "Specify the evils if there are any, Mr. Lovegood?"

L. "1. They excite envy in the children. Those who are not selected to speak envy those who are.

"2. They encourage pride of spirit and pride of dress— that is, pride of talent in the speakers; and pride of dress, because the girls and young ladies are often dressed as for a show.

"3. They are destructive of spiritual interest in the school, especially in seasons of revival.

"4. They create confusion and disorganization in the school, owing to the attention given to preparation and to efforts to enlist children in the sale of tickets, etc.

"5. They have a reactionary tendency, throwing the school backward for weeks after they are over.

"6. They are mere money-making affairs, and to make them popular with irreligious persons the pieces selected are often irreligious and of evil tendency."

F. "Would you advise parents to withdraw their little ones from these nurseries of piety, Mr. Lovegood?"

L. "If contamination and damnation, instead of salvation, assuredly. As I remarked previously, five distinguished Presbyterian elders, of the city of New York, told me, with tears, 'We are compelled to keep our children out of Sunday-school altogether because of the swarms of pious novels which infests the shelves.' The church is helping the world—projecting it into amusements. Novels lay the groundwork for gambling, in the church and out of it. Let me specify more definitely how Satan is gaining the ascendency. The use of wine—not to say strong liquors, at the dinner-table, is not unfrequently in so-called Christian homes. Attendance at the opera or theater is no more classed among interdicted amusements. The sons and daughters of Christian households are trained in dancing-schools, permitted to give juvenile balls, engage in various dissipating amusements that turn away the heart from Christ and from God.

"Opposition to these indulgences is pronounced Puritanism, and Christianity is to be made so tolerant that such time-honored phrases as self-crucifixion, self-denial, keeping the body under, spiritually-minded, and the like, are to be cast out of the Christian vocabulary. Piety is no longer to be armor-clad, armed in the battle-field; but is to be clothed in gay dressing-gowns, slippered, lodged in well-stuffed easy-chairs. The road to heaven is to be traveled in railway-cars, with ample accommodations for the world, the flesh, and the devil, in suitable portions of the train.

"That this spirit of self-indulgence is cherished and defended in and by numerous Christian families, is undeniable. That it is increasing is equally true, and will become general, if not sternly checked."

F. "Are you not, Mr.—"

L. "Hold! a moment, Mrs. Fickle, I was about to say, during the past summer, I saw ministers in high standing play hours at croquet, and in a large parlor, lead the assembly in 'amusement' at charades, conundrums, and other like sports, and with no misgivings preach and administer communion a Sabbath after. We are growing in the wisdom that attains flowers without thorns—and without fruit. We are adopting a cross disarmed of its nails and wreathed with roses, a flowery bed of ease, whereon to be carried to the skies. In absence of the music of heaven, we are lulled and charmed by the music of the opera. The sword of the Spirit, 'sharp and piercing to the dividing asunder of joints and marrow,' is muffled with flowers of poppy, a wand of sensuous soothing and spiritual numbness. I clip the following from the *Boston Journal* of March 4th :

" ' The Young Men's Christian Association of Meriden, Conn., purposes to erect a new building. In addition to two stores, the building will contain a bowling-alley, coffee and refreshment room, library, conversation and amusement room, and gymnasium. There will also be a hall arranged *for private theatricals*, etc.'

" ' Private theatricals' will be found but a stepping-stone to the public theater, and though members in some respects may have ' a form of godliness,' it will be manifest that they are ' lovers of pleasure more than lovers of God.'

" The festivals of various names connected of late years with churches of different denominations are working to the same end. Who can draw the line between the church and the world on such occasions? No thorough, enlightened Christian can be satisfied that festivals are Christ-like in which 'grab-bags,' 'guess-cakes,' 'post-offices,' and similar means are resorted to for the purpose of raising money for church-building, etc. Only imagine such a festival held in the apostolic age : Paul, for example, putting his hand into a bag and pulling out a rag-baby amid a roar of laughter; Peter paying out a few cents (for he would not be likely to have much silver and gold unless he got it by miracle, as he did the money to pay his tax) for a piece of cake—hoping to be lucky enough to find a ring in it: 'the beloved disciple' charged an exorbitant price for a letter in the church post-office—which he pays rather than to appear mean by refusing to do it; or a large number of the primitive disciples appealing to the flesh by announcing a turkey or an oyster-supper at a hotel, for the purpose of getting money out of the men of the world, and having a good time themselves!"

F. "Excuse me, Mr. Lovegood, I must be off; every moment is gold till our 'Sociable' is consummated. May we not have the pleasure of seeing you present, your wife and daughters on the occasion?"

L. "How can you consistently press your invitation after what has been said? I would as soon attend a theater, a Saratoga hop, a horse race or that club-house of the prince of gamblers."

F. "Christians at Saratoga do attend these places of amusement; not a few, and some sanctified ones. What harm in looking on if so be they don't hop themselves, bet, lay a wager, or take a pledge at the horse race or clubhouse?"

L. "'Be not conformed to this world, but be ye transformed.' 'Love not the world nor the things of the world. If any man love the world the love of the Father is not in him.' 'Know ye not that the friendship of the world is enmity with God? whosoever, therefore, will be a friend of the world is the enemy of God.'

"'Ye also, as lively stones, are built up a spiritual house, an holy priesthood, to offer up spiritual sacrifices, acceptable to God by Jesus Christ. Ye are a chosen generation, a royal priesthood, an holy nation, a peculiar people ; that ye should shew forth the praises of him who hath called you out of darkness into his marvellous light."—*Pet.* ii. 5, 10.

"'Whatsoever is not of faith is sin.' 'Be ye holy, for I am holy.' 'Abstain from all appearance of evil.'"

F. "Are you not a little squeamish, Mr. Lovegood? Some of the most distinguished divines, eminent pulpit orators (one in Brooklyn especially), look upon some of Paul's writings as obsolete, out of date, particularly those referring to self-denial, worldly conformity, etc."

L. "Explain, Mrs. Fickle, if you have facts touching this false teacher, hold him up to the public gaze in his naked deformity, as a beacon of warning!"

F. "Mind you, Mr. Lovegood, I do not say he is false, but the doctrine advanced by him is, 'that the women of this age who profess to follow Christ are not required to put off their trinkets and adornments. St. Paul, in this and other matters he said, meant only contemporary women, as if pride in this exhibition of itself no longer existed.'"

L. "Is this Gospel? I read the Scriptures differently, and believe that when women approach the Lord's table, or go forward to meet Christ in any other duty, they are not allowed to robe themselves in the gaudy attire of the worldling. They are forbidden to do that at any time, and he is a faithful shepherd who keeps them within the lines.

"Consider the words of the apostle (from 1 *Tim.* ii. 9): 'I will also that women adorn themselves in modest apparel, with shamefacedness and sobriety, *not with broidered hair, or gold, or pearls, or costly array.*' (Also 1 *Pet.* iii. 3.) But go on, Mrs. Fickle."

F. "This same popular preacher declared publicly from the pulpit in Brooklyn, that 'Paul's precepts were only local, and entitled to the ridicule of this age!' Speaking of the drama or stage, he said, 'he would not, to save his right hand, have the theatres of the city closed, because of their power to prevent evil!'"

L. "Is it surprising that with such teachers and teaching the 'Internationals' and the masses keep away from religion, and are wheeling into line to fight it as a thing to be hated and despised? Truly 'one sinner destroyeth much good.'

"But from what source did you gather this important information, Mrs. Fickle?"

F. "From 'The N. Y. Daily Witness' and other periodicals. 'Mine eyes have seen it, mine ears have heard it.'"

L. "You see, or ought to see, pleasure rules the hour. It is fearful to witness the inroads which worldly pleasure is making upon Christianity.

"That the church is rapidly conforming to the spirit and pleasures of the world none can deny. The most alarming feature is that prominent preachers lead the way, and the people blindly follow."

F. "To calm your fears, Mr. Lovegood, do away with your scruples, or over-much righteousness, let me assure you our 'sociable' is to be respectable, genteel. Not a breath has been breathed as yet about 'ring cakes,' grab boxes, post-offices, and the like, or winding up with a drama or game! Besides, our pastor will be on hand, and if suitable opportunity offer, he will begin or close our exercises with prayer."

L. "This offering prayer before or after spending the night, 'till cock crowing, in cackling nonsense, feasting to gluttony, serving the devil in various ways, I look upon as the worst feature in the case—solemn mockery!—little short of blasphemy! saddling your abominations on the Almighty!

"Suppose Aaron had offered a prayer before or after he and the rest of the idolaters danced around the golden calf, saying: 'These be thy gods, O Israel!' would it not have added to his guilt ten fold? See Ex. xxxii. 2, 3, 4.

"You recollect well, Mrs. Fickle, what rascally things took place at that tin-wedding!"

F. "When and where, Mr. Lovegood?"

L. "In Brooklyn. The scene was disgraceful beyond expression. After spending a large part of the night in sensuous hilarity, triphammer, nonsensical garrulity, and when about to wind up, the pastor comes forward and displays his clerical wit, the merry Andrew or buffoon, 'mid roars of laughter, in the presence of both saints and sinners, then to cap the climax of iniquity—prayer was offered! The same was true at the supper or banquet given to deify a certain bishop, at a rum-selling, gambling hotel in Chicago, Ill. 'For the time past of our life may suffice us to have wrought the will of the Gentiles, when we walked in lasciviousness, lusts, excess of wine, revellings, banquetings, and abominable idolatries.'

"Those familiar with the facts in these cases, assure us that the whole proceedings were ridiculous in the extreme, shockingly disgusting, enough to cause angels to weep, and Satan to blush! How is the gold become dim! how is the most fine gold changed!

> "'Will ye play, then, will ye dally
>   With your music and your wine?
> Up! it is Jehovah's rally!
>   God's own arm hath need of thine!'

"The festivals or sociables you are planning and endorsing, Mrs. Fickle, *are stumbling-blocks to the world!* Sinners are eagle-eyed—they see and know these festivals are gotten up for selfish purposes; that their chief object is money-making and not soul-saving. Consequently they lose confidence in religious professors, and become more given up to the service of sin and Satan. Exhort sinners to faith, repentance, and newness of life, they point us directly to these dark spots, beguiling unstable souls, sporting themselves with their own deceivings! Impenitent sinners, instead of looking to the Bible, to the Lord Jesus Christ for the truth, for the religion of purity and love, as they ought to, and as God commands them to do, they look upon ungodly church-members, and judge of religion as they see it embodied in these dry bones, in those having a name to live and are dead, having a form of godliness, but, by wicked works, denying the power thereof! Thus the world is reeling on, like a drunken man, to dark damnation!

"I object to them because they are stumbling-blocks to young converts, the lambs of the flock; one special cause of their backsliding, losing their first love. How can it be otherwise? A fearful woe is pronounced against those who offend or cause God's 'little ones' to stumble. (See Math. xviii. 6.)

"They wound the hearts of God's chosen people. The most consistent, consecrated, humble, devoted disciples of Jesus are always grieved at this method of raising money for religious objects. They see and know with sorrow the evil effects on the church and the world.

"'If meat make my brother to offend, I will eat no flesh while the world standeth, lest I make my brother to offend. 'Give none offence, neither to the Jews nor to the Gentiles, nor to the church of God.' 'Even as I please all men,' says Paul, 'in all things, not seeking mine own profit, but the profit of many, that they may be saved.' 'Whether, therefore, ye eat or drink, or whatsoever ye do, do all to the glory of God.'—1 *Cor.* x. 31, 32, 33.

"Again, they are special hindrances to revivals. Soul-saving is out of the question, so long as these fairs, tea-parties, or festivals, are on the docket. And when these upheavings are over, the undue excitement for weeks in the preparation of luxuries, fancy articles of little or no value—the late hours, the gluttony, the surfeitings, the foolish talkings and jestings—who is prepared for prayer, praise, or to labor in a revival, to urge sinners to repentance, temperance, and holy living? Samson is shorn of his locks. Often when God is near to bless, revive His work, pour out His Spirit graciously, convict and convert sinners; when inquiring souls are weeping between the porch and the altar; just at this crisis Satan comes in, stirs up the people—cold, formal, backslidden church-members*—for a fair, donation, tea or strawberry party, a pic-nic, oyster-supper, a feast of some kind, to turn away the attention from things pertaining to life eternal, hope everlasting! Thus the Holy Spirit is grieved, takes His flight, the revival is scattered to the four winds!

"'The fact that "fairs" make the procurement of means to pay for a house of worship or to purchase a Sunday-school library, simply a matter of buying and selling, resolves itself into a weighty objection to their propriety. They are departures from the New Testament method of

---

* Is it not invariably true that none but backsliders or formalists, having a name to live and are dead, ever dream of pushing these cars of Satan?

meeting the pecuniary necessities of the church, and so far forth must operate against the spirit of self-denial, liberality, and faith which that method calls into action.

"'Whatever is done by a church, or by a portion of the members *for* it, should be so done as neither to sacrifice nor to obscure that which distinguishes the church from the world. How totally fairs, festivals, or tea-parties fail to meet this requirement, we need not tarry to depict. They are scenes of mirthfulness and levity, in which men can trace nothing that distinguishes the church from the world.'

"Besides, the precedent of making God's house a house of merchandize, is a dangerous one. When we see the whole world on fire with sin and Satan, shall we add fuel to the flame by our example? 'Behold how great a matter a little fire kindleth.'

"'The course of evil
Begins so slowly, and from such light source,
An infant's hand might stop the breach with clay;
But let the stream get deeper, and philosophy,
Aye, and religion too, shall strive in vain
To turn the headlong current!'

"What! compromise with the devil, to obtain the devil's money to build up God's cause? This is worse than the game of Tetzel's selling indulgences; only on a smaller scale. Does the blessed Lord desire his children to go begging of Satan's emissaries, impenitent sinners, rebels against God to uphold his kingdom? When? and where such a proposal or consent?

"The sin of Jeroboam, son of Nebat, who made Israel to sin, become idolaters, by setting up two golden calves, one in Bethel and the other in Dan, (1 *Kings* xii. 28, 29,) is nothing compared to this idolatry and witchcraft in our churches!—*Acts* xvii. 30.

"'Behold thy gods, O Israel, which brought thee out of the land of Egypt.'

"Multitudes of God's faithful ones are beginning to awake to this superabounding 'iniquity which God knoweth.' T. Dewitt Talmage, of the Brooklyn Tabernacle, says: 'Do you wonder that churches built, lighted, or upholstered by such processes as that, come to great financial and spiritual decrepitude? The devil says: "*I* helped build that house of worship, and I have as much right there as you have;"—and for once the devil is right.

"'We do not read that they had a lottery for building a church at Corinth or Antioch, or for getting up a gold-headed cane, or for an embroidered surplice for St. Paul. All this I style ecclesiastical gambling. More than one man who is destroyed can say that his first step on the wrong road was when he won something at a church fair.'

"President C. G. Finney, of Oberlin, the revivalist, alluding to these revival-killers and soul-destroyers, remarks thus:

"'Often when it comes the time of year to work, when the evenings are long, and business is light, and the very time to make an extra effort—at this moment somebody in the church will give a party and invite some Christian friends, so as to have it a religious party. And then some other family must do the same, to return the compliment. Then another and another, till it grows into an organized system of parties, that consume the whole winter.

"'This is the grand design of the devil, because it appears so innocent and so proper to promote good feeling, and increase the acquaintance of Christians with each other.

And so, instead of prayer-meetings, they will have these parties. The evils of these parties are very great. They are often got up at great expense; and the most abominable gluttony is practised at them.

"'But it is said they are Christian parties, and that they are all, or nearly all, professors of religion who attend them. And furthermore, they are often concluded with prayer. Now I regard this as one of the worst features about them; that after the waste of time and money, the excess in eating and drinking, the vain conversation and nameless fooleries with which such a season is filled up, an attempt is made to sanctify it and to palm it off upon God, by concluding it with prayer! Say what you will, it would not be more absurd, or incongruous, or impious to close a ball or a theatre with prayer.

"'But I shall advise any congregation who are calculating to have a circle of parties, in the meantime to dismiss their minister, and let him go and preach where the people would be ready to receive the word and profit by it, and not have him stay and be distressed, and grieved, and killed by attempting to promote religion among them, while they are engaged, heart and hand, in the service of the devil! Professors should never get up anything that may divert public attention from religion. In relation to giving parties, say what you please about their being an innocent recreation, I appeal to any of you, who have ever attended them, to say whether they fit you for prayer, or increase your spirituality, whether sinners are ever converted in them, or Christians made to agonize in prayer for souls.'"

☞ PRICE $2.25 per 100 copies, at the office of the—"Home Thrusts," "Shining Light," "The Sword that Cuts, the Fire that Burns," "Apples of Gold in Pictures of Silver,"—303 West Twentieth street, New York. (*Orders thankfully received.*)

Landscape.

AMUSEMENTS AND RECREATIONS.

" As bird from fowler's share set free,
 Soaring sings 'Sweet Liberty!'
 As the roe from the hunter's hand,
 Darting, bounds o'er stream and land ;
 So, from Satan's slavish band,
 So, from this world's iron hand
  Our soul's set free!"*

Recreation is a demand of our nature, and is profitable not only for *young* people, but for children of larger growth also. The important question is, What kind of amusement should be allowed? The taste for games of hazard is growing upon our people, until gambling is rapidly becoming a national vice, and it is, therefore, questionable whether any game of "chance," however innocent it may seem in itself, has not in it a tendency to cultivate a desire for the excitement of technical gambling.

" A man's heart deviseth his way; but the Lord directeth his steps."—Prov. xvi. 9.

---

* " Why do ye spend money for that which is not bread, and your labor for that which satisfieth not? Hearken diligently, and eat ye that which is good, and let your soul delight itself in fatness. Ho! every one that thirsteth, come ye to the waters, and he that hath no money; come ye, buy and eat; yea, come, buy wine and milk without money and without price."—Isa. lv. 2, 1. "O that men were wise, that they understood this!"

A PIOUS FATHER INSTRUCTING HIS SON IN WAYS OF WISDOM.

BEAUTIFUL! BEAUTIFUL!!

Young readers, is not this beautiful, exquisitely?—delightfully interesting? What more so? Look at it, listen, listen—hark! "My son, forget not my law; but let thine heart keep my commandments; for length of days and long life and peace shall they add to thee.

Let not mercy and truth forsake thee: bind them about thy neck; write them upon the tablets of thine heart: so that thou find favor and good understanding in the sight of God and man." *Prov.* iii. 1-4.

SPYING THE NAKEDNESS OF THE LAND.

Conversation between Mr. TIMEWELL *and* Mr. SERVILITY.
(No. 12.)

"And when Moses saw that the people were naked, (for Aaron had made them naked unto their shame, amongst their enemies)."— *Ex.* xxxii. 24.

T. "You're in time, friend Servility; so far so good. This scene is the closing one—the finale. Another interview we may not have till at the bar of the Highest, where the secrets of your heart and mine will be revealed.

"'For God shall bring every work into judgment, with every secret thing, whether it be good, or whether it be evil.'—*Ecc.* xii. 14.

"I beseech you, therefore, suffer the word of exhortation."

S. "Speak, Mr. Timewell."

T. "Your name is Servility—you continue in the 'Ring,' move in a circle, and will doubtless, while you live, move, have your being. The Ethiopian change his skin! or the leopard his spots! When?—where?

"'Because sentence against an evil work is not executed speedily, therefore the heart of the sons of men is fully set in them to do evil.'—*Ecc.* viii. 11."

S. "What now calls forth your vindictiveness?"

T. "'Correction is grievous unto him that forsaketh the way: and he that hateth reproof shall die.'—*Prov.* xv. 10.

"Rebuke a wise man, and he will love thee. Give

instruction to a wise man, and he will be yet wiser : teach a just man, and he will increase in learning.'—*Prov.* ix. 9."

S. " I'm in the dark—I know not to what you allude."

T. " 'Do ye indeed speak righteousness?—do ye judge uprightly?' 'Yea, in heart ye work wickedness.'—*Psa.* lviii. 2.

" You shut up the kingdom of heaven against men, for you neither go in yourself, nor suffer you them that are entering to go in. What wickedness greater, this side perdition ?

" Mark these whited sepulchres that tithed mint, anise and cumin, ' and omitted the weightier matters of the law— judgment, mercy, and faith ;' blind guides, which strained at a gnat and swallowed a camel—and what fearful judgments denounced by our blessed Lord upon them !

" ' Fill ye up then the measure of your fathers. Ye serpents, ye generation of vipers, how can ye escape the damnation of hell ?'—*Math.* xxiii. 32, 33."

S. " I'm still in the dark, Mr. Timewell."

T. " None are so blind as those that will not see. ' If we say that we have fellowship with him, and walk in darkness, we lie, and do not the truth.'—1 *John* i. 6.

S. " Is not every man considered innocent till proved guilty ?"

T. " I speak what I do know, testify to what I have seen. Call to remembrance that course of lectures you publicly announced—on amusements—' the lust of the flesh, the lust of the eyes, and the pride of life ?' "

S. " What of them ?"

T. " What of them ! Indeed ! Did you obey God ? assume the apostolical ? or play the coward, the sycophant ? On theatricals you laid aside your gloves for a little space, bristled up porcupinely, swelled like Esop's frog, declaimed rousingly against these bubblings of the pit, moral leprosies, sink holes, and hot-beds of lewdness. This you could do safely, and not infringe or trespass on your popularity, or the receiving of honor from men; you could thunder and flash lightnings in the face and eyes of what satan himself would not be afraid to do, and keep inside the "ring." But, mark you, friend Servility, when you came to novels, romances, popular works of fiction, religious white-lying, publishing and puffing; secret conclaves, the 'pic-nics' of the day, fashionable choirs; popish church building; the broidered hair, the 'gold, pearls, and costly array,' 'the tinkling ornaments,' the 'cauls and round tires,' like the moon; 'the chains, and the bracelets, and the mufflers, the bonnets, and the ornaments of the legs, and the head-bands and the tablets, and the ear-rings; the rings and nose jewels; the changeable suits of apparel, and the mantles, and the wimples, and the crisping pins; the glasses, and the fine linen, and the hoods, and the vails.'—*Isa.* iv. 19, 23.

"What now, stand the fire? Nay, you winced, succumbed, conferred with flesh and blood; daubed here, daubed there, bowed the knee to Baal; else you held your peace; hushed rebuke like a dumb dog that 'cannot bark, sleeping, lying down, loving to slumber.'—*Isa.* lvi. 10, 11. 'Your glorying is not good.'

"Wherefore these conservative plasters, this covering of sin? staring you full in the face heaven-daring?

"You knew you were before an audience that would not endure sound doctrine, that had, for a long time, after their own lusts, heaped to themselves teachers having itching ears—that turned away their ears from the truth and were turned 'unto fables.'—2 *Tim.* iv. 1–5.

"'If thou forbear to deliver them that are drawn unto death, and those that are ready to be slain : If thou sayest, Behold, we knew it not: doth not he that pondereth the heart consider it? and he that keepeth thy soul, doth not he know it? and shall not he render to every man according to his works?'—*Prov.* xxiv. 11, 12.

"Your example, Mr. Servility, is death in the pot—death spiritual—its damnation!

"Were God to deal with very many teachers in Israel in our popular churches in New York and out of it as he dealt with Ananias and Sapphira for keeping 'back part of the price,' how many dead corpses think would be found in pulpits here and there? And you among the rest, Mr. Servility, for you withhold the truth, refuse to declare God's full council—'*all the words of this life*'—clear your skirts of blood! Horrible!

"'Therefore as the fire devoureth the stubble, and the flame consumeth the chaff, so their root shall be as rottenness, and their blossom shall go up as dust : because they have cast away the law of the Lord of hosts, and despised the word of the Holy one of Israel.'—*Isa.* v. 24."

S. "Why make mountains of mole-hills, Mr. Timewell? Thousands of the most eminent divines in our day never dream of referring to those parts of Scripture in Isaiah and St. Paul alluding to fashionable gayety, personal adornments, tinkling ornaments, 'mantles and wimples' you speak of. Some distinguished pulpit orators totally discard these passages as applicable to modern and intellectual refinement. By your over-much righteousness you unchurch one-half, if not two-thirds, of our most elegant church members—regular communicants."

T. "'He that diggeth a pit shall fall into it; and whoso

breaketh a hedge, a serpent shall bite him. Surely the serpent will bite without enchantment, and a babbler is no better.'—*Ecc.* x. 8, 11.

"'There is a generation that are pure in their own eyes, and yet is not washed from their filthiness.'

"'Add thou not unto his words, lest he reprove thee, and thou be found a liar.'

"'For I testify unto every man that heareth the words of the prophecy of this book, If any man shall add unto these things, God shall add unto him the plagues that are written in this book:

"'And if any man shall take away from the words of the book of this prophecy, God shall take away his part out of the book of life, and out of the holy city, and from the things which are written in this book.'—*Rev.* xxii. 18, 19.

"Beware how you tamper with God's word; better a mill-stone were tied to your neck, and yourself hurled into a sea bottomless!

"'Well spake the Holy Ghost by Esaias the prophet unto our fathers, saying, Go unto this people, and say, Hearing ye shall hear, and shall not understand; and seeing ye shall see, and not perceive: For the heart of this people is waxed gross, and their ears are dull of hearing, and their eyes have they closed; lest they should see with their eyes, and hear with their ears, and understand with their heart, and should be converted, and I should heal them.'—*Acts* xxviii. 25, 26, 27.

"Fashion rules the world—curses the world! I've gone no farther in brandishing God's two-edged sword in the face and eyes of this idolatrous age than one of your own conservatives, or 'Ring' folks."

S. "To whom do you allude?"

T. "The good Dr. Crosby ventures to step one foot out of the 'Ring' for a moment, and say by pen what it seems he fears to say in the presence of his gayly-dressed and fashionable audience!"

S. "What is it? Out with it."

T. "'If I were called to point out,' says Dr. Crosby, 'the most alarming sins to-day—those which are most deceitful in their influence, and most soul-destroying in their intimate effects—I would not mention drunkenness, with all its fearful havoc; nor gambling, with its crazed victims; nor harlotry, with its hellish orgies; but the love of money on the part of men, and the love of display on the part of women. While open vice sends its thousands, these fashionable and favored indulgences send their ten thousands to perdition. They sear the conscience, incrust the soul with an impenetrable shell of worldliness, debauch the affections from every high and heavenly object, and make man or woman the worshiper of self. While doing all this, the poor victim is allowed by public opinion to think himself or herself a Christian; while the drunkard, the gambler, or the prostitute is not deceived by such a thought for a moment.'

"'Moreover the Lord saith, Because the daughters of Zion are haughty, and walk with stretched forth necks and wanton eyes, walking and mincing as they go, and making a tinkling with their feet:

"'Therefore the Lord will smite with a scab the crown of the head of the daughters of Zion, and the Lord will discover their secret parts.

"'In that day the Lord will take away the bravery of their tinkling ornaments about their feet, . . .

"'And it shall come to pass, that instead of sweet

smell, there shall be stink ; and instead of a girdle, a rent ; and instead of well-set hair, baldness; and instead of a stomacher, a girdling of sackcloth ; and burning instead of beauty.

" 'Thy men shall fall by the sword, and thy mighty in the war.

" 'And her gates shall lament and mourn ; and she being desolate shall sit upon the ground.'—*Isa.* iii. 16–26.

" 'If our gospel be hid, it is hid to them that are lost : in whom the god of this world hath blinded the minds of them which believe not, lest the light of the glorious gospel of Christ, who is the image of God, should shine unto them.'—2 *Cor.* iv. 3, 4."

"The Accursed Thing!"

The Israelites are smitten at Ai.

"But the children to Israel committed a trespass in the accursed thing."—*Josh.* vii. 1.

THE army of Joshua could not prosper while Achan was in the camp. The ship's crew must have been lost had not Jonah been thrown overboard.

If God's people could not prosper with only one Achan in the camp, how can they now with many Achans in the church ? The children of Israel were smitten before their enemies for Achan's sake ; and, until the guilty one was brought to punishment, the heart of the people was as water, and they could not stand before their enemies. The trespass of Achan cost the entire defeat of the Hebrew army, and the lives of thirty-six men, besides that of all his own family.

"Apples of Gold," 303 West Twentieth Street, New York.

BUSY FOLKS, OR LITTLE FOLKS BUSY.

LITTLE FOLKS BUSY? BUSY AS A BEE THAT GATHERS HONEY FROM EVERY OPENING FLOWER.

KEEP them still? No, you can't. It's work, work, from sunrise to sunset. How much, think you, does a little child daily? can you tell? It is doing this, doing that—tottering here, tottering there—climbing up here, kneeling down there, running to another place, but never still. Twisting and turning, rolling and doubling, as if testing every bone and muscle for their future uses. It is very curious to watch it. One who does so will understand the deep breathing of the little sleeper, as, with one arm tossed over its curly head, it prepares for the next day's gymnastics. Tireless through the day, till that time comes, as the maternal love that accommodates itself, hour after hour, to its thousand wants and caprices, real and imaginary.

Winning the Hearts of Little Folks.

"Love is the little golden clasp
That bindeth up the trust;
Oh, break it not; lest all the leaves
Shall scatter and be lost."

THE heart of a child is easily won. Love begets love. Love children and they will love you. Let children feel that you care for them, that you are interested in all that interests them, that you sympathize with them in all their little sorrows, rejoice with them in all their little joys, that you are their friend, and you have the key to their hearts.

Smile upon a child: have you not won its heart? Does it not smile in return? Do not its eyes follow you? Does not its face sadden as you disappear, and smile when you come again? Does that smile cost you anything?

It is sweet to have children love us. It is sweet to know that they delight to nestle upon our bosoms, and that their little arms long to clasp about our necks. It is sweet to feel the soft clinging tendrils of their honest hearts intertwining, cosily and trustingly, in among the stouter and chillier tendrils of our own.

Love is the grand secret in domestic education. Give your children a genial, loving atmosphere in which to grow. Love precludes not decision or correction, but is prompt in the execution of both.

Deal with your children as God deals with his. Do not meet their anger with your anger, their petulance with your own, or their obstinacy with wilfulness still greater. Overcome evil with good. When God called himself a father, he chose a name which he designed to be significant of overflowing love, tender mercy, and long-continued forbearance.

Parents, "provoke not your children to wrath."

> "A word, a look, has crushed to earth
> Full many a budding flower,
> Which, had a smile but own'd its birth,
> Would bless life's darkest hour."

A heavenly countenance is the highest commendation, the most conclusive argument for the character of him who earns it. One glimpse of an angel's face would probably do more to impress us with the beauty of holiness than many an eloquent sermon an hour long. Stephen's radiant face was a powerful auxiliary to his discourse. The shining face of Moses, when he came down from the Mount, was proof to the Israelites that he had seen the Lord.

If this be true with an audience of adults, how much more with children! Sensitive as they are, and often affected, they cannot tell why or how, and gazing steadfastly as they do, with no sense of impropriety, into the face of their parent or teacher, it is almost unavoidable that his image should be reproduced in them.

> "Then deem it not an idle thing
> A pleasant word to speak;
> The face you wear, the thoughts you bring,
> A heart may heal or break."

What will not love do? Who can describe its powerful subduing influences? Who ever accomplished anything by reproaches, or violence, or harsh measures? You gratify a private and dark passion in your own heart, and arouse a darker one in another bosom. Oh, try the mighty efficacy of love! One smile of genuine sympathy is worth all your purse to a beggar. "Beloved, let us love one another; for love is of God; and every one that loveth is born of God, and knoweth God."—1 *John* iii. 7.

Parents, commend your little ones whenever they do right, perform that which is good and praiseworthy. Whenever they are quick to obey cheerfully, express your grateful approbation; tell them how pleased you are at any improvement in well-doing. Your child has been very pleasing and obedient through the day. Just before putting him to sleep for the night, you take his hand and say: "My son, you have been very good to-day. It makes me very happy to see you so kind and obedient. God loves children who are dutiful to their parents, and he promises to make them happy."

This approbation from his mother is to him a great reward. And when with a more than ordinarily affectionate tone you say, "Good-night, my dear son," he leaves the room with his little eyes full of feeling. And when he closes his eyes for sleep he is happy, and resolves that he will always try to do his duty.

> "Good-night is but a little word,
> Yet beautiful though brief,
> And falls upon the gentle heart
> Like dew upon the leaf."

Mothers, train your daughters *to be mothers!* Think what a mother ought to be in every relation of life—social, domestic, public, at home and abroad, by day and by night. Think of Washington's mother, Samuel's, Timothy's, the mother of our Lord. Mothers *cannot* be good mothers, unless taught to be good mothers from their infancy. If all mothers were good mothers, would not our world soon be a paradise?

The Bible lays down four great rules, involving four great elements of successful religious training of children: *prayer, example, instruction,* and *restraint.* And it is doubted if a solitary case can be found when all these have been united, where the child has not followed in the footsteps of the pious parent.

Disobedience to parents is the beginning of all crime! How infinitely important then that the habits of disobedience should never be formed.

It is only from the Bible we learn that God is love; that his character is spotlessly holy. There we are informed that our first duty, our chief interest, is to acquire a character in righteousness and benevolence like God's.

"Apples of Gold," 303 West Twentieth Street, New York.

NOVEMBER.

"The leaves are fading and falling,
 The winds are rough and wild,
The birds have ceased their calling;
 But let me tell you, dear child,

"Though day by day, as it closes,
 Doth darker and colder grow,
The roots of the bright red roses
 Will keep alive in the snow.

"And when the winter is over,
 The boughs will get new leaves,
The quail come back to the clover,
 And the swallow back to the eaves.

WOMAN AT HOME.

Home is the throne of empires on which woman sits, the sceptre with which she wields the destiny of nations. All that is dear and holy, noble and divine, in society or the nation, centres back to home, where woman presides as the angel of love.

If she would seek the honor of exerting an influence which shall last after the present order of the universe is changed, a philanthropist whose name, though not lauded by the fickle multitude, shall be remembered by the good and pure in the ages of eternity, let her not, for any social interest or cause, neglect the hallowed duties of home, but watch over them with jealous trust, with devotional constancy, with unruffled vigilance, to keep that home the nursery of all the virtues, the sanctuary of the heart's deepest loves, the "holy of holies," where the divine presence may shine forth in her looks, and be manifest in her actions.

Home is woman's true sphere. There is nothing in this wide world that will confer greater honor upon her than for her to make that home a type of what society should be, and of what heaven is in the graces of exalted character. As a wife, she should be to her husband a guardian angel; as a mother, charged with the high trust of directing the child, she should see that, like the work of the skilful artist, she moulds it "true to nature," beautiful and pure.

> "Nor steel nor fire itself hath power,
> Like woman in her prayerful hour!"

The poet has disclosed the whole secret of woman's conquering power. Fair in her virtue, smiling in her goodness, she wields an influence which a mailed warrior never could.

HIS FINGERS ARE COLD, AIN'T THEY? TERRIBLE!

Poor boy without mittens, don't you pity him, little folks? Winter? Certainly it is. See the snowflakes falling.

SNOW, EMBLEM OF PURITY.

"There is something so *pure* in the falling snow,
　As it comes on its wings so light,
And mantles the valleys and plains below
　In a robe of spotless white;
That I love to gaze thro' the misty air,
　Where the broad flakes are at play,
And offer a silent, earnest prayer,
　That my heart was as pure as they;
That every thought and wish might be
The emblem of such purity."

ATTEMPTS TO POISON CHILDREN.

"It is now a well-known fact, that in most of our large cities—probably, also, in most of our large towns and villages—there are well-laid plans, systematically and persistently followed, for poisoning children—of both sexes, and of all social conditions—not indeed with arsenic, or strychnine, or Paris green, but with obscene books. To such an extent have these endeavors gone, that there are publishing firms with large capital invested, with many agents and dealers, constantly employed in producing and circulating the most abominably corrupting publications. These are of different sizes, and skilfully adapted to attract attention, being designed mostly for children and youth from ten to eighteen years of age. They are put into the hands of hundreds and thousands of school children going to and from school, with the injunction to tell no one about them, and especially not to let their parents see them, and the place where they can get more is carefully told. Children receive the books with their gaudy pictures, wholly ignorant of their nature and purpose; and by the time they actually learn their vileness, their minds are corrupted. What a horrible crime is this! And yet, for the sake of gain, there are found men enough who will engage in the publication and distribution of these polluting and destroying works. Many of the social vices and misfortunes of maturer years are the direct fruits, grown and ripened, from the reading of obscene books in childhood."

We clip the foregoing from a daily issue. Religious

writers, and puffers of religious novels or white lies! see what you have done—are still doing.

> "How can ye! While the cause ye nurse,
>   Which madness, crime, and misery brings;
> How can ye dry the river's course,
>   Unless you stop its rising springs?"

The thought is painful in the extreme that pure and innocent childhood should be corrupted with the vices of maturer years, and of more experienced depravity. What monsters of evil are they that do the work!

Look again.

The Traffic in Obscene Literature.

"A meeting took place last evening at No. 107 East Twenty-eighth street, for the purpose of inaugurating a society for the suppression of the trade in and circulation of obscene literature. Alderman Wilder pointed out the necessity of having an amendment to the act of 1868 passed, so that the evil complained of could be remedied. This was agreed to, and the meeting adjourned till Friday, March 1st."

Why not begin where Satan begins—with religious novel-writers and puffers?

A lack of reverence for the Word of God is the *one* great sin of Christendom. A certain tyrant of Rome used to wish the Roman people had but one neck, that he might dispatch them at a blow. You, friend, whether in the pulpit or out of it, continuing to traffic in religious fiction, have but one neck; namely, disrespect for God's Word. If a man have just reverence for his Word, he will commit none of the sins you are committing.

"He that being often reproved hardeneth his neck, shall suddenly be destroyed, and that without remedy."

December has not left us yet, little readers. You see—

COLD winter is here, and all nature looks drear,
    The streamlets in ice-fetters bound;
The leaves on the trees are all yellow and sere,
    And the snow-mantle covers the ground:
The tempest now darkens the face of the skies,
    And the sharp, whistling storm-winds with terror arise.

How cheerless and sad is the home of the poor,
    When the storm rages mournfully round!
When the northern wind blows, how hard to endure
    The privations which ever are found
In the home of the needy, where poverty dwells,
And the breast fill'd with anguish, painfully swells!

PUTTING RAZORS TO CHILDREN'S THROATS.

A BLESSED gospel minister, whose eyes are open to see what Satan is doing, through his active agents—ministers and religious editors—said a short time since, "that parents might just as well take a razor and cut their children's throats, as to allow them to read the corrupting literature of the day."

Is this declaration, startling as it is, too strong or too bold? Not in the least. If parents have made up their minds fully to kill their sons and daughters any how (as many seem to have), why not dispatch business—make quick work of it! This killing by inches or piecemeal, is the most painful and cruel of all deaths!

This same Christian minister goes on to say: "Thousands of the youth of our land are annually swept down to hell by poisonous literature. And yet books and papers of that character are to be found upon the tables of professed Christians. Some think them harmless, and permit them to ruin their own children. Fathers and mothers, look after your children, and see what they are reading. Banish all pernicious books and papers from your houses, and furnish your children with an abundance of such as are calculated to make them wise and good. They may plead for novels, and try to convince you that they are as harmless as they are charming. Beware of that thought! Hearken to the testimony of those who have watched the influence of novel-reading.

"Goldsmith, himself a novel-writer, says: 'Above all, never let your son touch a novel or romance. How delusive, how destructive, are these features of consummate bliss! They teach the youthful mind to sigh after beauty and happiness that never existed, to despise the little good that Fortune has mixed in our cup, by expecting more than she ever gave.'

"Rev. John Foster, an eminent Baptist minister in England, says: 'Novels are doing incalculable mischief. I wish we could collect them all together, and make one vast fire of them. I should exult to see the smoke of them ascend like that of Sodom and Gomorrah: the judgment would be as just.' The fearful results of novel-reading are a standing warning against the practice. Let the pulpit and the press speak out boldly, and arouse the unsuspecting."

Let your mind pierce through the vista of the next twenty years—the children now will be men and women then—the long procession of drunkards, criminals, and prostitutes that now degrade our world, will have passed away to "that borne from whence no traveler returns;"—but with the same influences at work, there will be few, *if any*, gaps made;—our workhouse will be crowded as they are now—our gaols will be crowded as they are now—drivelling sots and raving maniacs will abound on every hand as they do now;—a long train of lecherous harlots will infest our streets even as they do now. And where will they come from?—where, but from our children? Fathers!—mothers! your children are in danger;—run to their rescue! The most potent agency in effecting their ruin will be through the medium of a corrupt press in the hands of whom?

KILLED WITH A HATCHET: OR FEASTING ON LIES.

"LOUISVILLE, *December* 28, 1871.—The inquest on the body of Mrs. Klanzar, killed with a hatchet by her daughter-in-law, Mrs. Weissert, last Saturday, revealed the probability that the murderess is deranged on the subject of crime, from reading cheap novels and the flashy literature of the day. Many such books and papers were found in her room, and proved that she had been in the habit of poring over them incessantly."

THE case of Mrs. Weissert is a common one, though it rarely happens that the brutality and ferocity of a criminal can be so easily traced to their real cause. Could the public know how many of the suicides, murders, rapes and assaults of all kinds are due directly to the brutal and lascivious pictures and anecdotes of sensational newspapers upon diseased and morbid imaginations, there would be a reaction that would speedily drive those infamous weeklies from the market. But comparatively few people, it would seem, ever think of giving those newspapers their proper place among the causes of crime. Murders, seductions, and the other tragedies of every-day life, go on increasing from year to year; the vile print-makers and publishers work harder and harder, and grow richer and richer, while the law that would arrest and imprison the beggar-boy for stealing a bone, shuts its eyes secretly to the stream of vileness that goes out on every express train from New York to poison and brutalize the minds of the young and weak, and to place before the already debauched young men of every town and village an incentive to crime, surpassing in influence even the dram-shop or the brothel.

This woman in Louisville who was incited by sensational reading to commit murder, stands to-day as the type of a disease, for the existence of which society is responsible. Where do these sparks of hell-fire begin? Who kindled them?

This woman, doubtless, commenced her downward career on white lies, or religious novels penned and puffed by back-slidden, money-loving church members, trying to serve two masters—Christ and Belial! Then, when her taste was formed for the light and visionary, where now?—under the complete control of the devil!*

After feasting on white lies, she was prepared to take her fill on black lies, till given over to the vilest sins, to work all manner of iniquity with greediness! Finally, imbue her hands in blood!

Satan is at the bottom of this craziness. No one in his right mind will presume to write, read, sell, advertise, or puff these missiles of the pit. It is the worst kind of derangement or lunacy.

"The prince of the power of the air, the spirit that worketh in the children of disobedience," has many agents in his employ.†

A book or paper lives not only while its author lives, but long after the hand which wrote it has turned to dust, and if it is a bad book or periodical, it is one of the most malignant forces on the earth.

---

* Dr. Ray, of the Butler Insane Asylum, of Providence, R. I., attributes the increase of insanity to "excessive indulgence in the reading of novels, which have, of late years, swarmed from the presses of New York, Philadelphia and Boston.

† Let a committee be appointed to wait on ministerial writers and puffers of white lies, to cease their satanic agency and this work of desolation, and ruin ceases to exist—and not till then.

EDUCATING LITTLE MARY.

BEWARE OF THE SERPENT'S SUGAR-COATED POISONS—POPULAR WORKS OF FICTION.

Upon no class of persons does the habitual reading of this branch of our literature exert a more pernicious influence than upon the young men connected with our colleges and other institutions of learning. We have heard it asserted by those whose positions enable them to judge intelligently in this matter, that there is scarcely an instance on record where a young man, who habitually and regularly peruses works of fiction during his undergraduate course, ever received that degree of mental discipline which is necessary for a successful entrance upon the great duties of life, and which it is the aim of a collegiate course to furnish. And, indeed, it is hard to conceive how the case should be otherwise; for, besides the enormous waste of time, which is a necessary consequence of any considerable indulgence in novel reading, the mind accustomed to follow some sentimental hero or heroine through all sorts of silly, unheard-of adventures, and to revel amid scenes of fancied pleasures and happiness, takes little delight in attempting to grapple with the more profound truths of philosophy and mathematics, even when it is not wholly incapacitated to do so.

It is a lamentable fact, that at least half of the young men who graduate each year at our colleges, hardly possess even the rudiments of a sound and substantial education. Many, after spending three or four years within the walls of a university, possess, in return for their time and money, little besides their "diploma,"

A Savor of Life—A Savor of Death.

READING-ROOMS, PUBLIC AND SUNDAY-SCHOOL LIBRARIES,

> "Good books and papers live while we are dead
> Light on the darkened mind they shed,—
> Good seed they sow from age to age,
> Through all this mortal pilgrimage ;
> They nurse the germs of holy trust,
> They wake untired when we are dust."

Good books and papers preach; bad books and papers preach. One is a savor of life to life, the other of death to death! One preaches salvation, the other damnation!

Look at this subject, friends; turn it over, view it on every side; peep into Sunday-school libraries, public reading-rooms—what do you see? Scorpions, adders that sting, serpents that bite, Satanic transformations, the old serpent the devil, with cloven-foot concealed!

Do you ask what harm books and papers will do tinctured with romance and folly? The same harm that personal intercourse would with the bad men who wrote them. "That a man is known by the company he keeps," is an old proverb; but it is no more true than that a man's character may be determined by knowing the books he reads. If a good book can't be read without making one better, a bad book cannot be read without making one worse. A person may be ruined by reading a single volume. Bad books are like ardent spirits, they furnish neither aliment nor "medicine"—they are "poison." Both intoxicate—one the mind, the other the body. The thirst for each increases by being fed, and is never satisfied: both ruin—one the intellect, the other the health, and together, the soul. The makers and venders of each are equally guilty and equally corrupters of the community; and the safeguard against each is the same total abstinence from all that intoxicates mind or body.

The love of fiction is a growing appetite, and one which generally wastes more time than any other. It produces a distate for healthful mental food, and a dislike to strengthening mental exercise. However good the tone of fiction may be, or its moral, the habit of craving fiction, once formed, cannot be prevented from gratifying itself with those novels and romances of the day, which may well be described as "Satanic literature." The person who enters upon a course of novel-reading may be said to be rapidly unfitting himself for a noble and useful life. Then, all this reading is positively worse than useless. We have no faith in the effect of teaching moral truth by fiction. No real knowledge is stored by it. After reading a thousand novels, the youth may be still unfurnished with the most necessary information.

Nothing should find lodgment for a moment in our families, Sabbath-school libraries, reading-rooms, or on our centre-tables, but the salt of the earth, light, heavenly, intellectual and spiritual, life-giving, soul-kindling; such reading as elevates, purifies, and sanc tifies. Family-books and papers should be of the purest kind; nothing should be introduced that tends in the least to pervert or corrupt the rising generation. It is truly painful to see in some reading-rooms popular works of fiction, novels, romances, and works positively infidel in their tendency.

Such libraries and reading-rooms are a curse instead of a blessing to the community. Many a young man has been ruined for time and eternity by this corrupting literature.

No book or periodical, whatever its merits in other respects, which takes the name of God in vain, uses it profanely or irreverently, which contains a profane oath, an impure or libidinous thought, or speaks lightly of the Word of God, should ever be allowed in a family or reading-room. A parent ought never to allow a fascinating writer to say that, behind the screen to the eye of a child, which he would not permit any one to breathe into the ear.

Byron, Scott, Shakspeare, Dickens, Beecher, are, more or less, defiled by profane and impure allusions, dashes or exclamations, that offend the ear of modesty and virtue. What Christian father or mother woul allow Shakspeare, if he were now alive, to associate with a blooming circle of sons and daughters, or read his plays, just as they now stand in the best editions? Is it possible for them to pass through the youthful mind and not leave a foul stain behind? Read the "Personal Recollections of Charlotte Elizabeth," and see how narrowly she escaped the loss of both body and soul by poring over Shakspeare's corrupting fascinations.

Are not editors and publishers rolling up a fearful account for facilitating the circulation of these reptiles, now flooding and cursing the land? Unless some means can be devised to arrest this rapidly-augmenting currency of licentious and semi-infidel literature, its demoralizing effects every where manifest, we are *lost! lost!* Cease? When will this curse of all curses cease, that poisons the fountains of mercy, eats out the life-blood of spiritual life and salvation, ushering millions into the gulf bottomless? When will this death of deaths cease? Never, till God in mercy opens the eyes of religious editors to see the enormity of their guilt in offering polluted bread upon his altar!

"And if ye offer the blind for sacrifice, is it not evil? and if ye offer the lame and the sick, is it not evil? Offer it now unto thy governor; will he be pleased with thee, or accept thy person? saith the Lord of hosts."--Mal. i. 7-8.

"O ye priests, this commandment is for you. If ye will not hear, and if ye will not lay it to heart, to give glory unto my name, saith the Lord of hosts, I will even send a curse upon you, and I will curse your blessings; yea, I have cursed them already, because ye do not lay it to heart."—Mal. ii. 1-2.

"I hate the work of them that turn aside. He that worketh deceit shall not dwell in my house: he that telleth lies shall not tarry in my sight."—Psal. ci. 6.

Cast your eye, if you can, beloved brother and sister,

into the reading-room at the Cooper Institute—the "Young Men's Christian Association," in New York, and into libraries of a similar character in every city, what do you see? Some twenty, thirty, fifty, or more young men and women poring over what? The good, the solid, the virtuous, the pure, the elevating in these libraries, or the froth and scum of the pit?—the veriest trash Satan could concoct. The truth is, the taste of very many of the rising age is already formed for the devilish, and after the devilish they will go.

Bonfire, burn up one-half of the books and periodicals in these public libraries and reading-rooms—more yet, two-thirds at least. God of mercy, truth and love, speed the day—hasten the burning, scorching, consuming flames!

SOWING? YES, WE ARE.

"*And whatsoever a man soweth, that shall he also reap.*"—Gal. vi. 7.

" We are sowing, we are sowing,
   In eternity to reap ;
Day by day are harvests growing
   For us after death's long sleep.

" We are sowing, we are sowing,
   Thoughts are seeds cast in a field ;
Every act that we are doing,
   Every word its fruit shall yield.'

CAN'T FOLKS AND WON'T FOLKS;

—OR—

Lying Folks and Folks that will lie, keep on lying.

" Let the lying lips be put to silence."—*Psa.* xxxi. 18.

" Can't?" Who says you can't, friend, God or you. If God says you can stop lying, and you say you can't, what is this but making God a liar? God tell, you, Mr. Liar, writer, and puffer of lies, to stop this lying, repent, do works meet for repentance. But you say "no, I can't," that is you *won't!* The can't in your case means won't *emphatically.* So we understand it, so does God, and he will deal with you accordingly. Look out for breakers, Mr. Liar.

God tells sinners that tell lies and keep on telling them, in the church and out of it, to stop lying, writing lies, puffing lies, selling lies and reading lies. Then, in the face and eyes of Omnipotent, merciful grace, and heavenly pleading, what say these same liars? "We can't stop lying." That is you *won't*—can't means won't. God tells ministers that write lies for money, the accursed lust of gain, to stop this wicked lying and speak truth. What now do you hear from these lying lips? "Can't?" Yes, that is, "we *won't;* we love money, we love popularity, and lie we must—lie we will." And is it not precisely so with religious editors who puff these same ministerial lies? If teachers in Israel dressed in robes sacerdotal, tell lies and write lies, preach lies, what harm, pray, in religious editors doing the very same thing! The lies that this watchman on Zion's top wrote, are good, religious lies. So the pulpit man writes the good lies, and the good Christian editor takes his share of stock in this lying business. Thus one religious liar in high standing, helps on another good, religious liar of high distinction. When these religious liars are told to stop this lying, writing and publishing lies, for mercy's sake, weepingly, what the response? the same as before, "we can't, this is our every day business, it's our meat and our drink, our bread and our butter, what every body does we do, it's popular to lie, and cash is made by it, and we have been so long accustomed to writing and printing lies, it is just as natural and pleasant to us as it is to sit around a luxurious table and partake of a hearty meal. Indeed to speak truth once, we can't stop lying. We feed on lies, sleep on lies; we lie down lying and rise up lying. We go out and come in with lies on our lips. We take our seat in the ministerial or editorial chair with pen in hand, and the first thing that pops up in our noddle is a lie, and we put it on paper *quick!* then another and another, in rapid succession, and as soon as possible we send forth these newly concocted lies, for the good of the community at large. The business has become lucrative, as the public taste is now pretty well formed or educated on fiction, or lies in a religious form, no harm is thought of it ; all classes, old and young, parents and children, ministers and people, Sunday-schools and all, go in heart and hand for these religious lies. And, to speak the truth again, we can't help going forward as we have been going, kill or no kill. Curse the world, little folks and big, lead them step by step into forbidden paths, even down to the pit of woe everlasting, what of it? If we go down to hell for writing, publishing and selling either white lies or black lies, wo be to millions!

250   CAN'T FOLKS AND WON'T FOLKS.

We risk it any how; we love lying and telling lies, and after them we go. To be sure we know what God says about liars, lies and lying, and what becomes of those who do lie and keep on telling lies, in Revelations xxi. 8 :"

"But the fearful and unbelieving, and the abominable, and murderers, and whoremongers, and sorcerers, and idolaters, and all liars, shall have their part in the lake which burneth with fire and brimstone : which is the second death."

"Home Thrusts," 303 West Twentieth Street, New York.

Serpents that Bite—Adders that Sting!

"How shall I speak thee, or thy power address,
Thou god of our idolatry, the Press!
Like Eden's dread probationary Tree—
Knowledge of good and evil is from thee!"

KINDLING HEAVENLY FIRES;

—OR—

Some of the Lord's Dealings with George Muller.

The word of God is a fire, a sword—

> "Where'er it enters in,
> Is sharper than a two-edged sword,
> To slay the man of sin."

"My heart was hot within me; while I was musing the fire burned; then spake I with my tongue."—*Psa.* xxxix. 3.

"His word was in mine heart as a burning fire shut up in my bones."—*Jer.* xx. 9.

What blessed food for reflection is the word of God! Take a passage of Scripture, and dwell upon it, interweaving it with all the day's duties. Reflect upon it, and it will be continually developing in sweetness and power. Prayer and reflection will make plain what seemed obscure at first.

George Muller, of the Orphan Asylum, Bristol, England, whose wonderful faith is attracting the attention of the whole world, to kindle heavenly fires in his own soul, has had recourse to this musing or meditating in the word, "the sword of the Spirit." He says:

"The first thing I did, after having asked in a few words the Lord's blessing upon his precious word, was to begin to meditate on the word of God, searching, as it were, into every verse to get blessing out of it; not for the sake of the public ministry of the word, not for the sake of preaching on what I had meditated upon, but for the sake of obtaining food for my own soul. The result I have found to be almost invariably this : that after a very few minutes my soul has been led to confession, or to thanksgiving, or to intercession, or to supplication ; so that, though I did not, as it were, give myself to *prayer*, but to *meditation*, yet it turned almost immediately more or less into prayer. When thus I have been for a while making confession, or intercession, or supplication, or have given thanks, I go on, into prayer for myself or others, as the word may lead to it, but still continually keeping before me that food for my own soul is the object of my meditation. The result of this is that my inner man almost invariably is sensibly nourished and strengthened, and that by breakfast time, with rare exceptions, I am in a peaceful, if not happy state of heart."

"Faith cometh by hearing, and hearing by the word of God." This unreserved and perpetual adherence "to the word and the testimony," is the secret of the faith of George Muller, that has sounded out from the rising sun to the setting thereof. And what has not this faith in the promise of God wrought? Reader, cast your eye upon those five orphan houses and the lands adjacent. Step into these five orphan houses—what do you behold? 2,050 orphans under his care, fed, clothed and educated. Consider the day-schools, Sunday-schools, schools for adults, in which instruction is given upon Scriptural principles, by teachers professing faith in the Lord Jesus.

Look at the 150 missionaries sent out into various parts of the world, the thousands on thousands of Bibles going forth annually into the dark corners of the earth—the millions on millions of Gospel tracts (not novels) flying on the wings of the wind, "leaves for the healing of the nations." How is this marvellous work of benevolence grace and salvation, carried forward? by what means? How are means obtained? By begging? sending forth agents to collect funds from believers and unbelievers? By getting up a fancy fair, tea or strawberry party, a soiree or an oyster supper? Or by faith and prayer, prayer and faith! No being has ever been solicited for a farthing, but God alone. "More things are done by prayer than this world dreams of." Has brother Muller or his family lacked anything? Have the thousands of orphans for thirty-eight years lacked food, raiment, heavenly inculcations? Have the numerous missionaries with no stated salaries lacked anything?

"And he said unto them, When I sent you without purse, and scrip, and shoes, lacked ye any thing? And they said, Nothing."—*Luke* xxii. 35.

"Ask and it shall be given." God stirs up the hearts of his people in answer to the prayer of faith to contribute. Donations for this "light-house," this "city set on a hill," have flown in from all parts of the world, from the widow's mite, to eight hundred pounds or more.

Reader, here's a lesson for me, for you, for every one naming the name of Christ. Brother Muller tells us it's not for every one to build orphan houses, to do exactly what he is doing in the various benevolent operations, but it *is* the blessed privilege of *every disciple* of the Lord Jesus to "walk thus by faith and not by sight."

"Trust in the LORD, and do good, so shalt thou dwell in the land, and verily thou shalt be fed."—*Psa.* xxxvii. 3.

Mr. Muller says: "I repeat here again, what has been stated in the previous Reports, for the sake of those who do not know it, that in November, 1830, I was led to give up my salary in connection with the ministry of the Gospel, and during these 35 years and 6 months I have never had any salary nor other stated income, either in connection with the ministry of the Word, or as Director of the scriptural knowledge institution for home and abroad. If, however, one or the other of the readers should suppose, that, on that account, I have been a sufferer or loser, my reply is, that it has been the very reverse. The Lord, whose servant I am, and whom I delight in serving, having condescended to employ me now for more than forty years, has amply, most amply, provided for me, by putting it again and again into the hearts of his children to give to me of their means. Had I with never so much earnestness sought to provide well for myself, I should not, in all human probability, have succeeded half as well, as God, without my seeking, has done it for me. I take pleasure in bearing this testimony for God, to the honor of His name. But I cannot send this forth, without again cautioning any who may read it, against doing the same by way of imitation. Let any one trust in God, as I by His grace did, and have Scriptural warrant for doing so; and the Lord will surely honor this confidence in Himself; but, as assuredly as any one professes to trust in God, his profession of faith will be tested, and greatly tested, even as mine was; and then it will be soon seen, whether the trust in God is real or not. When I took this step, in November, 1830, I determined, really, truly, solely, habitually, by God's help, to look to Him, and under no circumstances, either directly or indirectly, to make known my present position, however needy, to my fellow men, in order that the hand of God might be seen, when He helped. In this way I have continued ever since; and, by the help of God, purpose to continue to the end of my course. Now, because many, who have professed to look to the Lord alone for their temporal supplies, have failed in this, and have made their wants known to their fellow men, to induce them to help them, they have thus failed in obtaining the wholesome food for their faith, and their faith has become weaker instead of stronger. But, further, no one, I judge, can be truly happy in such a path, except he be content, to the end of his course, to remain only a steward for God; so that, if he be intrusted by Him with more than he needs, he be willing to give it back to God, who gave it to him. Let these two points be carried out, in an humble prayerful state of heart, and happy and blessed will that servant of God be. All whom I have known to have acted thus, have, without a single exception, done well; but those, who merely said that they trusted in God, without doing it, and who therefore did not act as stated above, sooner or later broke down. God looks for reality. Faith may be weak at first, but it must be real.

"The reader who desires to know further particulars as to the reasons which led me into this course of life, will find them in my Narrative, Part I, pages 68 and 69."

No Contracting Debts.

"Owe no man anything but love."

Mr. Muller goes on to say in his last Report (1871): "As from the beginning, so now also, we would under no circumstances contract debts, but act according to God's mind, by first obtaining the needed means for the contemplated enlargement; for if *we* are the persons through whom God will do His work, and if *His time* has come for us to do His work, He will certainly, in answer to believing prayer, give to us the needed pecuniary means.

"With regard to pecuniary supplies to carry on the various operations in connection with the Institution, we have obtained from the beginning above five hundred thousand pounds, as the result of prayer and faith, which, we trust, is a plain proof, that waiting upon God for means is not in vain. It also shows, that the work of God may be carried on, on the above principles, not only whilst small, but when it is large, yea very large.

"The reader, who is unacquainted with the previous Reports, may ask, And what has been accomplished, through the five hundred thousand pounds, which have come in for this Institution? To such our answer is: Twenty-three thousand children, or grown-up persons, have been taught in the various schools, *entirely* supported by the funds of the Institution, besides the tens of thousands who have been benefited in the schools, which were *assisted* by its funds; more than sixty-four thousand Bibles, eighty-five thousand Testaments, and one hundred thousand smaller portions of the Holy Scriptures, in various languages, have been circulated since the formation of the Institution; and thirty-nine millions of tracts and books, likewise in several different languages, have been circulated. There have been, likewise, from the earliest days of this Institution, missionaries assisted by its funds, and of late years more than one hundred and fifty in number. On this object alone above one hundred and four thousand pounds have been expended from the beginning. Also 3575 orphans have been under our care, and five large houses, at an expense of one hundred and fifteen thousand pounds, have been erected and fitted up, for the accommodation of 2050 orphans. As to the spiritual results, I will here say nothing; indeed eternity alone can unfold them; yet, even in so far as God has been pleased to allow us to see already the results of our service, we have reaped most abundantly, and do so more and more with every year, whilst going on in the work.

"The fourth object of the Institution is, the circulation of such publications as may be calculated, with the blessing of God, to benefit both believers and unbelievers. As it respects *tracts for unbelievers*, I especially aim after the diffusion of such, as contain the truths of the Gospel clearly and simply expressed; and as it respects *publications for believers*, I desire to circulate such as may be instrumental in directing their minds to those truths which, in these last days, are more especially needed, or which have been particularly lost sight of, and may lead believers to return to the written Word of God.

"There has been laid out for this object, from May 26, 1870, to May 26, 1871, the sum of £917 15s. 1d.; and there have been circulated within the last year more than two millions and eight hundred and seventy-two thousand (exactly 2,872,301) tracts and books. The sum total which has been expended on this object, since November 19, 1840, amounts to £19,837 19s. $0\frac{1}{2}$d.

"The total number of all the tracts and books, which have been circulated since Nov. 19, 1840, is about thirty-nine millions (exactly 38,893,712).

"More than two millions three hundred and eighty-three thousand of the tracts and books, circulated during the past year, were given away *gratuitously*. Hundreds of believers have been engaged in spreading them abroad, not merely in many parts of England, Scotland, and Ireland, but in various other parts of the world. I give now, as an encouragement for this service, the following extracts from letters received from individuals to whom these tracts were sent. (These extracts unintentionally omitted.)

"For the sake of younger believers in Christ, I make the following remarks with reference to their service in seeking to circulate the Holy Scriptures and tracts:

"What, then, have we to do as Tract or Bible distributors? 1. Never to reckon our success by the number of Bibles, or Testaments, or Tracts, which we circulate; for millions of Bibles, Testaments and Tracts might be circulated, and little good result from our efforts. 2. We should, day by day, seek God's blessing on our labors in this particular; and on every tract or copy of the Holy Scriptures which we give, we should, as much as possible, ask God's blessing. 3. We should expect God's blessing upon our labors, and confidently expect it; yea, look out for His blessing. 4. We should labor on in this service, prayerfully and believingly labor on, even though for a long time we should see little or no fruit; yea, we should labor on, as if every thing depended on our labors, whilst, in reality, we ought not to put the least confidence in our exertions, but alone in God's ability and willingness to bless, by His Holy Spirit, our efforts for the sake of the Lord Jesus. 5. And what will be the result of laboring on patiently in such a spirit? We find the answer in the epistle to the Gallatians vi. 9: 'Let us not be weary in well-doing; for for in due season we shall reap, if we faint not.' Observe, in *due* season. The whole of our earthly pilgrimage is a sowing time, though we may be allowed to see now and then, already in this life, fruit resulting from our sowing to a greater or less degree; but if it were not thus, or if comparatively but little fruit were now, in this life, reaped, the *due* season is coming. At the appearing of our Lord Jesus all will be made manifest; our reward of grace will be given to us for our patient service then; and in the prospect of that day we have patiently to continue in well-doing. But this patient continuing in well-doing calls for much prayer, for much meditation on the Word of God, and for much feeding on the work and person of our Lord Jesus, in order that thus our spiritual strength may be renewed day by day.

"Tract distributors *who can afford to pay for publications*, and who desire to procure them from us, may obtain *Tracts* for this purpose with a discount of one-half, or 50 per cent. from the retail price, and *Books* with a discount of 25 per cent. or one-fourth from the retail price. I state this, as many believers may not like to give away what does not cost them anything, and yet may, at the same time, wish to obtain as much as possible, for their money. Applications for this would need to be made verbally or in writing to Mr. James L. Stanley, at the Bible and Tract Warehouse, No. 34 Park-street, Bristol. To him, also, application may be made for specimen packets, containing an assortment of the tracts and small books which are kept. By sending 3s., 5s., 7s., or 10s. in postages to Mr. Stanley, packets will be sent to any part of England, Wales, Ireland, Scotland, Jersey, Guernsey, etc., containing specimens to the amount of the postages which are sent.

"A catalogue of the various books and tracts sold at the above Warehouse of the Institution, with their prices, may be had there, by applying either personally or by letter to Mr. Stanley. There are now kept on sale 950 different books, large and small; and 773 different tracts, which number is continually added to. During the last year many new books and tracts were introduced.

5. The fifth object of the Institution is, to board, clothe,

and Scripturally educate *destitute* children who have lost *both* parents by death.

"At the commencement of the last period there were 1722 orphans in the New Orphan Houses No. 1, No. 2, No. 3, No. 4, and No. 5. During the past year 308 orphans were admitted into the five houses now in operation; so that the total number on May 26, 1871, would have been 2030, had there been no changes; but, of these 2030, twenty-nine died during the past year. This number of deaths is exceedingly small, if it be remembered that three-fourths of all the orphans under our care lost one or both parents in consumption, which we know from the official certificates; and, especially, that we had several hundred of the orphans ill in scarlet fever. Eight of those who died were decidedly resting upon the atoning death of the Lord Jesus for salvation, and some of them had known the Lord a good while; of a few others, besides, we were not without hope. Twenty-five out of the two thousand and thirty were either returned to their relatives, as we could not train them for service or apprentice them on account of their physical, mental or moral state; or relatives, whose temporal circumstances had improved since they placed them with us, desired now, or felt it their duty, to provide for them. Ninety-nine girls were sent out for service, eight of whom had known the Lord some time, before they left. Thirty-two boys were sent out to be apprenticed, seventeen of whom had been previously brought to the knowledge of the Lord Jesus; 185 are therefore to be deducted from the 2030, so that we had on May 26, 1871, only 1845 orphans under our care, viz., 280 in No. 1, 356 in No. 2, 450 in No. 3, 450 in No. 4, and 309 in No. 5. The total number of orphans, who have been under our care, since April 11, 1836, is 3575.

"I notice further the following points respecting the orphan work:

"1. The girls, who are received into the establishment, are kept till they are able to go to service. Our aim is to keep them till they shall have been sufficiently qualified for a situation, and, especially also, till their constitution is sufficiently established, as far as we are able to judge. We uniformly prefer fitting the girls for service, instead of apprenticing them to a business, as being, generally, far better for their bodies and souls. Only in a few instances have female orphans been apprenticed to businesses, when their health would not allow them to go to service. If the girls give us satisfaction, while under our care, so that we can recommend them to a situation, they are fitted out at the expense of the establishment. The girls, generally, remain under our care till they are about 17 years old. They very rarely leave sooner; and, as we receive children from their earliest days, we have often had girls 13, 14, yea, above 17 years under our care. They are instructed in reading, writing, arithmetic, English grammar, geography, English history, a little of universal history, all kinds of useful needlework and household work. They make their clothes and keep them in repair; they work in the kitchens, sculleries, wash-houses and laundries; and, in a word, we aim, after this, that, if any of them do not do well temporally or spiritually, and do not turn out useful members of society, it shall at least not be *our* fault. The boys are, generally, apprenticed when they are between 14 and 15 years old. But *in each case* we consider the welfare of the *individual* orphan, without having any fixed rule respecting these matters. The boys have a free choice of the trade they like to learn; but, having once chosen, and being apprenticed, we do not allow them to alter. The boys, as well as the girls, have an outfit provided for them ; and any other expenses, that may be connected with their apprenticeship, are also met by the funds of the Orphan Establishment. It may be interesting to the reader to know the kind of trades to which we generally apprentice the boys, and I therefore say, that, during the last twenty-two years, all the boys who were apprenticed, were bound to carpenters, or carpenters and joiners, cabinet makers, basket makers, shoe makers, tailors and drapers, plumbers, painters and glaziers, linen drapers, printers, bakers, grocers, hairdressers, ironmongers, tin-plate workers, confectioners, hosiers, builders, millers, gasfitters, smiths, outfitters, provision dealers, sail makers, upholsterers, wholesale grocers, chemists, seed merchants, umbrella makers, or electro plate manufacturers. The boys have the same kind of mental cultivation as the girls, and they learn to knit and mend their stockings. They also make their beds, clean their shoes, scrub their rooms, go errands, and work in the garden ground round the Orphan Establishment, in the way of digging, planting, weeding, etc.

" 2. Without any sectarian distinction whatever, and without favor or partiality, the orphans are received *in the order in which application is made for them*. There is no interest whatever required to get a child admitted, nor is it expected that any money should be paid with the orphans. Three things only are requisite : *a*, that the children should have been lawfully begotten ; *b*, that they should be bereaved of *both* parents by death ; and *c*, that they should be in needy circumstances. Respecting these three points, strict investigation is made, and it is expected that each of them be proved by proper documents ; but that being done, children may be admitted from any place, provided that there is nothing peculiar in the case that would make them unsuitable inmates for such establishments as the New Orphan Houses. I state here again, that no sectarian views prompt me, or even in the least influence me, in the reception of children. I do not belong to any sect, and I am not, therefore, influenced in the admission of orphans, by sectarianism; but from wheresoever they come, and to whatsoever religious denomination the parents may have belonged, or with whatever religious body the persons making application may be connected, it makes no difference in the admission of the children. The new ophan houses on Ashley Down, Bristol, are not *my* orphan houses, nor the orphan houses of any party or sect; but they are God's orphan houses, and the orphan houses for any and every destitute orphan who has lost *both* parents, provided, of course, there be room in them.—I particularly request that persons would kindly refrain from applying for children who only virtually are orphans, but who have not lost *both* parents by *death*, as I shall be obliged to refuse them admission, without exception; since this orphan-work has been from the beginning only for destitute children who have *neither father nor mother*.

"3. The New Orphan House No. 1 is fitted up for the accommodation of 140 orphan girls above eight years of age, 80 orphan boys above eight years, and 80 female orphans from their earliest days, till they are about eight years of age. The infants, after having passed the age of eight years, are removed into the department for older girls. The New Orphan House No. 2 is fitted up for 200 infant female orphans, and for 200 older female orphans. The New Orphan House No. 3 is fitted up for 450 older female orphans. The New Orphan House No. 4 is fitted up for

210 boys of eight years old and upwards, 208 infant boys under eight years of age, and 32 older girls, to do the household work—450 in all. The New Orphan House No. 5 is fitted up for 210 infant female orphans, and for 240 older female orphans.

"4. The New Orphan House No. 1 is open to visitors every Wednesday afternoon, the New Orphan House No. 2 every Tuesday afternoon, the New Orphan House No. 3 every Thursday afternoon, the New Orphan House No. 4 every Friday afternoon, and the New Orphan House No. 5 every Saturday afternoon; but the arrangements of the establishments make it needful, that they should be shown at those times only. No exceptions can be made.—The first party of visitors will be shown through the houses at half-past two o'clock, God permitting; the second at three o'clock; and, should there be need for it, the third and last party at half-past three o'clock.—As it takes at least one hour and a half to see the whole of each establishment, it is requested that the visitors will be pleased to make their arrangements accordingly before they come, as it would be inconvenient should one or the other leave, before the whole party has seen the house.—From March 1st to Nov. 1st there may be three parties shown through the houses every Wednesday, Tuesday, Thursday, Friday and Saturday afternoon; but from Nov. 1st to March 1st two parties only, at half-past two and three o'clock, can be accommodated, on account of the shortness of the days.

"5. Persons who desire to make application for the admission of orphans, are requested to write to me and address the letter to my house, No. 21 Paul-street, Kingsdown, Bristol, England.

"6. I again state, as regards the funds, that the income for the orphans has been kept distinct from that for the other objects, and I purpose to keep it so for the future. Donors may therefore contribute to one or other of the objects exclusively, or have their donations equally divided among them all, just as it may appear best to themselves. If any of the donors would wish to leave the application of their donations to my discretion, as the work of God in my hands more especially may call for it at the time, they are requested, kindly to say so, when sending their donations.

"7. *Without any one having been personally applied to for anything* by me, the sum of £349,342 6s. 1½d. has been given to me for the orphans, *as the result of prayer to God*, since the commencement of the work, which sum includes the amount received for the building fund for the five houses. It may also be interesting to the reader to know that the total amount, which has been given for the other objects, since the commencement of the work, amounts to £140,205 13s. 8½d.; and that which has come in by the sale of Bibles, since the commencement, amounts to £4,806 16s. 9½d.; by the sale of Tracts, £9,931 10s. 10¼d.: and by the payment of the children in the day schools, from the commencement, £3,627 13s. 1½d. Besides this, also, a great variety and number of articles of clothing, furniture, provisions, etc., have been given for the use of the orphans.

"The average expense of one orphan, during the past year, was £12 17s. 6d. This includes every expense, without exception.

"Having been often asked for a form how to leave a legacy for the orphan work, or any other part of the Institution, I think it well to give here a proper form drawn up by a legal practitioner, accustomed to such matters.

"*Form of a Legacy for the orphan work.*— "I give to George Müller of Bristol, or such other person or persons as shall, when this legacy shall become payable, be the director or directors of the New Orphan Houses on Ashley Down, Bristol, the sum of   , to be paid out of such part of my personal estate as shall be legally applicable thereto ; and to be applied by the said George Müller, or such other director or directors for the purpose of such New Orphan Houses, and his or their receipt shall be a sufficient discharge to my executors."

"To avoid mistakes, delays, and other difficulties, I would request that all letters for me should be directed to my house, No. 21 Paul-street, Kingsdown, Bristol, England.

Bristol, July 21, 1871.   GEORGE MULLER."

Lamps do not talk—they simply shine. A lighthouse sounds no drum, it beats no gong, and yet far over the waters its friendly spark is seen by the mariner. So should it be with religion, which should be proclaimed and made known by its quiet works rather than by loud or frequent protestations.

"Take heed that ye do not your alms before men, to be seen of them : otherwise ye have no reward of your Father which is in heaven. Therefore, when thou doest thine alms, do not sound a trumpet before thee, as the hypocrites do, in the synagogues, and in the streets, that they may have glory of men. Verily I say unto you, they have their reward. But when thou doest alms, let not thy left hand know what thy right hand doeth ; that thine alms may be in secret : and thy Father which seeth in secret, himself shall reward thee openly."—*Math.* vi. 1–5.

---

303 West Twentieth Street, New York.

KINDLING HEAVENLY FIRES.—(No. 2.)

"Read the Bible; it will point you
To bright scenes of bliss on high,
Where there's rest for all the weary,
And our loved ones never die."

THE Bible holds the first place among the means of implanting and promoting divine life in the soul; and the Christian who fails to keep in some way the great truths of the Bible steadily before his mind, will find the vigor of his graces departing. No other reading will serve as a substitute for reading the Bible. No other study or meditation will answer the purpose of the word of Christ, dwelling in us richly in all wisdom. If we look for religion to be revived, our expectation will be realized, only by the mind of the Church being brought in steadier contact with the lively oracles. When the Christian mind awakes from its comparative coldness to a higher state of vitality and devotedness, the word of God invariably does the work of an instrument of the quickening. And when conviction of sin, and those struggles of mind which are wont to precede conversion, are experienced by the impenitent, it is the contents of the Bible which have introduced them; and that religious experience which holds the Bible at a distance, or that does not stand immediately connected with some fact or principle of the divine word, is spurious.

The habitual reading of the Bible, joined with prayerful meditations, becomes then a duty of the first importance. That eminently devoted and faithful servant of Christ, Cotton Mather, born 1762, to kindle heavenly fires in his soul resorted to a method similar to that of George Muller, musing and meditating in God's word, prayerfully, till his whole being was gospelized. Christ was ever present with him—"The way, the truth, and the life." "The fairest among ten thousand, and the one altogether lovely." He says: "The thoughts of Christ are become exceedingly frequent with me; I meditate on His glorious Person, as the eternal and the incarnate Son of God: and I behold the infinite God as coming to me, and meeting with me in this blessed meditation. I fly to Him on multitudes of occasions every day, and am impatient if many minutes have passed without some recourse to Him. Every now and then I rebuke myself for having been so long without any thoughts of my Saviour; how can I bear to keep at such a distance from Him? I then look up to him, and say, O my Saviour, draw near unto me! O, come to dwell in my soul, and help me to cherish some thoughts wherein I shall enjoy Thee; and upon this I set myself to think of what He has done, (is doing,) and what He will do, for me: I find the subject inexhaustible, and after I have been thus employed in the day, I fall asleep at night in the midst of some meditation on the glory of my Saviour; so I fall asleep in Jesus, and when I awake in the night, I do on my bed 'seek Him whom my soul loveth;' (on awaking) the desires of my soul still carry me to Him who was last in my thoughts when I fell asleep."

"Mark the perfect man, and behold the upright; for the end of that man is peace."—*Psa.* xxxvii. 37.

> "The chamber where the good man meets his fate,
> Is privileged above the common walks of life,
> Quite on the verge of heaven."

Josiah in his Kingly Robes.

He was lovely and Godfearing from a child. In reformatory measures he exceeded his great and good grandfather Hezekiah.

"Josiah was eight years old when he began to reign, and he reigned thirty and one years in Jerusalem: And he did that *which was* right in the sight of the LORD, and walked in all the ways of David his father, and turned not aside to the right hand, or to the left."—2 *Kings* xxii. 2.

When the book of the law was found dusted over, he wept, rent his clothes. He saw at a glance why the whole head was sick, the whole heart faint, why the curse of God rested upon the whole nation.

"And it came to pass when the king had heard the words of the book of the Law, that he rent his clothes." What now? continue to lie in sackcloth and weep? Nay, but up and *on*—turn and overturn, cast out Satan here, cast out Satan there, smash idols and grind them to powder here, smash idols and grind them to powder there! O! for such rulers, such ministers, to "rise up against evil-doers, stand up against the workers of iniquity," fire, hammer and sword men, to storm the fort of Satan, load and fire, load and fire! Where are they? Echo cries, "Where?"

No king set himself more earnestly to destroy every vestige of idolatry out of the land. Among other things, he defiled the altars of the idols at Bethel, by burning upon them the bones from the tombs of their deceased priests; as had been foretold more than three centuries before.— 1 *Kings* xiii. 2.

Wherever the Law was read, enforced, treasured in honest hearts, there was light, hope, peace, prosperity. The very Heaven of heavens smiled, and shed down its richest fragrance. Their barns were filled with plenty, their presses burst with new wine; fear fell upon the nations round about, and even their enemies were at peace with them, and brought them presents.

When the holy Scriptures were laid aside, dusted over, forgotten, or neglected, what now? Darkness, spiritual death, idolatry, superstition, will-worship. The whole head was sick, the whole heart faint. It was so then, it is so now.

> "The worth of truth no tongue can tell,
> 'Twill do to buy but not to sell;
> A large estate that soul has got,
> Who buys the truth, and sells it not." *

---

* How was this eminent Bible reformer educated, on what kind of mental food was he nourished or fed? chaff, husks, swine's food? novels, romances—"Little Corporal," "Mother Goose," "The House that Jack Built?" Satan as yet, had not so much as dreamed of this hellish stratagem to ruin souls. "As is the tree, so is the fruit."

> "Happy the soul that reads the page
> That guides our youth and cheers our age;
> Yea, blessed evermore is he,
> O Lord, who learns to come to thee."

LIGHT UNDER A BUSHEL—NOT ON A CANDLESTICK;

—OR—

Yoking Believers with Unbelievers, Christ with Belial!

Is this Bible? "Ye are the light of the world. A city that is set on an hill cannot be hid," saith the Lord of glory to his disciples. "Neither do men light a candle and put it under a bushel, but on a candlestick; and it giveth light unto all that are in the house. Let your light so shine before men, that they may see your good works, and glorify your father which is in heaven."—*Mat.* v. 15, 16.

Jesus says: "I spake openly to the world. . . . . and in secret have I said nothing."—*John* xviii. 20.

Why not be content and follow the Master? "For ye were sometimes darkness, but now *are ye* light in the Lord: walk as children of light."—*Eph.* v. 8. "What I tell you in darkness that speak ye in light."

Then again, Christian friends, why yoke yourselves with unbelievers, enemies of the cross of Christ? Is this Bible?

"Be ye not unequally yoked together with unbelievers: for what fellowship hath righteousness with unrighteousness? and what communion hath light with darkness? And what concord hath Christ with Belial? or what part hath he that believeth, with an infidel? And what agreement hath the temple of God with idols? for ye are the temple of the living God, as God hath said, I will dwell in them, and walk in *them,* and I will be their God, and they shall be my people. Wherefore come out from among them, and be ye separate, saith the Lord, and touch not the unclean thing, and I will receive you. And will be a Father unto you, and ye shall be my sons and daughters, saith the Lord Almighty."—2 *Cor.* vi. 14–18.

Under the Mosaic economy, we learn the same moral principle. "Thou shalt not sow thy vineyard with divers seeds: lest the fruit of thy seed which thou hast sown, and the fruit of thy vineyard, be defiled. Thou shalt not plough with an ox and an ass together. Thou shalt not wear a garment of divers sorts, as of woolen and linen together."—*Deut.* xxii. 9–11; *Lev.* xix. 19.

These Scriptures will suffice to set forth the moral evil of an unequal yoke. It may, with full confidence, be asserted that no one can be an unshackled follower of Christ who is, in any way, "unequally yoked."

Get your neck out of this unequal yoke, else how be received? God cannot fully and publicly own those who are unequally yoked together with unbelievers, for, were He to do so, it would be an acknowledgment of the unequal yoke. He cannot acknowledge "darkness," "unrighteousness," "Belial," "idols," and "an infidel." How could he? Hence, if I yoke myself with any of these, I am morally and publicly identified with them, and not with God at all. I have put myself into a position which God cannot own, and, as a consequence, He cannot own me; but if I withdraw myself from that position—if I "come out and be separate" —if I take my neck out of the unequal yoke, then, but not until then, can I be publicly and fully received and owned as a "son or daughter of the Lord Almighty."

This is a solemn and searching principle for all who feel that they have unhappily gotten themselves into such a yoke. They are not walking as disciples, nor are they publicly or morally on the ground of sons. God cannot own them

Their secret relationship is not the point; but they have put themselves thoroughly off God's ground. They have foolishly thrust their neck into a yoke which, inasmuch as it is not Christ's yoke, must be Belial's yoke; and until they cast off that yoke, God cannot own them as His sons and daughters.

Now, there are four distinct phases in which "the unequal yoke" may be contemplated, viz., the domestic, the commercial, the religious, and the philanthropic. Some may be disposed to confine 2 *Cor.* vi. 14, to the first of these; but the apostle does not so confine it. The words are, "be not unequally yoked together with unbelievers." He does not specify the character or object of the yoke, and therefore we are warranted in giving the passage its widest application, by bringing its edge to bear directly upon every phase of the unequal yoke; and we shall see the importance of so doing, ere we close these remarks, if the Lord permit.

I. And, first, then, let us consider the domestic or marriage yoke. What pen can portray the mental anguish, the moral misery, together with the ruinous consequences, as to spiritual life and testimony, flowing from a Christian's marriage with an unconverted person? I suppose nothing can be more deplorable than the condition of one who discovers, when it is too late, that he has linked himself for life with one who cannot have a single thought or feeling in common with him. One desires to serve Christ; the other can only serve the devil: one breathes after the things of God; the other sighs for the things of this present world: the one earnestly seeks to mortify the flesh, with all its affections, and desires; the other only seeks to minister to and gratify these very things. Like a sheep and a goat, linked together, the sheep longs to feed on the green pasture in the field while, on the other hand, the goat craves the brambles which grow on the ditch. The sad consequence is that both are starved. One *will* not feed on the pasture, and the other *cannot* feed upon the brambles, and thus neither gets what his nature craves, unless the goat, by superior strength, succeeds in forcing his unequally-yoked companion to remain amongst the brambles, there to languish and die.

The moral of this is plain enough; and, moreover, it is alas! of but too common occurrence. The goat generally succeeds in gaining his end. The worldly partner carries his or her point, in almost every instance. It will be found, almost without exception, that, in cases of the unequal marriage yoke, the poor Christian is the sufferer, as is evidenced by the bitter fruits of a bad conscience, a depressed heart, a gloomy spirit, and a desponding mind. A heavy price, surely, to pay for the gratification of some natural affection, or the attainment, it may be, of some paltry worldly advantage. In fact, a marriage of this kind is the death-knell of practical Christianity, and of progress in the divine life. It is morally impossible that any one can be an unfettered disciple of Christ with his neck in the marriage yoke with an unbeliever. As well might a racer in the Olympic or Isthmæan games have expected to gain the crown of victory by attaching a heavy weight or a dead body to his person.

Then, as to its effect upon children, it is equally sad. These are almost sure to flow in the current with the unconverted parent. "Their children spoke half in the speech of Ashdod, and could not speak in the Jews' language, but according to the language of each people." There can be no union of heart in the training of the children; no joint and mutual confidence in reference to them. One desires to bring them up in the nurture and admonition of the

Lord; the other desires to bring them up in the principles of the world, the flesh, and the devil: and as all the sympathies of the children, as they grow up, are likely to be ranged on the side of the latter, it is easy to see how it will end. In short, it is an unseemly, unscriptural, and vain effort to plough with an "unequal yoke," or to "sow the ground with mingled seed;" and all must end in sorrow and confusion.

II. We shall now consider "the unequal yoke," in its commercial phase, as seen in cases of partnership in business. This, though not so serious an aspect of the yoke as that which we have just been considering, inasmuch as it can be more easily got rid of, will, nevertheless, be found a very positive barrier to the believer's testimony. When a Christian yokes himself, for business purposes, with an unbeliever—whether that unbeliever be a relative or not—or when he becomes a member of a worldly firm, he virtually surrenders his individual responsibility. Henceforth the acts of the firm become his acts, and it is perfectly out of the question to think of getting a worldly firm to act on heavenly principles. They would laugh at such a notion, inasmuch as it would be an effectual barrier to the success of their commercial schemes. They will feel perfectly free to adopt a number of expedients in carrying on their business, which would be quite opposed to the spirit and principles of the kingdom in which he is, and of the Church of which he forms a part. Thus he will find himself constantly in a most trying position. He may use his influence to christianize the mode of conducting affairs; but they will compel him to do business as others do, and he has no remedy save to mourn in secret over his anomalous and difficult position, or else to go out at great pecuniary loss to himself and his family. Where the eye is single, there will be no hesitation as to which of these alternatives to adopt; but, alas! the very fact of getting into such a position proves the lack of a single eye; and the fact of being in it argues the lack of spiritual capacity to appreciate the value and power of the divine principles which would infallibly bring a man out of it. A man whose eye was single could not possibly yoke himself with an unbeliever for the purpose of making money. Such an one could only set, as an object before his mind, the direct glory of Christ; and this object could never be gained by a positive transgression of divine principle.

This makes it very simple. If it does not glorify Christ for a Christian to become a partner in a worldly firm, it must, without doubt, further the designs of the devil. There is no middle ground; but that it does not glorify Christ is manifest, for his word says, "be not unequally yoked together with unbelievers." Such is the principle which cannot be infringed without damage to the testimony, and forfeiture of spiritual blessing. True, the conscience of a Christian, who transgresses in this matter, may seek relief in various ways—may have recourse to various subterfuges—may set forth various arguments to persuade itself that all is right. It will be said that, "we can be very devoted and very spiritual, so far as we are personally concerned, even though we are yoked, for business purposes, with an unbeliever." This will be found fallacious, when brought to the test of the actual practice. A servant of Christ will find himself hampered in a hundred ways by his worldly partnership. If in matters of service to Christ he is not met with open hostility, he will have to encounter the enemy's secret and constant effort to damp his ardor, and throw cold water on all his schemes. He will be laughed at and despised—he will be continually reminded of the effect which his enthusiasm and fanaticism will produce in reference to the business prospects of the firm. If he uses his time, his talents, or his pecuniary resources, in what he believes to be the Lord's service, he will be pronounced a fool or a madman, and reminded that the true, the proper way for a commercial man to serve the Lord is to "attend to business, and nothing but business." A man must be either the one or the other. If I am a Christian, my Christianity must show itself, as a living reality, in that in which I am; and if it cannot show itself there, I ought not to be there; for, if I continue in a sphere or position in which the life of Christ cannot be manifested, I shall speedily possess nought of Christianity but the name, without the reality—the outward form without the inward power—the shell without the kernel. I should be the servant of Christ, not merely on Sunday, but from Monday morning to Saturday night. I should not only be a servant of Christ in the public assembly, but also in my place of business, whatever it may happen to be. But I cannot be a proper servant of Christ with my neck in the yoke with an unbeliever; for how could the servants of two hostile masters work in the same yoke? It is utterly impossible; as well might one attempt to link the sun's meridian beams with the profound darkness of midnight.

For want of space we are obliged to omit the third item, the religious phase of the unequal yoke, and come directly and lastly to what is termed the philanthropic phase of the unequal yoke. Many will say, "I quite admit that we ought not to mingle ourselves with positive unbelievers in the worship or service of God; but, then, we can freely unite with such for the furtherance of objects of philanthropy—such, for instance, as feeding the hungry, clothing the naked, reclaiming the vicious, in providing asylums for the blind and the lunatic, hospitals and infirmaries for the sick and infirm, places of refuge for the homeless and houseless, the fatherless and the widow; and, in short, for the furtherance of everything that tends to promote the amelioration of our fellow creatures, physically, morally, and intellectually."

This, at first sight, seems fair enough; for I may be asked, if I would not help a man, by the road-side, to get his cart out of the ditch? I reply, certainly; but if I were asked to become a member of a mixed society for the purpose of getting carts out of ditches, I should refuse—not because of my superior sanctity, but because God's word says, "Be not unequally yoked together with unbelievers." This would be my answer, no matter what were the object proposed by a mixed society. The servant of Christ is commanded "to be ready to every good work"—"to do good unto all"—"to visit the fatherless and the widows in their affliction;" but then, it is as the servant of Christ, and not as the member of a society or a committee in which there may be infidels and atheists, and all sorts of wicked and godless men. Moreover, we must remember that all God's philanthropy is connected with the cross of the Lord Jesus Christ. That is the channel through which God will bless—that the mighty lever by which He will elevate man, physically, morally, and intellectually. "After that the kindness and philanthropy ($\varphi\iota\lambda\alpha\nu\theta\rho\omega\pi\iota\alpha$) of God our Saviour toward man appeared, not by works of righteousness which we have done, but according to his mercy he saved us, by the washing of regeneration, and renewing of the Holy Ghost; which he shed on us abundantly through Jesus Christ our Saviour."—*Titus* iii. 4–6. This is God's philanthropy. This is His mode of ameliorating man's condition. With all who understand its worth the Christian can readily yoke himself, but with none other.

The men of the world know nought of this, care not for it. They may seek reformation, but it is reformation without Christ. They may promote amelioration, but it is amelioration without the cross. They wish to advance, but Jesus is neither the starting-post nor the goal of their course. How, then, can the Christian yoke himself with them? They want to work without Christ, the very One to whom he owes everything. Can he be satisfied to work with them? Can he have an object in common with them? If men come to me and say, "we want your co-operation in feeding the hungry, in clothing the naked, in founding hospitals and lunatic asylums, in feeding and educating orphans, in improving the physical condition of our fellow mortals; but you must remember that a leading rule of the society, the board, or the committee, formed for such objects, is that the name of Christ is not to be introduced, as it would only lead to controversy. Our objects being not at all religious, but undividedly philanthropic, the subject of religion of Christ must be studiously excluded from all our public meetings. We are met as *men*, for a benevolent purpose, and therefore Infidels, Atheists, Socinians, Arians, Romanists, and all sorts, can happily yoke themselves to move onward the glorious machine of philanthropy." What should be my answer to such an application? The fact is, words would fail one, who really loved the Lord Jesus, in attempting to reply to an appeal so monstrous. What!

benefit mortals by the exclusion of Christ? God forbid? If I cannot gain the objects of pure philanthropy, without setting aside that blessed One who lived and died, and lives eternally for me, then away with your philanthropy, for it, assuredly, is not God's but Satan's. If it were God's, the word is, "He shed it on us abundantly THROUGH Jesus Christ," the very One whom your rule leaves entirely out. Hence your rule must be the direct dictation of Satan, the enemy of Christ. Satan would always like to leave out the Son of God; and, when he can get men to do the same, he will allow them to be benevolent, charitable, and philanthropic.

But, in good truth, such benevolence and philanthropy ought to be termed malevolence and misanthropy, for how can you more effectually exhibit ill-will and hatred toward men, than by leaving out THE ONLY ONE who can really bless them, for time or for eternity? But what must be the moral condition of a heart, in reference to Christ, who could take his seat at a board, or on a platform, on the condition that that name must not be introduced? It must be cold indeed; yea, it proves that the plans and operations of unconverted men are of sufficient importance, in his judgment, to lead him to throw his Master overboard, for the purpose of carrying them out. Let us not mistake matters. This is the true aspect in which to view the world's philanthropy. The men of this world can "sell ointment for three hundred pence, and give to the poor;" while they pronounce it *waste* to pour that ointment on the head of Christ! Will the Christian consent to this? Will he yoke himself with such? Will he seek to improve the world without Christ? Will he join with men to deck and garnish a scene which is stained with his Master's blood? Peter could say, "Silver and gold have I none; but such as I have give I thee: in the name of Jesus Christ of Nazareth, rise and walk." Peter would heal a cripple by the power of the name of Jesus; but what would he have said, if asked to join a committee or society to alleviate cripples, on the condition of leaving that name out altogether? It requires no great stretch of imagination to conceive his answer. His whole soul would recoil from such a thought. He only healed the cripple for the purpose of exalting the name of Jesus, and setting forth its worth, its excellency, and its glory, in the view of men; but the very reverse is the object of the world's philanthropy; inasmuch as it sets aside His blessed name entirely, and banishes Him from its boards, its committees, and its platforms.

May we not, therefore, well say, "Shame on the Christian who is found in a place from which his Master is shut out?" Oh! let him go forth, and, in the energy of love to Jesus, and by the power of that name, do all the good he can; but let him not yoke himself with unbelievers, to counteract the effects of sin, by excluding the cross of Christ. God's grand object is to exalt His Son—"that all should honor the Son even as they honor the Father." This should be the Christian's object likewise; to this end he should "do good unto all;" but if he join a society or a committee to do good, it is not "in the name of Jesus" but in the name of the society or committee, without the name of Jesus. This ought to be enough for every true and loyal heart. God has no other way of blessing men, but through Christ; and no other object in blessing them but to exalt Christ. As with Pharaoh of old, when the hungry Egyptians flocked to his presence, his word was, "go to Joseph;" so God's word to all is, "come to Jesus." Yes, for soul and body, time and eternity, we must go to Jesus; but the men of the world know Him not, and want Him not; what, therefore has the Christian to do with such? How can He act in yoke with them? He can only do so on the ground of practically denying his Saviour's name. Many do not see this; but that does not alter the case for those who do. We ought to act honestly, as in the light; and even though the feelings and affections of the new nature were not sufficiently strong in us to lead us to shrink from ranking ourselves with the enemies of Christ, the conscience ought, at least, to bow to the commanding authority of that word, BE NOT UNEQUALLY YOKED TOGETHER WITH UNBELIEVERS.

May the Holy Ghost clothe His own word with heavenly power, and make its edge sharp to pierce the conscience, that so the saints of God may be delivered from everything that hinders their "running the race that is set before them." Time is short. The Lord Himself will soon be here. Then many an unequal yoke will be broken in a moment; many a sheep and goat shall then be eternally severed. May we be enabled to purge ourselves from every unclean association, and every unhallowed influence, so that, when Jesus returns, we may not be ashamed, but meet Him with a joyful heart and an approving conscience.

NOTE—We are indebted to a work entitled "The Unequal Yoke," for the most important ideas in this article. For further light on this important subject we refer our readers to a recent volume by C. G. Finney, late President of Oberlin College, Ohio, on "Free Masonry."

Beloved reader, after prayerfully perusing the foregoing, how can you or any one with grace in the heart, with Bible in hand, look upon secret oath-bound societies as anything but the scaffoldings of Babel, the climbing up to heaven some other way, and all connected with them, in the pulpit or out of it, anything but "thieves and robbers?" Look at the first three oaths of secrecy of one of these philanthropic societies—never to be divulged on pain of having "my throat cut across," "my left side opened and my heart torn out ;" and to have my body severed in twain and my bowels burned in the midst."

And is it possible? can it be? that religious statesmen, Vice-Presidents of the United States, professing Godliness, grave doctors of divinity, bishops, elders, deacons, class-leaders. Reverends advocating the doctrine of Gospel purity, a holy life, entire sanctification, in the face and eyes of Omnipotent grace and bleeding mercy, place their signatures to an instrument concocted and framed—where and by whom? infernals in perdition or out of it?

Here's a problem unsolved, never to be solved this side the pit bottomless. It's mystery on mystery from first to last. It begins in mystery, continues in mystery, ends in mystery; and doubtless it will be *forever* a mystery, both to men and angels. Mysteries never cease. There always have been mysteries, and doubtless there always will be mysteries, while time exists and eternity rolls on! There are mysteries in nature, in science, in religion, in things temporal, and in things spiritual; mysteries in heaven, and mysteries on earth.

And yet, amid all the mysteries above and below, in heaven and in hell, in time and in eternity, we know of no mystery so great and so mysterious a mystery as the one underconsideration.

Surely, devils in hell and out of it, wonder with amazement and hellish joy at their success in making converts.

CHRIST! CHRIST! CHRIST!!

It must be. Do anything for Christ without Christ? Could Paul? Not a thought, not a syllable of good, no preaching, praying, converting; doing this, doing that. It was Christ with Paul, at early dawn, at noon-day, at setting sun, all the time, lying down, rising up, going out, coming in. Christ was his food, meat and drink, *all in all*. Every breath breathed was Christ. Here's the great secret of success in Paul's labors, in synagogues, from house to house, by the river side, when tossed on the billows deep. It was Christ in his soul, deep down, burningly, that filled him with love that no waters quenched, that gave him power, spiritual, holy boldness. It was through Christ he endured hardness as a good soldier of the cross, suffered persecution, received forty stripes five times save one.

Here we fail, halt, stumble, sicken, die! Pigmies, mere skeletons in piety, dwarfs, dead branches, barren fig trees, a valley of dry bones? How else, but fit for burning without Christ in us savingly, the hope of glory? Here's where we miss it, sadly, shockingly! Here's where ruin begins, desolation, damnation! We are perishing, dying the death for want of Christ. Look here, look there, in this pulpit, in that pulpit, any Christ heard or seen? Hark! hear that prayer, that exhortation, what now? Christ, holy unction, sparks heavenly, tongues of *fire?* Listen to the conversation to the house of worship and returning therefrom, what is it, Christ? *all the way*, soul kindlingly? Do hearts burn within them while they talk about Jesus, as the hearts of those who walked to Emmaus? and Christ drew near and went with them? "And they said one to another, Did not our heart burn within us, while he talked with us by the way, and while he opened to us the Scriptures?"—*Luke* xxiv. 32.

How in Sunday-schools? is Christ *the* first and *the* last, the *always?* How at family worship, in the domestic circle, around the fire side, the table spread with heaven's bounties? No Christ, no family order, no Gospel training, no soul, no life, no holy unction, no tongue of *fire!* The Gergesenes didn't want Christ.—*Mat.* viii. 24. Wherefore? They were not disposed to give up their "ill-gotten gains," their devilish traffic in swine's flesh. They "besought him to depart out of their coasts." He took them at their word, left them to their own destruction, entered into a ship, passed over, and came into his own city.—*Mat.* ix. 1. What better are we than these same Gergesenes if living in lust? lust of the flesh, of the eyes, the pride of life?

Preaching Christ Crucified is Salvation.—*Col. i.* 28.

Prayers may be good, sermonizings may be good, orthodoxly,* here and there, in big congregations and in little, but if Christ is wanting, fire, heavenly, pentacostal, what but sounding brass, and tinkling cymabals are they? "Without me," said Christ, "ye can do nothing." "I am

---

* Orthodoxy may be in form both in writing and preaching, smooth and beautiful, and nobody is hit or hurt, no two-edged sword to slay the man of sin is drawn. Sinners in their sins are not disturbed, Satan is not roused. Proof positive this of prophesying smoothly. A pure Gospel, preached as Paul preached it, exposes popular sins everywhere, rouses the devil to opposition and persecution. Who is for the Lord? Who?

"Many sermons, ingenious, may be compared to a letter put in the post-office without a direction. It is addressed to nobody, it is owned by nobody, and if a hundred

the way, the truth and the life: no man cometh to the Father, but by me."—*John* xiv. 6. Will the Holy Spirit accompany the truth preached without Christ is in it, first, midst, last, always? Can he? No man can call Jesus Christ Lord, but by the Holy Spirit.

Why did the Holy Spirit accompany the discourse of Peter on the day of Pentecost to the convicting and converting of three thousand souls? Because Jesus, the Christ, was Alpha and Omega, all the way from first to last. (See Acts, chapter ii.) Why was the preaching of Phillip blessed to the conversion of the Ethiopean eunuch? Because he began with Isaiah, and preached Christ, and the eunuch believed, was baptized and went on his way rejoicing. (See Acts, chapter viii.)

Notice the conversion of Paul. Christ himself, from heaven, preached Christ to this mad persecutor. What now? awakened and led to cry out, "*Who art thou, Lord?*" When the scales had fallen from his eyes, what did this same Paul do? Preach Christ? Henceforth and forever? From the very hour that he knew Christ, he determined to know nothing else save Jesus Christ, and him crucified. (See 1 Cor. ii. 1–5.) Why was Paul's labors blessed on Mar's hill, in the midst of idolatry, Epicurean and Stoical infidelity, to the awakening and converting of precious souls? Because he preached Christ and the resurrection.

---

people were to read it, not one of them would think himself concerned in the contents. Such a sermon lacks the chief requisite. It is like a sword which has a polished blade, a jeweled hilt, and a gorgeous scabbard, but yet will not cut. Truth, properly presented, has an edge, it pierces to the dividing asunder of soul and spirit, it is a discerner of the thoughts and intents of the heart." The *N. Y. Herald* says: " Every Monday morning in the year the *Herald* publishes Sabbath-day sermons whose chief or only merit is that they contain fine phrases, beautifully rounded paragraphs and polished sentences, but they do not contain Gospel truth enough to save a soul."

(See Acts, chapter xvii.) Why was Felix made to tremble, and king Agrippa to say, "Almost thou persuadest me to be a Christian?" Was it not because Christ was first and last, in Paul's experience and preaching? (See Acts, chapter xxvi.) Why did the Holy Spirit fall upon Cornelius and those with him, under Peter's ministrations? (See Acts x. 44, 45.) Was it not because Christ was the theme, the soul and the life of what Peter said?

The apostles and early disciples, after the tongue of fire was given pentecostally, were filled with this purifying, sanctifying grace of Christ. Their preaching was Christ, their praying was Christ; their singing, making melody in the heart to the Lord, was Christ; their conversations at home and abroad, lying down, rising up, going out, and coming in; around the fire-side, the table spread with heaven's bounties, were made up largely of Christ. The meditations of their hearts, and the answer of their tongues were Christ. Glorious! Is it so now? O where?

What the results of this having Christ and him crucified, always, everywhere, in the heart, the life, the every-day walk? Most glorious! Sinners in the gall of bitterness and in the bonds of iniquity, the most stubborn, hardened, self-willed, heaven-daring, blood-guilty, were awakened and converted, multitudinous! Saints were strengthened, built up in their most holy faith, rejoicingly. It was fire, fire, *fire!* Gospel *fire*, day in, day out. Not a sermon was delivered without Christ, first and last. The apostles began their discourses with Christ, and kept on with Christ, both from the Old Testament and the New. Is it so now? O where?

"The testimony of Jesus is the spirit of prophecy."—*Rev.* xix. 10. The very soul, the leading subject, the main design, therefore, of prophecy is to testify of Jesus. Hence he himself declares, "In the volume of the book it is written of me, Lo! I come to do thy will, O God: thy law is within my heart."—*Psa.* xl. 7, etc. He is the Alpha and Omega. From the first promise declared to Adam, *Gen.* iii. 15, the atonement of the great Redeemer is traced in lines of blood, throughout all the types and shadows of the Mosaic ritual, up to his cross, the substance and glory of them all. *Behold the Lamb of God, which taketh away the sin of the world.* It is to this stupendous FACT—THE GREAT ATONING SACRIFICE OF IMMANUEL—that all the previous parts of Scripture point and labor to arrive, and which the Holy Ghost, in the Epistle to the Hebrews, so beautifully exhibits.

The whole Bible might be labelled, "The Word of Christ," it is so full of Him; in all parts of it you find a word from Him, or a word about Him; take Him away from it, and it would be a book without a meaning. It has been well said, "What a babe's *clothes* are when the babe has slipped out of them into death, and the mother's arms clasp only the raiment—that would the Bible be if the Babe of Bethlehem, and the great truths that clothed His life and death, should slip out of it." But there is no possibility of putting Christ out of the Bible, for He is its very substance.

Thus, notwithstanding all the schemes of ungodly men, it will be with the name of Christ; it will still remain in the Bible to be as the light and glory of the sacred page, and thus the Bible will be to all generations what the star was to the wise men of the East—a light to guide mankind to the Saviour.

> "Of all the gifts Thy love bestows,
>   Thou Giver of all good!
> Not heaven itself a richer knows,
>   Than the Redeemer's blood."

Friends of the Lord Jesus, redeemed by his blood, preach Christ the Saviour. Men are lost! *lost!* without Christ. Sinners need salvation, and none can save them but Christ the Lord, who came to seek and save the lost. There is no other name given under heaven, nor among men, whereby sinners can be saved, except the Lord Jesus. He was promised in Eden. Patriarchs saw his day, and were glad. Prophets described with glowing eloquence his sufferings and death. Angels announced his birth, and sung with celestial melody to the wondering shepherds. He was the Son of God. John the Baptist heralded his approach, saying: "This was he of whom I spake: he that cometh after me, is preferred before me, for he was before me."— *John* i. 15. Multitudes thronged to hear him preach, and witness his miracle-working power. He healed the sick, gave sight to the blind, strength to the lame, speech to the dumb, hearing to the deaf, joy to the sorrowful, peace to the troubled, forgiveness to the guilty, life to the dead, and preached the Gospel to the poor.

Preach Christ Jesus. The Bible is full of him. All the rays of divine truth connect and centre in him, like the rays of light in a focus. No man can preach the Bible, unless he preaches Jesus. Just as the rivers run to the sea, so do all the lines of promises and predictions lead to Jesus. Just as the sun is the centre of the solar system, so Christ is the centre of the system of Christianity. This radiance shines in every sacred text.

Preach Christ, and him crucified, now at the right hand of the Father. The holy prophets and apostles did. Their minds were full of him. Wherever they went they proclaimed him. He was the sum and substance of their preaching. When Philip heard the eunuch reading the prophecy of

Isaiah, he began at the same Scripture and preached Jesus. When he went down to Samaria, he preached Christ unto them. When Peter found the company assembled at the house of Cornelius, he preached peace by Jesus Christ. When Paul was converted and baptized at Damascus, he did not stop to confer with flesh and blood. In the synagogues he preached Jesus, that he is the Christ, and ever afterward Jesus was the theme of this great apostle. Hear him. "We preach not ourselves, but Christ Jesus the Lord, and ourselves your servants for Jesus' sake." "I determined to know nothing among you, save Jesus Christ, and him crucified." "Whom we preach, warning every man, and teaching every man in all wisdom ; that we may present every man perfect in Christ Jesus."

Beloved readers, in the assembly of the saints or out of it, preach Christ. But be sure, first of all, that you know him as your personal Saviour, your all and in all. "If Christ be in you, the body is dead because of sin, but the spirit is life, because of righteousness."

If Christ is in you the hope of glory, then you can preach him. Down with self, and exalt Jesus, come life, come death. Persecuted? Suppose you are, friend, even unto death. Did Christ come to send peace on earth or a sword? No true minister of the Lord Jesus fails to stir the sediment of carnal hearts, provoke the enmity and opposition of proud, fashionable, money-loving souls, "lovers of pleasure more than lovers of God." Those who tell us the offence of the cross, or persecution, has ceased—that the great battle for truth and righteousness is fought, and that henceforth the church is to move on smoothly and prosperously, "on flowery beds of ease," are not the ones to stand at the cannon's mouth, place themselves in the battle's front, beard the lion in his den, wage open warfare with the combined powers of earth and hell. Satan is not very likely to trouble those that shun the cross, are at ease in Zion, oppose agitation, cry "peace, peace," when there is no peace, bow the knee to a time-serving age, loving the praise of men more than the praise of God.

> "What wants the age? Heart-earnest men
> To spread the truth, the truth defend ;
> Such on the earth we need again
> As God in ancient times did send."

Ministers are like the pole on which the brazen serpent was erected ; they are useful so long at they *hold up the object of faith,* Jesus Christ. Hide behind the cross, and let the people see nothing but JESUS. Preach his life ; preach his death ; preach his resurrection ; preach his ascension ; preach his coming ; preach his reign ; preach all about him ; keep preaching him. Preach him not only in the pulpit, but out of it ; preach him in every thought, word and action. Preach him from house to house : keep back no part of the price. Neglect no opportunity to preach Jesus. Do this, and thou shalt be a good minister of Jesus Christ, nourished in the words of faith and of good doctrine.

> "And what, O what is good?
> 'Tis first to seek the favor of thy God ;
> Let thy will blend with his, and honor him
> By walking in the way thy Saviour trod."

Address.... **Author of "DIGGING ROOTS," "SHINING LIGHT," Etc**
No. 303 West Twentieth Street, N. Y.

TALKING WITHOUT SAYING ANYTHING!

> "If wisdom's ways you wisely seek,
> Five things observe with care:
> *To* whom you speak, *of* whom you speak,
> And *how*, and *when*, and *where*."

TALK, and nothing to say? No, you shouldn't, friend. Stop, close your lips, hush till you have something to say. This talking when nothing is said, alas! how common, how dreadful! We hear it at the table, around the fire-side, in social gatherings, here and there, by the way-side, no end to it. How much precious time is lost—worse than lost!

"He that hath knowledge spareth his words: and a man of understanding is of an excellent spirit. Even a fool, when he holdeth his peace, is counted wise: *and* he that shutteth his lips *is esteemed* a man of understanding."—*Prov.* xvii. 27, 28.

The Psalmist prayed earnestly for a watch to be placed at the door of his lips. He promised the Lord also that he would bridle his tongue, especially in the presence of the wicked or ungodly. "The tongue of the wise useth knowledge aright." "A wholesome tongue is a tree of life." "The lips of the wise disperse knowledge." "The heart of the righteous studieth to answer; but the mouth of the wicked poureth out evil things."—*Prov.* xv. 28. "Be more ready to hear, says Solomon, "than to give the sacrifice of fools." "Be not rash with thy mouth, and let not thy heart be hasty to utter anything before God, for God is in heaven and thou upon earth: therefore let thy words be few." "A fool's voice is known by a multitude of words."

James says: "If a man offend not in word, the same is a perfect man, able also to bridle the whole body." These passages from inspiration of God are applicable both to prayer and conversation.

"The words of a wise man's mouth are gracious: but the lips of the fool swallow him up." "The tongue is a little member and boasteth great things." "Put away from thee a froward mouth, and perverse lips put far from thee." "In the multitude of words there wanteth not sin." "He that keepeth his mouth, keepeth his life."

"The only edged tool that becomes sharper by constant use, is the tongue. It is often a sting full of deadly poison. It is both an offensive weapon—a shield and a spear. Some carry dirks in their pockets, others in their mouths. The tongue of the malignant is like a masked battery, which makes us feel fire when we can't see smoke. There's never a spur for the tongue in all the Bible, but many a bit. As a condition of longevity physicians say: 'Keep the head cool and the feet warm.' This is Peter's recipe for a long and happy life: 'He that will love life and see good days, let him refrain his tongue from evil, and his lips from speaking guile.' Physicians are accustomed to judge of the state of the body by the condition of the tongue, assuming as a settled principle that there is an intimate connection between the state of the tongue and the tone of the system. The apostle James adopts a similar course. To judge of soul-health, he looks at the tongue. If any man offend not in word, his moral health is perfect. On the other hand, if any one seem to be religious while the tongue is unbridled, that man's soul is sick. Read the third chapter of

James. What a delineation of the soul-sickness of the race!

> 'A child of *words* and not of *deeds*,
> Is like a garden full of weeds.'"

Have you nothing edifying or profitable to communicate? Well, then, *say nothing*—hold your peace.

Never talk merely for the sake of talking. Hush! Lift up your heart silently, in prayerful ejaculations, for wisdom, pure, gentle, easy to be entreated, full of mercy and good fruits, without partiality, and without hypocrisy; that the words of your mouth and the meditations of your hearts may be acceptable to God, edifying, administering grace to the hearers.

Again: never open your lips when unduly excited or ruffled. Keep still! look up. The art of silence is a great art, both with the old and the young.

Keep your mouth as with a bridle. Learn to be silent under oppositions, provocations, rebukes, injuries, or persecutions. It is better to say nothing, than to say anything in an angry or excited manner, even if the occasion should seem to justify a degree of anger. By remaining silent, the mind is enabled to collect itself, and calls upon God in secret aspirations of prayer. And thus you will speak to the honor of your holy profession, as well as to the good of those who have injured you, when you speak from God.

> "Whene'er the angry passions rise,
>   And tempt our thoughts and tongues to strife;
> To Jesus let us lift our eyes,
>   Bright pattern of the Christian life."

The right government of the tongue is a subject of vital importance, and which we cannot disregard with impunity.

"If any man among you seem to be religious, and bridleth not his tongue, that man's religion is vain." "By thy words thou shalt be justified, and by thy words thou shalt be condemned."

The cure of an evil tongue must be in the heart. The weights and wheels are there, and the clock strikes according to their motion. "Out of the abundance of the heart the mouth speaketh." Words are the index of the heart.

In short—when our hearts are right we shall never want for topics of conversation, which will "please our neighbor for his good to edification." "A good man, out of the good treasure of his heart, bringeth forth good things."

> "Trifle not; for from the fullness
> Of the heart the mouth doth speak,
> And from clear and rock-bound fountains
> Never will foul waters break."

A Quiet Spirit.

Of all the jewels that adorn the wearer, we have inspired authority for saying that the ornament of a meek and quiet spirit is, in the sight of God, of great price; and the question is one which is often asked by those who feel that they have it not, how shall we acquire this self-control? "If one could recall some of the bitter and uncharitable words that slip so easily from the tongue and which time cannot efface, how much suffering our loved ones might be spared!" How often the Scriptures call on men to consider, and wisdom bids her children ponder their steps and keep the door of their lips. The precious word is ever sounding to all burdened souls, "Come unto me." Christ alone can help.

Educating Little Folks—How? When?

"*Doing your very best*" are you, parent, in educating for glory eternal? Solemn thought, momentous! fearful! A Christian mother said to us rather tartly, when reproved for her remissness in family government: "I've done *the* very best I could, and still my children are what you see: they are wild, unruly, turbulent, selfish, graceless as graceless can be." We were startled! stood aghast! at the words flowing thus from her lips. Done your very best, have you, indeed, madam, in training your household for God? What meanest thou, dear woman, saddle your iniquity, the quintescence of the pit, on the Lord Almighty! Awful sin, blasphemous! What impenitent sinner more sinful, heaven-daring! What, make God a liar? What plea for serving the devil more common, more frequent in mouths foul as the pit! Obey God and live. Stamp down truth, beautiful, sparkling, glorious—die the death!

> "If self must be denied,
> And sin no more caressed,
> They rather choose the way that's wide,
> And strive to think it best."

Christian parent, God says—Devote your child to me under my revealed covenant, and I will accept the dedication. Train that child for me in humble faith, and I will aid your efforts. If you consent, I will be a God to you and your children after you.

Now with such a superadded pledge of divine co-operation, why should Christian parents fail in their training of their children for God and for usefulness? Must they not stand indictable before, not human laws only, but before the law and bar of God, if the early defection of their children prove that as parents, they have been recreant to their high, tender, and sacred obligations?

Parent, "Take heed to thyself, lest thou make a covenant with the inhabitants of the land, whither thou goest, lest it be a snare in the midst of thee."

"Blessed is the man that walketh not in the counsel of the ungodly."

> "O 'tis a lovely thing for youth,
> To walk betimes in wisdom's ways."

"Evil communications corrupt good manners."

> "Call the children early, parent,
> Call them at the dawn of day,
> Lead them in the narrow way."

How very common it is to hear from the lips of delinquents, by way of apology for sin and open disobedience "to the law and the testimony," "We do the best we can—we do the best we know how!" Parents excuse themselves in the same way when reproved for neglecting household duty.

"We have done the best we could—the best we knew how—in training our children, and yet they are wayward, disobedient, thoughtless, and fond of pleasure." Friends, this is strange talk. Is God a hard master? Does he require brick without straw? Has he said it, and will he not perform it—"Train up a child in the way he should go, and when he is old he will not depart from it?" And will you persist in saying, you have done to the best of your ability in obeying God in this precept, and your sons and daughters are, meanwhile, in the broad road that leads to destruction? Whom shall we credit, you or the God of truth, who cannot lie? "Yea, let God be true, but every man a liar." What saith the Lord on the subject of household training? What directions has he given, from Genesis to Revelation, on the duty of parents in rearing "the tender thought?" How readest thou, parent? Have you examined the writings of Moses prayerfully and carefully on the question before us? Likewise the sayings of Solomon, the inspired apostles, and the utterances of Jesus Christ, God's dear Son? Have you viewed critically the examples recorded by the pen of Holy Inspiration of consistent family training, and the unspeakable blessings resulting therefrom —the fearful curses that surely follow disobedience in the performance of this duty? The Bible is full of judgments and mercies touching this very thing. Instance the mercies accompanying obedience in the early training of Moses, Samuel, John the Baptist, and Timothy. It was said to the mother of Moses, "Take this child away and nurse it for me, and I will give thee thy wages." And how well this mother discharged her duty, the life and writings of Moses testify.

> "She asked not for it earthly bliss,
> Or earthly honors, wealth, or fame;
> The sum of her request was this,
> That it might love and fear God's name."

What untold blessings came upon Hannah, the mother of Samuel, for her faithfulness to her solemn covenant vow, in rearing her first-born in the fear and admonition of the Lord! The dedication of herself, and the male child whom she sought, was forever! Samuel was lent to the Lord in a perpetual and everlasting covenant ere he saw the light of the sun, or "curiously wrought in the lower parts of the earth." Who can reckon up in order the unspeakable blessings that crowned the labors of Joshebad and Hannah in this work of love? Who was Moses? who Samuel? what their lives? Light on earth! glory forever! All this for obedience, taking God at his word in household duty.

Again; parents, instance the example of Abraham? "I know him, saith the Lord, that he will command his children, and his household after him; and they shall keep the way of the Lord, to do justice and judgment, that the Lord may bring upon Abraham that which I have spoken of him." Abraham used not only persuasive means—mild, gentle, heavenly—in governing his household, but likewise commanding influence. "The rod and reproof give wisdom, but a child left to himself bringeth shame."

Look at John the Baptist. What was he? what his life from his birth? Among all those born of woman was there ever a greater? His parents, who were they? what their daily walk? They were both righteous before God, "walking in all the commandments and ordinances of the Lord blameless." Mark the course of Timothy from his childhood. How came he wise unto salvation? By whom? through whom? what medium?

These are a few recorded examples of truth and love by the pen of Infinite Wisdom, to show what has been, may be, should be. So it was, so it will be in every case, where the conditions of salvation are observed. The promise is sure. "Heaven and earth shall pass away, but my word shall not pass away." "Behold, to obey is better than sacrifice, and to hearken than the fat of rams."

Look now for a moment at the judgments, the curse of all curses, resting on those who disobey God in family training. What one thing troubled Jacob more than all his other troubles? Read the history of this good patriarch, and see what brought his gray hairs with sorrow to the grave prematurely.

Glance at Eli's household, what do you see—peace, joy, salvation, a little Eden, a heaven below, in the family circle? Nay, sons of Belial; wrath upon wrath; trouble here, trouble there, daily, nightly, till Eli fell backwards, and his neck snapped asunder, and his libidinous sons were hurled into an awful eternity, as in a moment. All this, and yet more, "because his sons were vile, and he restrained them not."

What sorrowed David's heart evermore—from first to last gave him trouble and vexation, even to his dying pillow? Was it not on account of parental neglect, false tenderness? Nothing gave King David half the trouble and grief at heart, during his long and successful reign, as his proud, ambitious, rebellious sons, whom he permitted to grow up in idleness, sin, and folly, to do as they pleased.

Like Eli, his sons were vile, and he restrained them not. It is said in 1 Kings i. 5, that David had not displeased his wicked son Adonijay at any time by saying, "Why hast thou done so?" As much as to say, "serve the devil when you please, as much as you please." Follow the same train of thought to the present, what do you see? the very same judgments, the very same mercies, in accordance with obedience or disobedience in family culture.

Eli was an accomplice in the crimes of his sons, because he connived at them. He knew his duty, and did it not. "For I have told him that I will judge his house forever, for the iniquity which he knoweth: because his sons were vile, and he restrained them not."—1 *Sam.* iii. 13. (See, also, 1 Sam. ii. 29-36.) Responsible for the sins of your children, as truly and certainly as God rules and reigns.

Sow to the wind, the whirlwind reap! Heaven and earth shall pass away: the word of truth, never. And yet, you parents, with all these examples of judgments and mercies staring you full in the face, assert or vouchsafe your innocence—that you are clear in the matter of paternal discipline; you have always done your best in training your children, and yet they stretch forth the puny arm of rebellion against the Most High—refuse to bow the knee to the sceptre of King Immanuel. "Beware, therefore, lest that come which is spoken of in the prophets."

"Behold, I will send you Elijah the prophet before the coming of the great and dreadful day of the Lord. And he shall turn the heart of the fathers to the children, and the heart of the children to their fathers, lest I come and smite the earth with a curse."—*Mal.* iv. 5, 6. "For I the Lord am a jealous God, visiting the iniquities of the fathers upon the children unto the third and fourth generation of them that hate me; and show mercy unto thousands of them that love me and keep my commandments."—*Ex.* xx. 5, 6.

The command, "Be ye holy, for I am holy," is applicable to every little son and daughter of Adam's fallen race.

> "If children thus earnestly seek him below,
> They shall see him and hear him above,
> In that beautiful place he has gone to prepare,
> For all who are washed and forgiven;
> And many dear children are gathering there,
> For of such is the kingdom of heaven."

Save all the little folks, you save the world. Let the "little folks" grow up wicked, proud, disobedient, (as most of them are growing up;) and the world becomes more and more wicked, an aceldama, a field of blood! as we now see it! Therefore lay the ax at the root. Begin where God begins.

God said to his ancient people, "Thou shalt teach these words which I command thee diligently unto thy children . . . when thou liest down and when thou risest up." Lead the children directly to Jesus—rest not till you are sure they are in his arms. Never let go their hands till then.

One thing is certain—none educated in a home of cheerful, consistent, heart-felt piety, the love of Jesus, regenerated and sanctified, can ever afterward be led to despise the religion of the Bible.

A child trained from infancy's early dawnings "in the way he should go" till the age of maturity or the leaving the paternal roof, God says, "*he will not depart from it.*"

Address..........Author of "LITTLE MARY IN A NUT-SHELL,"
No. 303 West Twentieth Street, N. Y.

A CLOSING, LOVING APPEAL TO EDITORS AND PUBLISHERS.

"A word spoken in season how good it is."—*Pro.* xv. 23.

"Open rebuke *is* better than secret love. Faithful *are* the wounds of a friend; but the kisses of an enemy *are* deceitful."—*Pro.* xxvii. 56.

"Let the righteous smite me: *it shall be* a kindness: and let him reprove me; *it shall be* an excellent oil, *which* shall not break my head: for yet my prayer also *shall be* in their calamities."—*Psa.* cxli. 5.

> "To conquer is a glorious thing:
> To dare in mind, in heart, in deed;
> 'Tis *great,* 'tis *glorious* to succeed!"

BELOVED in the chair editorial, you have friends, not a few, but, who among them all dearer, or more faithful than the one now addressing you? Who among your numerous friends say to you kindly, for mercy's sake "stop and think before you farther go?" "*A friend in need is a friend indeed.*"

"He that rebuketh a man, afterwards shall find more favor than he that flattereth with the tongue." "Let him know, that he which converteth the sinner from the error of his way shall save a soul from death, and shall hide a multitude of sins."—*James* v. 20.

For lack of timely outspoken, loving, God-fearing faithfulness in rebuking sin, we are perishing, dying the death! In brandishing the two-edged sword of God's truth against popular sins that cry aloud for vengeance, what are we in comparison with you if clothed in your right minds, sitting at the feet of the Lord Jesus? Yet, feeble as we are—

insignificant as we are—speak we must to be refreshed, for duty's sake, for Christ's sake.

> "For right is right, since God is God,
> And right the day *must win;*
> To doubt would be disloyalty,
> To falter would be sin."

Beloved editors and publishers, when you advertise and puff books and papers, what is it for—to please the Master? Can you, *dare* you put pen to paper in literary notices, till you *know* whether you are building the Lord's kingdom or Satan's? Only a short time since we said to a religious editor, "Friend, what could induce you to notice that vile sheet, made up more or less of lies?" "Why," said he, smilingly, "it was a mere compliment, everybody puffs it!" Serve the devil by way of compliment, or because others serve him! Another very pious editor slaughters by wholesale. Some four or five beautiful volumes are placed on his table for puffing. He gravely and sanctifiedly tells the public, he is pressed with duty, and has no time for critical examination, but from the contents he presumes they must be worthy of commendation. Besides, other good editors have puffed them, and forthwith he draws his bow at a venture, takes a leap in the dark, sink or swim, kill or no kill, for the Lord or for the devil, he lets fly! Could Satan desire an agent more to his liking? Thus the leprosy spreads—takes deep root.

Some publications in the book and periodical form begin with lies, keep on steadily and increasingly with lies and lying, page after page, all through, boldly, unblushingly, devilishly, letting everybody see and know they are the devil's faithful servants. Others again, conceal the cloven foot—the snake lies coiled unseen, everything outwardly appears beautiful and fair.

"There is a way which seemeth right unto a man; but the end thereof are the ways of death."

> "Far off, the road which leads to death
> Looks beautiful and fair."

Satan's ways are moveable, thou canst not know them. Read along—by and by, what do you see, the serpent with forked tongue? Not long since we saw a new book from the "American Tract Society," puffed here, puffed there, by religious editors, not excepting the "Female Guardian." Surely, thought we, this must be a valuable keepsake: we ventured to purchase several copies. What now? Satan in the beginning? No. Where then? in the middle? There the viper was sure! Oh! oh! what a devil! *what* a devil! His infernal nose is getting into every dish! Embrace him, clasp him to the bosom, who don't? what religious editor, novel writer, puffer and seller does not take stock in this lucrative business?

Look at the trash, heaps on heaps, the silliest of the silly, the foolishest of the foolish, the devilishest of the devilish, termed "gift books, Christmas or holiday presents for children," sent forth from religious book stores, advertised and puffed by religious editors! What a curse, *what* a curse! Is it a wonder that so many of our dear youth are lovers of pleasure—baptized infidels? sons and daughters of Belial? To advertise and puff these imps of Satan, placed on your tables by pious booksellers, what but serving the devil is it? What else, friends? Ashamed of it? Not a blush is on your cheeks. You bow the knee to Baal with heart-felt complacency, with as good grace and dignified composure as you sit down to a luxurious repast, brazen-facedly! "Such is the way of an adulterous woman: She eateth and wipeth her mouth, and saith, I have done no wickedness."—*Prov.* xxx. 20.

Sick at heart, on opening your weekly and monthly issues, and beholding your abominable time-serving, popularity-seeking, catering to a corrupt public taste; your receiving honor of men, while casting behind you the honor that cometh from God only! puffing meanwhile the very bubblings and scum of the pit, the rottenest of the rotten, the quintescence of hell—how otherwise than sick even to vomiting! Not only sick, but we fear greatly. We open your linsey-woolsy sheets tremblingly, lest venomous, hissing serpents, not a few with forked tongues and heads uplifted, run here, run there, biting or stinging to death, little folks and big folks, up stairs and down. Frequently we are *constrained* for mercy's sake, the safety of our family, little ones and great ones, to *scream out* piercingly: "*Beware of the snakes*, the coiled serpents! *run!* flee! escape for your life!"

These last mentioned, advertised and puffed by pious editors (snakes in the grass), are Satan's transformations, or angel devils. The former alluded to, the obscene, brazen-faced, openly and squarely, for death and damnation, "the world, the flesh and the devil." Which the most dangerous, the most to be feared and shunned? the lion devils or the angel devils? The American Tract Society, "The Christian Union," and other religious bodies (not a few), including many pious editors and publishers, repudiate the lion devils, but clasp the angel devils to their bosoms! This is all Satan asks, or wishes for. These angel devils, religious novels and tales, he well knows lead, unmistakably, to the lion devils, the most obscene and soul-polluting, publications.

It is through the imagination chiefly that society is corrupted. Most temptations would appeal in vain to the other faculties. The insinuating, tainting products of the Satanic press, the opera, the theatre, the gambling-hell, the dance-house, the ball, the extravagances of fashion, and the pleasures of dissolute society, all make the appeal to the imagination. There are poets who, with siren notes, charm the unsuspecting victim into the jaws of destruction —poets

——" Whose poisoned song
Would blend the bounds of right and wrong,
And hold with sweet but cursed art
Their incantations o'er the heart,
Till every pulse of pure desire
Throbs with the glow of passion's fire."

There are novelists and actors who, by similar methods, wield influences most potent for corruption and ruin. And all this measureless mischief is wrought through the imagination.

Repent of your wickedness, friends, do works meet for

repentance? When? At doom's day? Because sentence against your evil doings is not executed speedily, your *whole heart* is fully set in you to work wickedness with greediness! Tell the Lord Jesus of you? how awfully and shamefully you dishonor his name? trample bleeding mercy under your feet? We *have* told him, we *do*, we *shall*. *Beware*, friends, lest by and by he tear you in pieces. Read Proverbs, chapter I, beginning at verse 20, and go through the chapter, and see how terribly God deals with incorrigibles, the willfully stiff-necked and obstinate, "He that being often reproved, hardeneth his neck, shall suddenly be destroyed, and that without remedy."—*Prov.* xxix. 1. See your picture portrayed vividly? When told in love, a spirit of Gospel meekness, in strains sweet as angels use, weepingly, beseechingly, for Christ's sake, for the honor and glory of Him who shed his precious blood on Calvary, for the sake of precious immortals yet unborn, to stop this putting the shoulder to Satan's wheels—*stop* stretching every nerve in blotting out the life, the essence and quintessence of Gospel purity—any signs of life, hope, confession, restitution, or of ceasing to do evil? Do your stiff necks bend in the least? your callous, adamantine hearts soften or relent? Think, beloved editors and publishers, of proud Korah's troop, what became of them?—*Numbers* xvi; of Nadab and Abihu, that offered strange fire; what did God in their case? Send fire from heaven, burn them up?—*Lev.* x. how read ye?

"Though thou shouldest bray a fool in a mortar among wheat with a pestle, yet will he not depart from his foolishness."—*Prov.* xxvii. 22.

"Why should ye be stricken any more, ye will revolt more and more."—*Isa.* i. 5.

"Seest thou a man wise in his own conceit," what now? more hope for a fool? Solomon says so.

The devil is in this work of yours, friends, no mistake, sure as you live and breathe. And still you help the old serpent, stand side by side with him. Hail fellow, well met! Souls perish through your instrumentality? How many, think you, in the day of final reckoning, will date their downfall and everlasting ruin, through your puffing apparatus? Will it help you or these lost souls, spirits damned, by saying, "it was popular to puff Satan and his works, everybody puffed them?" Or what will it profit in taking the grog-seller's plea, "If I don't kill, somebody else will. If I don't poison souls to death, consign them to the pit bottomless, by dealing out liquid death, and distilled damnation, some one else will." Children, not a few, of those who traffic in strong drink, rum and tobacco, become inebriates, bloated sots, and find a drunkard's grave. Fathers, mothers, sons and daughters, all find a common hell of weeping, wailing, and gnashing of teeth. So may it be with these dealers in intellectual poisons, that intoxicate the mind, corrupt the heart, pollute the soul—sink it lower than the grave! "He that soweth to the flesh shall of the flesh reap corruption." "They have sown the wind, and they shall reap the whirlwind."—*Hos.* viii. 7.

> "Who sows to winds, the whirlwind reaps,
>   And life's great end confounds!
> Then be, ye stewards, wise to escape
>   The wrath that knows no bounds."

There is no offence upon the face of earth which causes such deep, overwhelming, heart-burning grief and sorrow, as does this one single crime of seduction, of leading the youth of our cities astray in paths of vice and sinful amusements, through the medium of novels, silly tales, fictitious writings.

> "Oh, if there be a doom more dread
>   Than others on the judgment-day,
> It sure must be for him who led
>   A pure and gentle heart astray.
> There may be pardon for the knave,
>   And mercy for the wretch that stole;
> But heaven, I fear, will ne'er forgive
>   The murderer of a human soul.

"And he said, Go and tell this people; Hear ye indeed, but understand not: and see ye indeed, but perceive not. Make the heart of this people fat, and make their ears heavy, and shut their eyes: lest they see with their eyes, and hear with their ears, and understand with their heart, and convert and be healed."—*Isa.* vi. 9, 10.

"Wo to him that coveteth an evil covetousness to his house, that he may set his nest on high, that he may be delivered from the power of evil. Thou hast consulted shame to thy house, by cutting off many people, and hast sinned *against* thy soul. For the stone shall cry out of the wall, and the beam out of the timber shall answer it. Wo to him that buildeth a town with blood, and stablisheth a city by iniquity. Behold, *is* it not of the LORD of hosts, that the people shall labor in the very fire, and the people shall weary themselves for very vanity?"

Address....*Author of* "*Digging Roots,*" *etc.*
        No. 303 West Twentieth Street, N. Y.

Sowing Good Seed!

Preaching Folks—Folks that Preach.

PREACH here, preach there—sow good seed here, sow good seed there.

> "Thou knowest not which may thrive,
>   The late or early sown;
> Grace keeps the precious germ alive,
>   When and wherever strown."

"As ye go, preach."—*Mat.* x. 7.

Begin with the rising sun, keep on with the king of day, from his rising to his setting thereof; preach in the morning, at noon-day, at even-tide. Husbands and wives preach? Yes. Parents and children? Yes. Little folks? *By all means* "Have ye not read, out of the mouth of babes and sucklings thou hast perfected praise?"—*Mat.* xxi. 16.

Parents, train your little ones to be preachers—missionaries of the cross; begin at home, in the nursery, by the fire-side, around the table, the family altar.

> "Keep the family altar burning—
>   Let the sacred flame be bright;
> Gather round it in the morning,
>   Gather round it every night.
>
> "Keep the family altar burning,
>   Let the children all be there;
> That they may receive the blessing
>   At the sacred hour of prayer."

Home work first, home work *all the time.* "Train up a child in the way he should go, and when he is old he will not depart from it."

> "Call the children early, parent,
> Give the little lambs thy care;
> See that they are folded safe."

"In the morning sow thy seed, and in the evening withhold not thy hand; for thou knowest not whether shall prosper, either this or that, or whether they both shall be alike good."

"Cast thy bread upon the waters, for thou shalt find it after many days."

Let your life speak for God, your every-day walk, every thought, word, deed, moving muscle. Preach by your pen —the "pen of a ready writer." Preach by silent messengers, leaves for healing the nations, Gospel books, tracts, periodicals.

> "Scatter ye seeds, and flowers will spring;
> Strew them at broadcast o'er hill and glen:
> Sow in your garden, and time will bring
> Bright flowers, with seeds to scatter again."

All we can do is to sow the seed in faith, water it with prayer as the dew of heaven.

> "Let us remember how
> The Holy One was doing good to all,
> And let us ever now,
> When on his name we call,
> Ask that his Spirit on our hearts may fall."

"Some seeds, doubtless, will fall by the wayside, some on stony places, some among thorns, but other into good ground."

www.ingramcontent.com/pod-product-compliance
Lightning Source LLC
Chambersburg PA
CBHW022042230426
43672CB00008B/1045